MW00344834

Change and Continuity in American Colleges and Universities

Change and Continuity in American Colleges and Universities explores major ideas that have shaped the history and development of higher education in North America and considers how these inform contemporary innovations in the sector.

Chapters address intellectual, organizational, social, and political movements that occurred across the nineteenth and twentieth centuries and have impacted the policies, scholarship, and practices enacted at a variety of public and private institutions throughout the United States. Topics addressed include the politics of racial segregation, the place of religion in higher education, and models of leadership. Through rigorous historical analyses of education reform cases, this text puts forward useful lessons on how colleges and universities have navigated change in the past and may do so in the future.

This text will be of interest to scholars, researchers, and students in the fields of higher education, administration, and leadership, as well as the history of education and educational reform.

Nathan M. Sorber is an associate professor of higher education administration at West Virginia University.

Perspectives on the History of Higher Education
Series editor: Nathan M. Sorber

Originally named *The History of Higher Education Annual*, this series was founded in 1981 as the sole national journal of higher education under the editorship of Edwin D. Duryea. The *Annual* was thereafter hosted by the University of Rochester under the editorship of Harold S. Wechsler. In 1992, the *Annual* moved to Pennsylvania State University with Roger L. Geiger as editor, and in 2004, it became *Perspectives on the History of Higher Education*. Over the last forty years, the series has offered key insights into the changes, continuities, and contexts of higher education in North America. It remains a place for scholars to challenge accepted interpretations of higher education history, and expand understandings of changing dynamics of universities and colleges, and their students, faculty, governance, leadership, policy, and organizations.

Books in this series include:

The Land-Grant Colleges and the Reshaping of American Higher Education
Edited by Roger L. Geiger and Nathan M. Sorber

Higher Education for African Americans Before the Civil Rights Era, 1900–1964
Edited by Marybeth Gasman and Roger L. Geiger

Iconic Leaders in Higher Education
Edited by Roger L. Geiger

Curriculum, Accreditation and Coming of Age of Higher Education
Perspectives on the History of Higher Education
Edited by Roger L. Geiger

For more information about this series, please visit: www.routledge. com/Perspectives-on-the-History-of-Higher-Education/book-series/ TRANPHHE

Change and Continuity in American Colleges and Universities

Lessons from Nineteenth and Twentieth Century Innovations

Edited by Nathan M. Sorber

Routledge
Taylor & Francis Group

NEW YORK AND LONDON

First published 2021
by Routledge
52 Vanderbilt Avenue, New York, NY 10017

and by Routledge
2 Park Square, Milton Park, Abingdon, Oxon, OX14 4RN

Routledge is an imprint of the Taylor & Francis Group, an informa business

© 2021 Taylor & Francis

The right of Nathan M. Sorber to be identified as the author of
the editorial material, and of the authors for their individual
chapters, has been asserted in accordance with sections 77 and
78 of the Copyright, Designs and Patents Act 1988.

All rights reserved. No part of this book may be reprinted
or reproduced or utilised in any form or by any electronic,
mechanical, or other means, now known or hereafter invented,
including photocopying and recording, or in any information
storage or retrieval system, without permission in writing from
the publishers.

Trademark notice: Product or corporate names may be trademarks
or registered trademarks, and are used only for identification and
explanation without intent to infringe.

Library of Congress Cataloging-in-Publication Data
Names: Sorber, Nathan M, editor.
Title: Change and continuity in American colleges and universities :
   lessons from nineteenth and twentieth century innovations / Edited
   by Nathan M Sorber.
Description: New York, NY : Routledge, [2020] | Series: Perspectives
   on the history of higher education | Includes bibliographical
   references and index.
Identifiers: LCCN 2020018609 (print) | LCCN 2020018610 (ebook) |
   ISBN 9780367358402 (hardback) | ISBN 9780429342080 (ebook)
Subjects: LCSH: Educational change—United States—History—19th
   century. | Educational change—United States—History—20th century. |
   Education and state—United States—History—19th century. |
   Education and state—United States—History—20th century. |
   Education, Higher—Aims and objectives—United States.
Classification: LCC LB2806 .C324 2020 (print) | LCC LB2806
   (ebook) | DDC 371.200973—dc23
LC record available at https://lccn.loc.gov/2020018609
LC ebook record available at https://lccn.loc.gov/2020018610

ISBN: 978-0-367-35840-2 (hbk)
ISBN: 978-0-429-34208-0 (ebk)

Typeset in Baskerville
by Apex CoVantage, LLC

Contents

Preface

Change and Continuity in American Colleges and Universities: Lessons from Nineteenth and Twentieth Century Innovations represents the 33rd volume in the *Perspectives on the History of Higher Education* series. Over the last three decades, this series has transformed the way scholars understand the history of American higher education, with several volumes introducing works by celebrated authors of leading books in the field. The current volume addresses the history of reform in higher education by exploring illustrative cases that capture institutional and system-wide transformations in response to intellectual movements and shifts in social, political, economic, and cultural contexts. It investigates how purposes and structures in American colleges and universities changed in response to an emerging market society, the rise of capitalism and industrialization, religious shifts and secularization, bureaucratization, progressivism, technology shifts, demographic change, and neoliberalism. This book provides historical perspective on how colleges have navigated reform in the past and offers an essential background for contemporary movements for innovation in American higher education.

The book includes cases that span the late nineteenth and twentieth century and address organizational reforms that prompted curricular change, community engagement, urban extension, policy innovation, racial integration, cross-university collaboration, and systemic reform. *Change and Continuity* considers developments across institutional types, including reforms at public and private universities, land-grant colleges, Catholic universities, research universities, community colleges, former teachers' colleges, urban universities, liberal arts colleges, and state higher education systems. This volume includes chapters by leading and emerging scholars in their respective fields and leading voices in the history of American higher education.

Spanning nearly four decades, *Perspectives in the History of Higher Education* has been a leading outlet for established and new scholars to present critical and path-breaking research on the history of education. Our authors have developed *Perspectives* chapters into transformative books in the field. These include Lynn Gordon's *Gender and Higher Education,*

Roger Williams's *Origins of Federal Support*, Timothy Cain's *Establishing Academic Freedom*, Marc Van Overbeke's *The Standardization of American Schooling*, Nathan M. Sorber's *Land-Grant Colleges and Popular Revolt*, A. J. Angulo's *William Barton Rogers and the Idea of MIT*, Margaret Nash's collection of works on women and higher education, Daniel Clark's *Creating the College Man*, Roger L. Geiger's *The History of American Higher Education* and *American Higher Education Since World War II*, and many more. The 33rd volume continues this tradition of advancing and challenging our understanding of higher education by publishing chapters that are part of larger contracted works on their respective subjects.

The editor wishes to thank the editorial board and reviewers for their contributions to this volume of *Perspectives on the History of Higher Education*. The editor also recognizes the assistance of Lorena Ballester in the early phases of production and thanks colleagues at West Virginia University and the Center for the Future of Land-Grant Education for supporting this effort.

1 Introduction

Nathan M. Sorber

Ours is a time of significant change, innovation, or "disruption" in higher education. Social, political, cultural, and economic shifts have transformed the landscape, as American colleges and universities grapple with and are shaped by forces of massification, privatization, and globalization while confronting rapid technological and demographic change, public skepticism on the value of higher education, rising costs, and increasing competition from a variety of higher education forms. Traditional – indeed ancient – corporate structures are facing increasing strain from demands for access, equity, relevance, and affordability while concurrently responding to societal pressures to support economic development, confront social ills from racism, sexism, homophobia, transphobia, and xenophobia, maintain free expression and inquiry, and solve generational problems from food security to global pandemics to climate change.

Contemporaries that highlight immense changes in higher education – failing and merging colleges, curricular changes and online delivery, alternative providers, political antagonism, increasing institutional stratification, etc. – tend to assert that these transformative forces are new and that colleges and universities are best characterized as "immune," "resistant," or "incapable" of change.[1] Such thinking is an oversimplification of the history of change in American higher education; it also leaves current debates devoid of historical context. The purpose of *Change and Continuity in American Colleges and Universities: Lessons from Nineteenth and Twentieth Century Innovations* is to provide historical cases that illuminate how higher education has confronted social, economic, and political change in the past, how reform movements were created, contested, and implemented, and how college processes, purposes, and structures were transformed across space and time.

American Higher Education History: Surveying Patterns of Change and Continuity

Historian Roger Geiger states, "We study the history of higher education because some things change, and some things do not change."[2]

History provides insights into those persistent aspects of higher education – those continuities – that prove amendable to shifting contexts and changing societal expectations. Equally important, history allows us to explore cases of change in the appropriate temporal grounding. Upon evaluating the summative lessons of multiple cases, we can wrest away the enduring from the ephemeral. We can highlight decisive shifts in mission, purpose, practices, and processes that situate colleges for new generations, new ages, and new ideas.

Despite present pronouncements of the unchanging character colleges and universities, higher education history is epitomized by both patterns of intractable resiliency and decisive alterations. American higher education can trace continuities from ancient lineages: traditional corporate forms, faculty governance, Oxford-styled residential education, or liberal arts curricula, to name a few. Yet nearly as soon as colleges took root in American soil, movement to adapt colleges to local conditions, to shifting intellectual currents, or to the transformation of political economy and society began to occur.[3] The earliest colleges arose in response to religious fragmentation and enthusiasm, as Protestant denominations were destabilized and developed new institutions during the Great Awakening. Many of the early colleges were steeped in classical languages aimed to educate ministers and ecclesiastical authorities, yet the infusion of enlightenment ideals at the onset of revolution transformed the curricula, structures, and missions of these colleges. Indeed, the new republic witnessed several states embracing "republican universities" as pivotal innovations for the new democratic experiment where students could develop into virtuous leaders that would put the public good before personal passion.[4]

The post-revolutionary decline of the economy, the expansion of popular democratic participation, and the anti-elitism of an awakening democratic spirit led to a prolonged period of public skepticism toward higher education in the early nineteenth century. Yet in this lacuna of public withdrawal, private colleges – oft supported by churches and local boosters – dotted the landscape as westward migration brought new settlements. There were only 15 colleges in 1820, but by 1840, this number would increase to 80, as frontier communities established higher learning institutions. On the one hand, these colleges adopted curricula and purposes of eastern colleges by providing a liberal arts education steeped in Latin and Greek as the "foundations of a superior education."[5] Yet on the other hand, as internal improvements like roads and canals began to integrate frontier communities, emerging markets reframed thinking around the value and uses of education for marketable ends. The multipurpose college arrived as an innovative grassroots alternative in higher education, as these institutions experimented on the edges of the liberal arts curriculum to offer "useful" knowledge in commerce, didactics (teaching), agriculture, and proto-engineering to both traditional and irregular (part-time and summer) students. Local pressure and conditions also brought more radical departures: the collegiate education of women in single-sex and coeducational settings, remedial and preparatory programs for the underprepared, manual and practical courses for part-time students, and access for African Americans.[6]

At the onset of the Civil War, federal and state governments made inroads into higher education with the passage of the Morrill Act of 1862 and the creation of land-grant colleges. There had been state universities since the time of the early republic, but the support of these enterprises was limited and erratic. The Morrill Act provided proceeds from the sale of federal land – made available through Native American dispossession – to the states to establish land-grant universities, while also requiring state governments to contribute. This greatly increased the number of public colleges and facilitated the expansion of state and federal funding. The land-grant colleges disrupted the higher education marketplace, affecting purpose, institutional capacity, access, clientele, and curriculum. The overarching goal of the Morrill Act was to use the resources of the federal government "to align higher education with economic and national development . . . with [land-grant] institutions premised on the advancement and dissemination of scientific knowledge . . . for the purpose of increasing agricultural and industrial productivity."[7] In a higher education landscape epitomized by denominational colleges with often fewer than 50 students, land-grant colleges and universities formed in every state and, over time, contributed to a considerable expansion in higher education participation. This potential for increasing enrollment was facilitated by the Morrill Act provisions that land-grant colleges would "promote the liberal and practical education of the industrial classes in the several pursuits and professions in life." Notwithstanding these stipulations, land-grant colleges struggled to increase access for the industrial classes in the early years due to students lacking the requisite academic preparation and the financial resources to pay the modest tuition and fees. However, land-grant preparatory programs and the rise of public secondary schools helped alleviate these admissions barriers, and the implementation of campus student employment programs and state scholarships provided financial aid that delivered a more egalitarian clientele. The land-grant colleges also shifted and broadened the curricular landscape in the later decades of the nineteenth century, building on the innovations of multipurpose colleges to advance applied scientific subjects like agriculture and engineering.[8]

Along with this transformative federal intervention, traditional higher education practices, purposes, and forms were disrupted by the burgeoning university model in Europe. Although the classics remained the staple of the early nineteenth century college, scientific study had made inroads. Traditional colleges like Harvard, Yale, and Dartmouth established separate scientific schools, polytechnics in urban settings and military schools introduced proto-engineering curricula, lyceums and agricultural colleges offered applied science, and many colleges experimented with offering a smattering of scientific subjects on the edges of the classical course of study. However, America lacked a true university for advanced scientific study, and many scholars had to travel to Germany to partake in higher education innovation. German universities, in particular, adopted the *Wissenshaft* ideals of advancing and disseminating knowledge as central tenets. As the German state became the guarantor of *lehrfreiheit* (the freedom to teach) and *lernfreiheit* (the freedom to learn), a higher education context arose that nurtured free inquiry and study. These conditions produced dramatic advances in knowledge with discoveries in chemistry, agricultural science, electromagnetism, mechanics, physics, history, geology, and botany, to name a few.[9]

Many of the expatriate scholars that returned stateside embracing *Wissenshaft* ideals became pioneers in building and leading new universities in America. Transformative leaders like Andrew Dickson White (Cornell), Evan Pugh (Pennsylvania Agricultural College), Samuel Johnson (Yale and Connecticut Experiment Station), Charles Eliot (Harvard), and Daniel Coit Gilman (Yale, California, and John Hopkins) are all examples of individuals that either studied in Germany or went abroad to learn about the system. Some of these individuals would guide the recently established land-grant institutions on a university trajectory, while others would lead new German-styled institutions supported by private funding.[10] For example, the private wealth of telegraph tycoon Ezra Cornell was combined with the state's land-grant funds and, under the visionary leadership of Andrew Dickson, a true university was created in upstate New York. Cornell University represented a clear departure in the higher education marketplace, quickly growing the nation's largest enrollment and offering a remarkable breadth of courses – liberal arts, social sciences, agriculture, engineering, and host of emerging professions and natural sciences. With its considerable resources, Cornell University could recruit leading scholars and teach subjects at the frontier of known knowledge. However, Cornell remained primarily an undergraduate institution; it would be the 1876 founding of Johns Hopkins University in Baltimore, Maryland, that would bring a conclusive shift of the paradigm.

The founding of Johns Hopkins University contributed to one of the most significant disruptions in American higher education history. Historians mark this event as the onset of an "academic revolution." Following the largest private gift to date and the recruitment of Daniel Coit Gilman as president, John Hopkins became the nation's first research university and purveyor of graduate education. The university invested in the latest research laboratories and apparatus, provided graduate fellowships for students and research sabbaticals for faculty, and standardized the American PhD as three years of intensive study capped with an original thesis. Hopkins was soon joined by other research-based universities backed by philanthropists, most notably the founding of Stanford University in Palo, Alto California and the Rockefeller-backed University of Chicago. In Chicago, President William Rainey Harper oversaw the creation of a university that was integrated with the development of the city, maintaining an impressive breadth of programs that incorporated advanced study and research. The University of Chicago developed and advanced a host of social science disciplines through research and engagement, including in the fields of sociology, education, political science, and economics.[11]

Traditional colleges needed to innovate to remain competitive for faculty and students in a landscape altered by the new universities. Throughout the 1870s, President Charles Elliot worked to reform Harvard, instigating a host of initiatives to transform curriculum, faculty work, and the structure of the college along with affiliated professional schools. The most profound change was the adoption of the elective system. Students were now free from the rigid strictures of the fixed course of study to pursue their interests, and faculty could forgo required sections of the traditional fare in favor of courses that aligned with a scholarly specialization. At Harvard and far beyond, the elective system not only expanded the appeal of the curriculum for students but created a mechanism where faculty researchers could evolve from generalists to specialists. Concurrent with these developments, the reform of professional schools was an equally dramatic albeit lagging higher education disruption during the academic revolution. Law and medical schools were typically proprietary ventures attended by non-college students, but reformers like Eliot brought these schools under the college's control. These efforts served to limit admission to college graduates, reorganize the curriculum on a scientific basis, and create a professional faculty under university control in lieu of proprietary practitioners.[12]

The creation of new and reformed universities at the turn of the century changed the structure of academic life, restructured the academic profession, and shifted our thinking about the purpose of higher education. It also sparked a multifaceted process of standardization, as higher education leaders, societal reformers, and philanthropic organizations sought to define the normative boundaries of higher education. The leading universities set standards that influenced the broader market: curriculum of two years of general study followed by two years of major specialization, the admittance of only high school graduates, graduate education, and a reformed academic profession.[13] Shedding the old order of a generalist faculty teaching all courses, universities organized into academic departments, a product of the advancement of specialized knowledge across multiple domains. This was facilitated by the rise of graduate education, the elective system, academic societies, scholarly journals, and academic structures that supported faculty research.

Universities also embraced faculty polices to encourage scholarship, notably "up or out" promotion processes, which would ultimately tie faculty rewards and recognition to specialized scientific communities. Faculty organized to protect their new professional identity with the founding of American Association for University Professors (AAUP) in 1915 that advocated, amongst other things, for academic freedom to teach and research.[14] Standardization was also advanced by philanthropic organizations like the Carnegie Foundation for the Advancement of Teaching and Rockefeller's General Education Board. These organizations committed to bring order and efficiency to higher education, providing matching funding for faculty pension programs and campus construction to those institutions that agreed to appeal to alumni for donations, build endowments, sever religious ties, and conform to elevated academic expectations. Outcomes included the adoption of standard admission criteria (i.e. agreed numbers of Carnegie Units), secularization of private higher education, and the development of alumni engagement and fundraising.

Amid the impressive university building – including the rapid creation of land-grant universities, philanthropic ventures, and reformed institutions – contemporaries expected the demise of the traditional colleges. Many called for the shortening of the undergraduate degree to more quickly progress to specialized instruction and others predicted the inevitable shuttering of many smaller colleges. Indeed, the rapid rise of specialized knowledge housed in a multitude of academic departments favored larger institutions, and in doing so, disrupted the market of multipurpose colleges. It became increasingly difficult for these older institutions to offer the breadth of knowledge that emerged during the academic revolution, as economies of scale favored big institutions. The "old older" of smaller multipurpose colleges either closed or reframed their purpose as liberal arts colleges. In fact, the undergraduate liberal arts or general college persisted as a viable higher education entity, representing a notable continuity during rapid change in the history of higher education.[15] The continuity of the American college alongside the rise of the university and specialized knowledge can be partially explained by the evolution of collegiate life and the place of the undergraduate experience in American society. By the end of the nineteenth century, American higher education witnessed a breathtaking expansion and elaboration of collegiate experiences, including fraternities and sororities, campus activities in drama, music, and the arts, student government, and college athletics.[16] Alumni with fond memories of this student experience soon became passionate supporters – both vocally and financially – and a public that had no previous connection to the colleges, increasingly followed and supported college sports – especially football.[17] In time, colleges grew concerned with extracurricular excesses and placed collegiate activities under the supervision of campus life administrators. With the undergraduate experience becoming a middle-class cultural rite of passage, the four-year degree persisted, fusing with advanced study and research in a single organization. In short, the academic and collegiate revolutions managed to coexist and represent dual forces of continuity and change.[18]

The twentieth century witnessed far-reaching transformations in American higher education, including those rooted in trends from previous decades. The first was the enduing impact of female higher education. Women's entrance and participation in higher education were developments that spurred new institutions and transformed others. In 1837, Mary Lyons founded Mount Holyoke; an inventive model that combined academic subjects – including collegiate-level coursework – and a system that required female students to complete all the domestic duties for the institution. Although such a system aligned with cultural norms regarding separate spheres for the sexes, Lyons sought to expand the female domain, proposing that roles as teachers, wives, mothers, and community organizers required a more thorough education. In a few decades, the seminary graduated over five hundred women and spawn "sister" institutions that adopted the Holyoke model. By the late 1850s, new institutions like Elmira College and Mary Sharpe College were officially offering the full BA curriculum to female students.[19] Concurrent with these developments, the demand for qualified teachers created opportunities for and justified the mission of female higher education. In addition, to provide instruction at a burgeoning sector of primary and secondary schools, states created normal schools that bridged secondary and higher education. With state support that subsidized tuition, normal schools became an important entry point into higher education for both men and women of limited means.[20] After the Civil War, the two greatest innovations in female higher education were the rise of endowed colleges for women and coeducation. The founding of colleges like Vassar with deep philanthropic support, brought institutions with the financial wherewithal to, in the words of Matthew Vassar, to become "an institution which should be to women what Yale and Harvard are to young men." These Seven Sisters institutions would set a standard of academic excellence and educate countless female leaders and trailblazers at the turn of the century. However, the future of higher education for women would exist primarily in coeducational colleges. While pioneering women at coeducational institutions faced numerous challenges, including a lack of housing, academic and social restrictions, and dismissive pushback from peers and faculty, their attendance, perseverance, and success changed higher education and society.[21] The second generation of women that arrived at the dawn of the twentieth century negotiated inclusion into academic and social life, and at times, created separate spaces that spurred their own collegiate revolution – women's organizations, student governments, sororities, and athletics. Women's participation would continue to grow in the twentieth century, reaching forty percent of enrollments many public colleges and universities by the 1920s, reaching parity with men in the 1950s, gaining entrance to the holdout Ivy's in the 1960s, and overtaking men in participation across higher education by the end of the century.[22]

Social, economic, and political pressures also moved higher education in the early twentieth century toward the concept of public engagement. In the 1890s, populist pressure on land-grant colleges and universities entwined with progressive era thinking for societal intervention and improvement led to outreach innovations that would come to be known as extension. Populist organizations critiqued land grants for elevated admission standards, high costs, for too few graduates becoming farmers, and for a lack of utility for the needs of farm communities. Special part-time programs, summer courses, home economic divisions, and direct extension agent outreach that disseminated knowledge to farmers, communities, and rural homes. In 1914, these efforts garnered government support through the Smith-Lever Act, which combined federal, state, and local funding to support extension programs. The extension innovation not only facilitated farm modernization, it also confronted a host of problems facing states and rural communities. Extension ideals would evolve beyond the traditional farming clientele and spur higher education engagement and service missions that leveraged higher education's knowledge production and dissemination to address persistent social problems affecting states and local communities.[23]

The early twentieth century also witnessed the increased participation of African American students into both integrated and racially segregated colleges. African American students had been attending Predominantly White Institutions, albeit in token numbers, as early as 1835 when progressive Oberlin College allowed admission irrespective of race. Missionary societies, abolitionists, and African American churches supported the founding of private Black colleges before the Civil War, and after the fighting ended, reconstruction legislatures created colleges for African Americans in several southern states. After years of failing to direct federal resources to African American higher education, the Morrill Act of 1890 stipulated that land-grant colleges would receive an influx of additional, regular appropriations, but state governments had to make provisions to direct portions of the funding to Black students. However, segregated systems were deemed to comply with the law, and Southern states founded a separate system of land-grant colleges (today referred to as public Historically Black Colleges and Universities (HBCUs) that would receive legal justification with the infamous *Plessy v. Fergusson* decision. HBCUs served African Americans, navigated a challenging Jim Crow context, and developed a unique higher education model to disrupt dynamics of power, racism, social, political, and economic inequities, and oppression. For decades after the Civil War, legal barriers, a dearth of funding, and violence limited access to all levels of education. Thus, the HBCUs created a model that spanned elementary, secondary, and higher education, while others like Tuskegee Institute focused on vocational programs. The HBCUs would not only produce the foundation of a Black middle class, this sector would educate the legal, social, and political reformers that would spark and guide the Civil Rights Movement.[24]

In addition to these innovations that expanded access to higher education across gender, class, and race and expanded missions beyond the campus, there were other developments triggered by rapid economic, social, and political developments and external geopolitical shocks. These systemic pressures included massification, federal intervention, and the expansion and elaboration of university research. Perhaps the most significant changes came from the increase in enrollment that began to take shape in the first decades of the twentieth century. In 1900, only 8 percent of 14–17-year-olds attended secondary education, but the number would balloon to 80 percent by 1940. Prompted by swelling ranks of high school graduates, higher education participation doubled between the world wars. This growth disrupted the traditional order and led to qualitative changes including new institutions and the rise of differentiated higher education systems.[25] New options emerged to appeal to new clientele including local, urban, and low-cost institutions. Two-year junior colleges affiliated with traditional colleges expanded access via community accessibility and lower costs and large municipal universities like the City College of New York brought higher education to the diverse populations of American cities.[26] The rise of these mass sector institutions led elite colleges and universities to distinguish themselves through selective (and in cases discriminatory) admissions, elevated standards, liberal arts and general education reform and robust spending on extensive residential experiences and faculty research. In time, this process would create a differentiated system of selective colleges and universities and open-access community colleges, regional public colleges, municipal institutions, and for-profit colleges. Reformers and state coordinators worked to demarcate boundaries and define activities across institutions to bring systemic order.[27]

The transformative effects on higher education from early massification would intensify after World War II, encouraged by the arrival of a knowledge-based, postindustrial economy and the federal and state interventions that followed.[28] The passage of the Servicemen's Readjustment Act (GI Bill) of 1945 provided free tuition for returning soldiers to access higher education and over one million veterans took advantage of the program in the 1940s and 1950s. Institutions had to build rapidly to accommodate the influx of students, and the student soldiers brought a scholastic seriousness to campus that translated into academic success and earned praise inside and outside of higher education. Soon after, the

President's Commission on Higher Education was calling for robust federal aid for non-soldiers as well, but Congress remained resistant to an expanded federal role throughout the 1950s. This left state governments to respond to the growing demands of the coming-of-age baby boomer generation for affordable access to higher education. States invested liberally in the late 1950s and 1960s to dramatically increase the capacity of public colleges and universities. The insatiable demand for higher learning also spurred the rapid founding of community colleges by local governments and school districts. The new community colleges grew at a breathtaking pace, providing low-cost, vocational education as well as collegiate courses to local students that could be transferred to four-year institutions. The federal government fully intervened in the massification of higher education with the passage of the Higher Education Acts of 1965 and the amendments that followed. The Higher Education Acts represented a sea change in federal involvement, ushering in a massive federal student aid program and accreditation regime that would lower access barriers for low-income students and hereafter entwine participating institutions to federal oversight and regulations. After much political wrangling, the federal aid program was designed to "follow the student," allowing public and private institutions to reap the benefits and maintain the continuity of the mixed system.[29]

The university sector was also transformed by the Cold War competition for technological advancement. After the launch of Sputnik and domestic concerns over falling behind the Soviets, federal policy directed research funding through agencies like the National Science Foundation, National Aeronautical and Space Agency and the National Institute of Health. The best-equipped universities with the top researchers were well-positioned to receive funding awards. In short order, the leading research universities that had already marked their place of prestige earlier in the century as members of the Association of American Universities (AAU) secured continuity in the hierarchy by acquiring a disproportionate share of federal research dollars that brought further investment in laboratories, facilities, and star faculty.[30]

By the 1960s, a modern multiversity of impressive size and breadth had emerged at the apex of American higher education with its complex and multifaceted structures. Yet the multiversity was just part of a differentiated order of universities, liberal arts colleges, regional public universities, community colleges, and technical schools that comprised the emerging mass higher education system. Moreover, while more students were attending higher education at higher rates than anywhere in the world, an underlying student unrest revealed the limits of accessibility and persistent discontinuities within higher education and the broader society.

The Civil Rights Movement was a campaign for racial equality that included civil disobedience, protests, resistance, moral suasion, judicial appeals, and political action. The movement included a direct challenge to segregated systems and inequities in education. Legal campaigns against segregation occurred across multiple states, challenging schools and colleges for failing to offer equitable educational offerings. In the 1940s, judicial victories came through applying the dubious "separate but equal" doctrine and securing African American access to professional and graduate education in states where separate advanced schools did not exist for African Americans. The *Brown v. Board of Education* decision of 1954 extinguished the legality of racially separate schools, but it would take a decade of further legal challenges, grassroots organizing, federal executive intervention, and the persistence of students to integrate Southern colleges and universities and change higher education.[31] Equally trying events occurred in Northern institutions for access and equality, including dramatic battles at nation's most elite institutions.[32] The Civil Rights Act of 1964 capped years of political activism to advance legal protections for African Americans, including in education.

Further radical change came in the 1960s as part of a broader cultural revolution in American society. The quiet, apolitical campuses of the 1950s were replaced with student protests that challenged the status quo on campus and beyond. Many protest leaders received their political baptism in the Student Nonviolent Coordinating Committee during the Civil Rights Movement and then returned to campuses for political confrontation through organizations like the Students for a Democratic Society. Fueled by continued racism, outdated higher education norms, and the burgeoning war in Southeast Asia, student demanded that higher education be a progressive actor for change in the social and political contests of the era. With extraordinary events like the Free Speech Movement in Berkley and anti-Vietnam protests capped by the tragedy at Kent State, higher education moved from political apathy or neutrality to activism and social confrontation. As campus political activism spread and cultural norms changed, higher education could no longer uphold campus paternalism, *in loco parentis,* nor remain bastions of social conservatism. Movements confronted practices and policies that limited opportunities across race, gender, class, and sexual orientation, new academic opportunities emerged through diverse hiring and curricular changes like Women's or Ethnic Studies, and legal changes forced non-compliant institutions to provide equal opportunities through the Civil Rights Act of 1964 and Title IX of the 1972 amendments to the Higher Education Acts.[33]

The remarkable enrollment expansion of the twentieth century came to an end in the 1970s, as the baby boomer generation passed through higher education. The stagnation in enrollment coincided with an economic downturn that brought higher prices, unemployment, and decreased state appropriations. The process would ebb and flow, but starting in the 1970s, higher education entered a new era epitomized by privatization, increased competition, decreasing state support, and technological advancement. The result has been significant changes to higher education administration, missions, funding models, and relations with social and economic systems. The period witnessed a rise of an administrative apparatus to leverage new technologies to manage process of strategic prioritization to allocate scarce resources, to comply with a growing matrix of government regulations and accreditation, and to manage activities like recruiting, fundraising, and marketing for a competitive environment. Indeed, dependency on tuition at both private and public institutions led to an arms race to secure the best students and faculty, leading to extravagant spending on research facilities, campus buildings, residence halls, and athletics. The most selective and resource-rich institutions jockeyed for "best college" rankings to signal value to student "consumers."[34]

By the end of the century, and punctuated by the Great Recession of 2009, higher education had realized its shift to privatization and polarization, and increasingly held a critical but precarious place in American society. Higher education is more central than ever to societal and economic agendas. University research has undergone major transformations, integrating with economic development strategies through workforce development programs, commercialization and technology transfer operations, innovation zones and technology parks, and a host of industrial and public/private research partnerships. Through research, teaching, and service, higher education is confronting a host of pressing problems: food security to climate change, health care to drug addiction, pediatrics to pandemics, and countless more. Access is increasingly available through traditional and online options. However, many deep challenges remain. Public skepticism of higher education is high and public financial support is low. There may be accessibility, but serious concerns persist with the rising cost of higher education and inequitable access along lines of race, class, and gender. Moreover, campus unrest continues as students and faculty challenge unequal spaces. The Great Recession of 2009 and the Pandemic of 2020 exacerbated challenging financial times for higher education, disrupting markets and spurring closures and mergers of less viable institutions. Yet the point remains that higher education is changing as it always has changed, at times decisively and drastically. As in the past, successful higher education innovation will likely come when stakeholders recognize and accept that change is imminent, and when leaders work to ensure continuity of core functions – the teaching, advancement, and dissemination of knowledge – while embracing new models, processes, and structures that allow higher education to achieve those missions for a new era.

Exploring Cases of Change and Continuity

The preceding survey of continuity and change in higher education is a broad outline of key moments of disruption in American higher education. The purpose of this volume is to further probe historical cases to advance and add nuance to this narrative. Of course, these cases are not exhaustive, but they do represent key events that will expand our understanding of how higher education navigated shifting contexts and reform movements in the past.

In Chapter 2, *The Academic Engineers, 1890–1920: Understanding a Cohort of Higher Education Reformers,* Ethan W. Ris explores the contributions of an "ideological community" of higher education reformers that constructed a shared vision of how to transform American higher education at the turn of the century. In tracing the contributions of this cohort of six "academic engineers," Ris explains how these reformers from elite universities and philanthropies directed their efforts for systemic order and efficiency "downward" to direct, define, and confine the activities of lower-tier institutions in the wake of the massification and differentiation of higher education.

Chapter 3, Christen Ogren's *An "Administrativ" Approach to Innovation: Two Teachers-College Presidents and Simplified Spelling in the Progressive Era,* chronicles the campaign for "simplified spelling" by two higher education reformers at teachers' colleges that would transcended their individual campuses to engage state and national audiences. The movement for simplified spelling was controversial, but it was aligned with Progressive Era principles of efficiency, rationality, and accessibility that reformers hoped would improve literacy, decrease children's instructional time, and save money on printing. Ogren explains how Homer Seerley of the Iowa State Teachers College and David Felmley of Illinois State Normal University were dedicated to the campaign for simplified spelling, but had to balance this commitment to a controversial reform with the cultivation of their institutions' public images. This case shows how higher education innovations can run afoul of public perceptions, and the challenges leaders face in navigating the intersection of intellectually valid reform movements and public pressure.

In Chapter 4, *Progressivism, John Dewey, and the University of Chicago Laboratory School: Building Democratic Community,* Sam F. Stack Jr. continues the book's exploration of Progressive Era reforms by investigating how John Dewey sought to disseminate the research and educational ideals developed at the University of Chicago to transform K–12 schooling. Dewey envisioned school as places for renewing community, nurturing active student interest and learning, and educating individuals for social change. Stack explores how John Dewey attempted to create an innovative educational laboratory – the Dewey Lab School – to bridge research and practice and to advance the educational ideals of the Progressive Era. Stack reveals how educational reform occurs through the partnerships between higher education and other educational institutions and through the research, teaching, and dissemination of educational theory and practice.

In Chapter 5, Bryan McAllister-Grande challenges traditional thinking on curricular reform in the first half of the twentieth century, *The Inner Restoration: Christian Humanists Fighting for the Supernatural Order, 1925–1955*. McAllister-Grande reveals that a religious system of thought – Christian humanism – maintained steady continuity in the college well into the twentieth century. Countering a historiography that assumed that the rise of science and secularism displaced the sacred in approaches to assessing knowledge, the author shows the enduring place of Christian humanism in curricula and curricular reform, humanities courses, and honors programs at Harvard, Yale, and Princeton. The work contributes new thinking on how college students wrestled with truth and epistemology in a post-World War II era of rapid intellectual change.

In Chapter 6, *"We Felt . . . That We Were Talking to Old Friends": Catholic and Protestant Colleges and their Cooperation for Curriculum Reform*, Kevin S. Zayed continues the book's analysis of curricular change by investigating an intriguing general education reform partnership between Protestant and Catholic colleges. The author argues that in the midst of rapid societal changes, secularization, and top-down reform movements seeking systemic transformation (as discussed by Ris in Chapter 2), Catholic and Protestant institutions put aside differences to cooperate on curricular reform in the 1930s and 1940s. Zayed shows how smaller institutions were able to participate in needed but expensive reform to survive (and even thrive) during the period, engaging in "philanthropically funded, experimental, and interinstitutional cooperation" while maintaining their institutional autonomy.

In Chapter 7, Kate Rousmaniere expands our understanding of racial desegregation in the provocative *"Desegregated but Not Integrated": Race and the Politics of Student Housing in American Higher Education History*. The author shows that the change process of racial desegregation went well beyond access. Indeed, this chapter explores how the exclusion from housing was often the most significant challenge facing African American students beyond initial desegregation and was a source of radical backlash amongst local communities. Rousmaniere explains how African American student activism emerged around housing, intersecting with broader Civil Rights struggles and linking with other campus equity issues of student rights, curriculum, and resources to move campuses toward real integration.

Finally, in Chapter 8, *Transforming the Mission with a Nontraditional Presidency: David C. Hardesty's Land-Grant Leadership at the End of the Twentieth Century*, Katlin Swisher provides a historical leadership study of one land-grant president in the face of shifting public perceptions of the role and value of higher education. During a 12-year career, the president worked to transform the land-grant mission in response to a changing market. With a campaign to create a consumer-oriented, "student-first" university, the university grew into a national brand in the wake of privatization, and in doing so, changed traditional public good conceptions of the land-grant model.

Notes

1. For examples of trade publication commentary on higher education unchanging character, see for example Robert M. Diamond, Why Colleges Are So Hard to Change, Inside Higher Ed (September 6, 2006); Steven Mintz, How Higher Education Is and Is Not Changing, Inside Higher Ed (August 8, 2019).
2. Roger L. Geiger, "The Ten Generations of American Higher Education," in *American Higher Education in the Twenty-First Century*, eds. Michael N. Bastedo, Philip G. Altbach, and Patricia J. Gumport (Baltimore, MD: Johns Hopkins University Press, [1998] 2011), 3.
3. Roger L. Geiger, *The History of American Higher Education: Learning and Culture from the Founding to World War II* (Princeton: Princeton University Press, 2015).
4. David J. Hoeveler, *Creating the American Mind: Intellect and Politics* (Lanham: Rowan & Littlefield Publishers, 2002).
5. David Potts, *Liberal Education for a Land of Colleges: Yale's Reports of 1828* (New York: Palgrave Macmillan, 2010).
6. Roger L. Geiger, "The Era of Multipurpose Colleges in American Higher Education, 1850–1890," in The *American Colleges in the Nineteenth Century*, ed. Roger L. Geiger (Nashville, TN: Vanderbilt University, 2000).
7. Nathan M. Sorber, *Land-Grant Colleges and Popular Revolt: The Origins of the Morrill Act and the Reform of Higher Education* (Ithaca, NY: Cornell University Press, 2018), quote 5.
8. On land-grant history, see Sorber, *Land-Grant Colleges and Popular Revolt;* Roger L. Geiger and Nathan M. Sorber, eds., *The Land Grant Colleges and the Reshaping of American Higher Education* (New Brunswick, NJ: Transaction Press, 2013); Nathan M. Sorber and Roger L. Geiger, "The Welding of Opposite Views: Land-Grant Historiography at 150 Years," in *Higher Education: Handbook of Theory and Research*, ed. Michael B. Paulson, Vol. 29 (New York: Springer Publishing, 2014), 385–342; On land-grant access and early aid programs see Nathan M. Sorber, "Early Land-Grant Colleges and Students in the Northeastern United States: A History of Regional Access and Mobility Patterns in Maine, Massachusetts, and New York, 1862–1878," *Agricultural History* 92, no. 1 (Winter 2018): 101–123; and Gregory J. Behle, "Educating the Toiling Peoples: Students at the Illinois Industrial University, spring 1868," in *The Land-Grant Colleges and the Reshaping of American Higher Education*, eds. Roger L. Geiger and Nathan M. Sorber (New Brunswick, NJ: Transaction Publishers, 2013), 73–94; On Native American dispossession at the foundation of the movement, see Margaret A. Nash, "Entangled Pasts: Land-Grant Colleges and American Indian Dispossession," *History of Education Quarterly* 59, no. 4 (November 2019): 437–467.
9. Charles Rosenberg, *No Other Gods: On Science and American Social Thought* (Baltimore, MD: Johns Hopkins University Press, 1997); Mark R. Finlay, "Transnational Exchanges of Agricultural Scientific Thought from the Morrill Act to the Hatch Act," in *Science as Service: Establishing and Reformulating the American Land-Grant Universities*, ed. Alan I. Marcus (Tuscaloosa, AL: University of Alabama Press, 2015); Harold Perkin, "History of Universities," in *International Handbook of International Higher Education*, eds. James J.F. Forest and Phillip G. Altbach (London, UK: Springer, 2006), 156–206.

10. Nathan M. Sorber, "Creating Colleges of Science, Industry, and National Advancement," in *The Land-Grant Colleges and the Reshaping of American Higher Education*, eds. Roger L. Geiger and Nathan M. Sorber (New Brunswick, NJ: Transaction, 2013), 41–72.

11. On the academic revolution, see Christopher Jencks and David Riesman, *The Academic Revolution* (New York, NY: Doubleday, 1968); on the new philanthropic universities, see Roger L. Geiger, *To Advance Knowledge: The Growth of American Universities* (New Brunswick, NJ: Transaction, 2004); Hugh Hawkins, *Pioneer: A History of Johns Hopkins University, 1874–1889* (Ithaca, NY: Cornell University Press); Willard Pugh, "A Curious Working of Cross-Purposes in the Founding of the University of Chicago," in *The American College in the Nineteenth Century*, ed. Roger L. Geiger (Nashville, TN: Vanderbilt University Press, 2000).

12. For the classic yet definitive account of Eliot and Harvard reforms, see Samuel Eliot Morrison, *Three Centuries of Harvard, 1636–1936* (Cambridge, MA: Belknap Press of Harvard University, 1936); see also Bruce A. Kimball, *The Inception of Modern Professional Education* (Chapel Hill: University of North Carolina Press, 2009), and Geiger, *The History of American Higher Education*, chapter 8.

13. Laurence Veysey, *The Emergence of the American University* (Chicago, IL: University of Chicago Press, 1965).

14. On faculty changes, see Roger L. Geiger, "Professionalization of the American Faculty in the Twentieth Century," in *Perspectives on the History of Higher Education*, ed. Roger L. Geiger, Vol. 31 (New Brunswick, NJ: Transaction, 2015).

15. Roger L. Geiger, "The Crisis of the Old Order: The Colleges in the 1890s," in *The American College in the Nineteenth Century*, ed. Roger L. Geiger (Nashville, TN: Vanderbilt University Press, 2000), 264–277.

16. John Thelin, *A History of American Higher Education* (Baltimore, MD: Johns Hopkins University Press, 2019).

17. Peter Dobkin Hall, "Noah Porter Writ Large? Reflections on the Modernization of American Higher Education," in *The American College in the Nineteenth Century*, ed. Roger L. Geiger (Nashville, TN: Vanderbilt University Press, 2000), 196–220.

18. W. Bruce Leslie, *Gentlemen and Scholars: College and Community in the "Age of the University"* (New Brunswick, NJ: Transaction Press, 2005); on college as middle class, cultural rite of passage, Daniel Clark, *Creating the College Man: American Mass Magazine and Middle-class Manhood, 1890–1915* (Madison, WI: University of Wisconsin Press).

19. On development in female higher education in the early nineteenth century, see Margaret A. Nash, *Women's Education in the United States, 1780–1840* (New York, NY: Palgrave Macmillan, 2005); Barbara Miller Solomon, *In the Company of Educated Women: A History of Women and Higher Education* (New Haven, CT: Yale University Press, 1985).

20. Christine A. Ogren, *The American State Normal School: "An Instrument of Great Good,"* (New York: Palgrave Macmillan, 2005).

21. On anti-coedism across two generations, see Charlotte Williams, *Conable: Women at Cornell: The Myth of Equal Education* (Ithaca, NY: Cornell University Press, 1977).

22. Solomon, *In the Company of Educated Women.*

23. See Sorber, *Land-Grant Colleges and Popular Revolt*, chapter 5; Scott J. Peters, "Every Farmer Should be Awakened: Liberty Hyde Baily's View of Extension Work," *Agricultural History* 80, no. 2 (Spring 2006): 190–219.

24. Marybeth Gasman and Roger L. Geiger, *Higher Education for African Americans before the Civil Rights era, 1900–1964. Perspectives on the History of Higher Education* (New Brunswick, NJ: Transaction Press, 2012).

25. On general process of massification, see Martin Trow, *The Transition from Elite to Mass Higher Education* (Paris: Organization for Economic Co-Cooperation and Development, 1974). See also Geiger, *The History of American Higher Education*, chapter 10.

26. See for example, Willis Rudy, *The College of the City of New York: A History, 1847–1940* (New York: Arno Press, 1977).

27. On the process of differentiation, see David Levine, *The American College and the Culture of Aspiration, 1915–1940* (Ithaca, NY: Cornell University Press, 1986); on discriminatory admission practices to preserve elite status across race, class, and gender, see Jerome Karabel, *The Chosen: The Hidden History of Admission and Exclusion at Harvard, Yale, and Princeton* (New York, NY: Houghton Mifflin Harcourt, 2005).

28. On economic changes, see Daniel Bell, *The Coming of Post-Industrial Society: A Venture in Social Forecasting* (New York, NY: Basic Books, 1973).

29. On expansion and transformation in the postwar era, see Roger L. Geiger, *American Higher Education Since World War II: A History* (Princeton, NJ: Princeton University Press, 2019), chapters 1–4.

30. Roger L. Geiger, *Research and Relevant Knowledge: American Research Universities Since World War II* (New Brunswick, NJ: Transaction 2004).

31. Peter Wallenstein, Stanley Harrold, and Randall M. Miller, *Higher Education and the Civil Rights Movement: White Supremacy, Black Southerners, and College Campuses* (Gainesville, FL: University Press of Florida, 2009).

32. Stefan M. Bradley, *Upending the Ivory Tower: Civil Rights, Black Power, and the Ivy League* (New York: New York University Press, 2018).

33. Roger L. Geiger, Nathan M. Sorber, and Christian K. Anderson, eds., *American Higher Education in Postwar Era, 1945–1970. Perspectives on the History of Higher Education* (New York, NY: Routledge, 2018).

34. Geiger, *American Higher Education Since World War II*, chapters 6 and 7.

2 The Academic Engineers, 1890–1920

Understanding a Cohort of Higher Education Reformers

Ethan W. Ris

In the historiography of American higher education, ideas and innovations have traditionally been associated with individuals. We think of iconic leaders as typically university presidents who have championed reforms, introduced curricula, marshalled resources, and built institutions. This line of interpretation can be useful, but it can also create a sense that change in higher education operates on a punctuated equilibrium basis; things hum along in our colleges and universities until a Charles Eliot, Clark Kerr, or John Sperling emerges to shake up the entire sector. It makes for compelling reading, both biographical and autobiographical, but it ultimately tells us little about the longitudinal patterns of reform and innovation in our colleges and universities.

In this chapter, I offer a different type of narrative by seeking to situate ideas within ideological communities of higher education leaders that develop and evolve over time. It is a taxonomic approach that seeks to build on Paul Mattingly's recent work on broad sociopolitical trends in higher education, which he describes as "varied generational cultures."[1] Here, however, the focus is not on culture but on reform ideologies, and specifically on one generation of ideas-driven reformers.

I term these reformers "the academic engineers," a cadre that I have described at length elsewhere.[2] Most active between 1890 and 1920, they were not actual engineers by training, but they consciously borrowed the language and ethos of engineering in order to pursue a nationwide program of systemization and efficiency in the higher education sector, particularly in its non-elite tiers. They pursued this program using the normative and coercive control promised by two new institutional forms: the permanently endowed philanthropic foundation and the research university. Many of the academic engineers could be found on the boards and the payrolls of the two first foundations established by Andrew Carnegie and John D. Rockefeller, Sr.: respectively, the Carnegie Foundation for the Advancement of Teaching (CFAT) and the General Education Board (GEB). Each was endowed with $10 million in the spring of 1905, with equivalent mandates to pursue systemic reforms of the nation's colleges and universities.

I have described the academic engineers as analogous to the "administrative progressives" described by David Tyack as architects of K12 school reform in the decades around the turn of the 20th century. Both groups (which had considerable overlap) believed in top-down control of educational institutions by disinterested "experts," with a focus on creating consolidated systems with economies of scale, as well as best practices borrowed from business and industry.

The academic engineers had four overarching goals. The first was creating a nationwide system of higher education; as one of their leaders explained in 1908, they perceived colleges and universities as "inefficient, superficial, lacking, expert supervision. They are disjointed members of what ought to be a consistent system."[3] They pursued this by attempting to enforce universal curricular and administrative standards and organizing institutions into distinct status categories. The second goal concerned wresting control of colleges and universities away from suspect stakeholders like religious denominations and elected legislatures, and placing it in the hands of experts who were in sympathy with the academic engineers' ideals. The third goal involved eliminating competition between institutions, so that scarce financial resources from tuition, philanthropists, and taxpayers would not be spread too thin. They pushed this agenda by encouraging institutions to consolidate with their neighbors or to drop to sub-baccalaureate status as junior colleges or secondary academies, as well as by directing their gifts to bolster the prospects of "strong" colleges and universities while letting others wither for lack of resources. Finally, they sought to create normative hierarchies, both at the national level (including with the quixotic push for a University of the United States at the top of a nationwide pyramid) and at the state level, with singular research universities, both public and private, capping state systems whose lower tiers were populated by baccalaureate and sub-baccalaureate colleges under the control of the universities. The academic engineers pursued this last mission primarily through legislative efforts.

Informed readers will immediately note that much of the academic engineers' agenda went unfulfilled. We do not have a nationwide system of higher education; religious orders and elected officials still are quite involved with the sector; and competition is rampant, with 4,000 institutions scrapping for scarce resources. This failure is one reason that the academic engineers, as a cohort, have not received attention from historians. Much has been written about many of them as individuals, as well more modest amounts about the foundations themselves, but this scholarship tends to miss the broad, ideological nature of higher reform during these decades.[4] Yet, as I will argue in this chapter's conclusion, the academic engineers established a lasting logic about the causes of and solutions to higher education's biggest problems. Their ethos continues to inform debates over the form and function of American colleges and universities.

This chapter is not focused on describing the activities of the academic engineers, which I have done elsewhere, but rather on whom they were, where they came from, how they formulated their theory of change, and what set them apart from other generations of reformers. I will start with that final concept, in defining their cohort as distinct from the institution builders who preceded them and the self-critics who followed them. I will then describe the origins and mechanisms of the two groundbreaking foundations that provided homes for the academic engineers. Next, I will explain their ethos, rooted in the logic of engineering and in their status as "outsiders" within the higher education sector. Finally, before my forward-looking conclusion, I will offer biographical portraits of six exemplary academic engineers, focusing on their outsider origins and their beliefs about systemic change. Two were the founding leaders of the foundations: Henry Pritchett of the CFAT and Frederick Gates of the GEB. Two others were staff members of the foundations: John Bowman of the CFAT and Abraham Flexner of both. Two are apparent anomalies who actually fit directly into the academic engineering cohort: Booker T. Washington and the banker Frank Vanderlip. Each of these men came from unlikely origins to become leading higher education reformers, and each shared the same vision of systemic, efficiency-minded, top-down transformation that defined the academic engineering movement.

Situating the Academic Engineers

One interpretation of successive waves of reform is a pendulum swing between self-criticism within the elite tier of higher education and top-down reforms pushed by the self-satisfied leaders of that tier. Within that crude framework, the academic engineers certainly represent the latter swing, bookended by swings toward self-criticism. In order to add nuance to that description, however, it is helpful to take a closer look at the generations of reformers that preceded and followed the academic engineers.

The earlier group has arguably attracted the most attention, and celebration. We can think of them as the institution builders, operating primarily between 1850 and 1890. They include the founding presidents of ambitious new research universities like Andrew Dickson White at Cornell (founded 1865), Daniel Coit Gilman at Johns Hopkins (1876), and G. Stanley Hall at Clark (1887). These leaders, and their benefactors, established new institutions to counter the dominant trends in nineteenth century higher education. They were joined by reformist presidents who sought to transform existing universities. This trend arguably began with Francis Wayland's curricular reforms at Brown in 1850, continued with Henry Tappan's presidency of Michigan starting in 1852, and certainly included the transformations of Harvard and Yale under the respective leadership of Charles Eliot (inaugurated 1869) and Noah Porter (1871).

All of these leaders enacted reform by building institutions – either from scratch or by turning a college into a university. And to that end, their reformist vision was primarily an internal one. Yes, Tappan's vision of graduate education and Eliot's elective system quickly spread to many campuses around the country. But that spread was driven by normative isomorphism, not by any coercive mechanisms. Their new ideas about higher education took the form of self-criticism, and their reforms were inwardly directed.

The institution-builders' intellectual "grandchildren" were once again inward facing. A generation of reformers active between 1920 and 1960 turned their critical lens on themselves. The best example is Robert Maynard Hutchins, whose strident denunciations were directed at his own University of Chicago as much as anywhere else. It also included James Conant of Harvard and his "Red Book" general education project, and Robert Gordon Sproul, who focused his energies as University of California President on maintaining the university as a cohesive whole, including by sanctioning loyalty oaths. It also includes non-presidents like the conservative critics William F. Buckley and Russell Kirk, who launched their careers by attacking their own alma maters. To be sure, reformers did not dominate the mid-century decades known as the "golden age" of American higher education; these were often minority opinions, less dominant than the authors of the mostly copacetic Truman Report. Still, the reformist critiques that did come out of the era were primarily internal, typically with elite institutions as their targets.

The academic engineers had a very different vision than the generations of reformers that preceded and followed them. Their reforms were directed downward; elite universities were not the problem, but rather the solution. But the idea was not to replicate the research university model throughout the higher education sector. Instead, they sought to control and restrict the ambitions of lower-tier institutions. Their goal was a stratified, pyramidal system of higher education, with a handful of elite universities at the top and a vast collection of inferior institutions organized below them.

Higher Education Reform and the Origins of the Endowed Foundation

The academic engineers viewed research universities as the nodes of their nationwide system of higher education, but their mechanism for creating such a system came in a new institutional form: the endowed philanthropic foundation. A small handful of permanent funds were established after the Civil War, dedicated to primary and secondary education: most notably, the Peabody Education Fund and the Slater Fund. These were minor, by comparison, to two massive endowed foundations created in 1905 at the height of the academic engineering movement. Significantly, these two foundations were the first established by the two leading names of the history of American philanthropy: Andrew Carnegie and John D. Rockefeller, Sr.

The academic engineers did not adopt the apparatus of the foundation for their purposes; they, personally, developed it. We remember Carnegie's philanthropy, of course, but usually in two phases. The first dates to 1889, and his preaching of the "gospel of wealth." This phase was dominated by Carnegie's personal gifts, out of his own pocket, most notably to build public libraries. Then, we advance to his 1911 establishment of the massive Carnegie Corporation, designed as a permanently endowed philanthropic foundation to continue distributing the interest on his money in perpetuity. But in between came the Carnegie Institute of Washington (1902) and the Carnegie Foundation for the Advancement of Teaching (CFAT; 1905), his first endowed, chartered non-profit organizations – both dedicated to higher education reform. The Carnegie Institute was more closely linked to an earlier era of reform, with a charge to strengthen the research capacities of existing universities.[5] Its founding president was an institution-builder in the twilight of his career: Daniel Coit Gilman of Johns Hopkins. The Carnegie Foundation, by contrast, was focused on top-down control of a nationwide system of higher education. Its founding president was a leading academic engineer: Henry Pritchett, who I will discuss at length later in this chapter.

Similarly, Rockefeller did not first enter institutionalized philanthropy in 1913 with the creation of the massive Rockefeller Foundation. His creation of the General Education Board (GEB) predated his namesake philanthropy by a decade. The GEB is primarily remembered by historians for its work in primary and secondary education, especially in the Southern states. For the first three years after Rockefeller endowed it with one million dollars in 1902, it indeed focused its activities in that area. In 1905, however, he eclipsed his founding gift with one for $10 million, earmarked exclusively for higher education reform.[6] At its helm, he placed another of the most visible academic engineers: Frederick Gates, who I will also discuss at length later.

The academic engineers established these foundations with ambitious goals of control and organization. After Rockefeller's $10 million gift to the GEB, Gates immediately proposed using the money to create a national system of higher education. His platform had four planks, emphasizing that colleges and universities "must be comprehensively and efficiently distributed," that they "must be related to each other harmoniously and helpfully and not hurtfully," that they "should be each within its assigned compass," and finally that "the scheme, as a whole and in all its parts, must be essentially stable and permanent and not temporary or fluctuating."[7] The goals were vaguely worded, but they amounted to a vision for a network of institutions spread evenly throughout the country so as not to compete with one another for students and resources, and so that stability would be ensured through generous, permanent endowments. Rockefeller's gift money would be used to cultivate well-built and well-situated institutions, and at the same time the GEB would deliberately deny resources to less promising ones, in the hopes that they would wither away.

The CFAT leaders were more specific, and from all appearances, they operated behind a veil of benevolence. Carnegie's $10 million gift was earmarked exclusively for awarding pensions to retiring college professors. As I have described elsewhere, Carnegie had no fondness for professors or their work.[8] The pension scheme was not actually borne from benevolence, instead operating primarily to clear out "dead wood" from the professoriate. In a letter announcing his gift, Carnegie wrote that without guaranteed pensions, "Able men hesitate to adopt teaching as a career, and many old professors whose places should be occupied by younger men, cannot be retired."[9] Gates echoed this in a circumspect assessment of the plan:

> The purpose of this fund is stated to be to increase the efficiency of college teaching. This it aims to do in part by pensioning off inefficient college teachers so that their places may be supplied with younger and better instructors and possibly the founder may hope, erroneously I think, that ultimately an abler class of young men will be brought into the teaching profession.[10]

CFAT's mission went well beyond cleaning up the professorate; it transparently sought to control and reform American higher education at a systemic level. From the start, Carnegie granted the foundation expansive power to promote systemization and standardization in the sector. The CFAT charter established firm criteria for admitting institutions into the pension system, and Carnegie's gift letter authorized the board to impose additional "terms and conditions" on participating schools, "in case two-thirds of the Trustees decide that times have so changed that the form specified is no longer the best way to aid the cause we have all at heart."[11] In a variation of Gates' vision for the GEB, Carnegie and Pritchett's goal was to deny resources and status to subpar institutions, whose choice would be to reform or perish. Within its first year of operations, the board announced a minimum definition of a "college," requiring that participating institutions have at least six full-time professors, an endowment over $200,000, and an admissions policy that required matriculating students to have completed a specific sequence of high school coursework. This final provision is of course the origin of the "Carnegie Unit."

The foundation was thus far more than a pension fund. As Pritchett explained in 1906, it was "a central agency in educational administration" that would promote the progressive ideal:

> The idea of the scope of the Carnegie Foundation for the Advancement of Teaching as a centralizing and standardizing influence in American education promises to outweigh in importance the primary purpose of the fund, great as that primary purpose is.[12]

A decade later, the longtime CFAT official Clyde Furst collectively credited his organization and the GEB with having transcended the interests of individual institutions in the spirit of social control:

> The educational foundations represent an even broader view of universities and colleges, approaching them not only through their institutional history and functions, but chiefly from the point of view of social need, so far as this can be apprehended. . . . [T]hey have preached the difficult doctrine that a college is known and rewarded according to its fruits, not according to its intentions or its desires.[13]

The Engineering Ideal in Higher Education Reform

History best remembers the Carnegie Foundation for the Advancement of Teaching for its famous "Bulletin Number Four" on medical education, also known as the Flexner Report. Less attention is extended to "Bulletin Number Five," also issued in 1910: a report titled "Academic and Industrial Efficiency." Its author, Morris Llewellyn Cooke, described by his biographer as the archetypal "progressive engineer," had a lifelong admiration for the "Social Darwinist" philosopher Herbert Spencer. (Carnegie was also an ardent disciple of Spencer.) However, he also had a closer guiding light in his neighbor in Philadelphia, Frederick Taylor, whose theory of "scientific management" electrified the American intellectual class in the first decades of the 20th century.[14] After a period of informal study, Taylor chose Cooke as his special assistant when he was elected president of the American Society of Mechanical Engineers in 1906. Cooke absorbed Taylor's gospel of scientific management and sought to extend it beyond the factory floor; as Christie writes, "to lead the way toward social betterment was, in his eyes, both the social responsibility and the professional opportunity of engineers."[15]

Engineering was both a set of skills and, as Taylorites soon came to argue, a philosophy for the administration of organizations and society itself. In a 1904 speech, Pritchett explained that "The engineer today is no longer a mere specialist; he is also the executive officer, the manager, the agent, the director of great business enterprises." The logic ran both ways: engineers could apply their vision to many different domains in need of reform, and administrators of all stripes, including those like Pritchett and Gates who had no training in the discipline, could also pick up the mantle of the engineer whenever it suited them.

Short of Taylor himself, Cooke was the ideal critic of American higher education as far as the academic engineers were concerned. Here was a clear-eyed, impartial judge, whose engineering expertise qualified him to make sweeping judgments about how to reorganize whole sectors of economy and society. In the preface to "Bulletin Number Five," Pritchett declared that the "standpoint" from which the author had conducted his investigation "is the same which Mr. Cooke takes when he examines a manufacturing concern." He explained that while the college should be

> viewed from a different standpoint than that of factory efficiency, it is still true that all large and continuing causes rest upon formal organization and upon some assumed machinery of administration. . . . In any event, only good can come to an organization – whether it be commercial, educational, or religious – when a friendly hand turns the light of public scrutiny upon its methods, resources and aims.[16]

Cooke lived up to the task. His introduction blithely declared that the challenges of American higher education were universal, and thus simple: "As a matter of fact, from the standpoint of organization, uniformity in collegiate management is a much easier problem than it is in most industries, because in any industry which I know about, the individual plants vary considerably more than do the colleges."[17]

That uniformity, however, extended only to the form of the American college, and not to its internal or external functioning:

> Perhaps the most notable feature of collegiate administration is the entire absence of uniformity or accepted standardization. . . . At nearly every institution progress has been made along certain lines, but generally it has been a 'lone fight;' one institution doing one thing and another doing another, without any of the mutual help and cooperation which is given in the business world.[18]

Cooke went on to detail numerous sins in institutional management, including an overreliance on faculty committees, an absence of rational financial accounting, and the inefficient use of buildings and classrooms.

Cooke was far from the only person applying the rhetoric of industrial efficiency to higher education. Charles F. Birdseye, a prominent New York lawyer and reformer whose son went on to found the Birdseye frozen foods empire, was blunt in a 1909 lament: "These terrible losses in educational efficiency and results come from the unwillingness of the American college to learn from and in part to pattern after the American factory."[19] In 1912, a group of actual engineers organized a symposium in Boston on "Scientific Management and Efficiency in College Administration." Some participants were harsh on leadership: "The manager of the factory knows that he knows nothing about the best way of running a factory and therefore calls in outside expert assistance; the manager of the college thinks he knows it all, and therefore has no need of advice."[20]

Others turned to the question of students, acknowledging that the college had some advantages ("It would be to any industrial organization an asset of untold value to have among its employees and esprit de corps at all approaching 'college spirit' ")[21] but also pointing out that many students squandered their college years on frivolous pursuits that wrecked their efficiency ratios, which were weighted down with heavy inputs in terms of time and tuition.

The academic engineers, however, thought not primarily about students and individual administrators, but about institutions and systems. Pritchett made this case in a 1906 speech that borrowed the term "prime mover" from engineering:

> A college is one of the prime movers in our social order. Into it is poured an enormous stream of human energy: the energy of devotion, of high scholarship, of unselfish service, and the potential energy of wealth. There is constantly being fed into it a never-ending stream of youth, impressionable, responsive, full of possibilities. It is the business of this educational prime mover to produce educated men and women, strong for citizenship, for scholarship, for the world's work. There can be no question that all colleges do produce some such men and women; but is the college an efficient prime mover in education? Is its product in proportion to the energy poured into it? Is its co-efficient of efficiency high or low?[22]

Pritchett would spend his career trying to answer those questions. And his position in control of a huge endowment made his answers particularly salient. Cooke took note of this in his report, explaining that efficiency was not just an end in itself, but rather a means to attract the attention of benefactors with deep pockets:

> Every one likes to feel that the money which he devotes to educational and charitable and philanthropic purposes is well expended; and other things being equal, that university or that department within a university, which has an organization making possible the highest efficiency will in the long run receive the greatest consideration from such public benefactors.[23]

That utilitarianism aside, the academic engineers took the engineering ideal seriously. They were of course not actual engineers (as Taylor and Cooke were), but they revered – even fetishized – engineering. The discipline, which had only been formalized in the 1880s,[24] spoke to the central goals of the effort to reshape the form and function of higher education. "Efficiency," above all, was a ubiquitous buzzword for the reformers. As Pritchett's quotation shows, they viewed colleges and universities as engines with inputs and outputs; conserving a low ratio of the former (financial assistance, both from philanthropic giving and from tax dollars) to the latter, (the production of human capital and useful knowledge) represented the pinnacle of academic engineering.

In prevalence, however, the word "system" may have even outranked "efficiency" in the rhetoric of the academic engineers. It spoke to a desire to emulate best practices from Taylorism and the great industrial trusts.[25] But more importantly, it spoke to their hunger for ongoing control of colleges and universities. Laurence Veysey claimed that the development of the American university had reaching a "stopping place" by 1910: "An architect [was] no longer needed, only a contractor."[26] That may have been true for the university itself, but certainly not for the yearned-for higher education "system." The individuals who were still passionately working toward reform in 1910 did not see the higher education sector as a static edifice. The institution-builders that came before them had indeed created some magnificent edifices, but new generation's goals were even more ambitious. They were neither architects nor contractors. They sought, instead, to craft a dynamic system – one that needed the constant tending of highly skilled engineers.

Insiders and Outsiders

Earlier, I emphasized that the generations of reformers who operated primarily before 1890 and after 1920 directed their critical gaze inwardly. As such, it makes sense that their ranks were dominated by the "insider" leaders of elite institutions, whose task was to both create and improve the acme of American higher education. The academic engineers, by contrast, were focused on reforming the entirety of the sector, with an overwhelming focus on its non-elite tiers. Therefore, I classify them as outsider reformers.

That is not to say that the academic engineers did not include institutional leaders. For example, perhaps no one fit the description of an academic engineer quite as well as Nicholas Murray Butler, president of Columbia and a longtime CFAT board member. In his many roles, however, Butler established himself primarily as a reformer not of Columbia itself, but of other, less elite, institutions. These included small colleges in greater New York that he brought into the orbit of Columbia, the New York public schools (whose systemic reform he led), and the vast array of colleges subject to the carrots and sticks of the Carnegie Foundation. He was joined on that board by William Rainey Harper, founding president of the University of Chicago. Harper was an institution-builder, but like Butler he was also heavily involved in reforming "lesser" institutions, including the Chicago public schools. His signature contribution to top-down reform, first discussed in a 1900 book, was the promulgation of the junior college.[27] This was perhaps the best example of the reformers' dream of populating the vast base of the higher education pyramid with subordinate institutions controlled by a few elite universities. In Harper's University of Chicago's "affiliation" scheme, small colleges gave up their autonomy to benefit from the expertise and articulation opportunities of the university.[28]

These university leaders within the academic engineering movement also tended to share another credential that lent them a prestigious form of "outsider" status: experiences pursuing graduate education in Germany. Whereas some of the earlier generation of reformers had investigated and openly expressed admiration of German universities, these individuals had actually spent real time there. One of their contemporary critics, Upton Sinclair, made this connection in his customary flamboyant language, linking their German training with their elitist reform dogma:

> one after another of these academic drill-sergeants – Butler of Columbia, Berlin – Lowell of Harvard, Berlin – Smith of Pennsylvania, Goettingen . . . Angell of Yale, Berlin – Wheeler of California, Heidelberg – Wilbur of Stanford, Frankfurt and Munich – every one of them learned the Goose-step under the Kaiser![29]

Among the other reformers I profile in the next section, Pritchett and Flexner also undertook graduate study in Germany.

Furthermore, with their commitment to the top-down reform of less prestigious institutions, the academic engineers positioned themselves as external critics, a position that aligned with the Progressive Era ideal of management by disinterested elites. Wallace Buttrick, who helped Gates run the GEB, habitually described his organization as "the layman's contribution to education."[30] Butler expressed this ethos in saying that "The United States is in sore need today of an aristocracy of intellect and service" – a counterpoint to insider know-how.[31] In the realm of colleges and universities, this meant the hierarchical authority of scientific management, as opposed to self-governance by educators. Furst explained that such "intellect" did not extend to professors, who "notably interrupt and waste the time of specialists in matters in which they are not expert. . . . Industrial organization would substitute a so-called functional management that would allow the specialist authority and freedom in the field in which he is expert, and free him from the claims of anything else."[32]

Semantics aside, many of the academic engineers were true outsiders, by merit of both their educations and their biographies. They shared that status, not coincidentally, with their primary benefactors. Carnegie was an immigrant with a grade school education. Rockefeller was born in poverty in far upstate New York, and his postsecondary education amounted to ten weeks at Folsom's Commercial College in Ohio. Although both would eventually donate the latter-day equivalent of billions of dollars to colleges and universities, they each were deeply skeptical of both the form and function of higher education. Accordingly, they had no qualms about surrounding themselves with allies who had similarly spotty academic backgrounds and outsider status.

The section that follows provides sketches of six exemplary academic engineers, each of them very prominent in their day and closely linked to the CFAT and GEB circles. All had haphazard postsecondary educations, and only two held bachelor's degrees. All were administrators: of foundations, businesses, institutes, and postsecondary institutions. All were geographical outsiders, having grown up in the Midwest or South before careers revolving around the business and philanthropic world of New York City. And finally, all shared the same forceful vision of top-down systemic reform that was the defining feature of the academic engineering movement.

Portraits of Exemplary Academic Engineers

Frederick T. Gates

The Reverend "Fred" Gates is best described as Rockefeller's *consigliere* on philanthropic matters, as well as the architect and leader of the GEB for its first decade. Rockefeller trusted Baptist ministers. Although Gates' pastoral days ended before the two met, he retained the spirit of the evangelical revivalism of upstate New York's "burned-over district," where both men were born before moving to the Midwest as children.

He was a striking character. Judith Sealander describes Gates as "arms waving, long white hair flowing wildly . . . characteristically banging a table with the flat of his hand" in meetings.[33] Ron Chernow describes his "prosecutorial zeal and ministerial fervor." John Boyer calls him "a tough-minded rationalist with little patience for soft-hearted social causes."[34] Raymond Fosdick, who worked with him as a young man, calls him a "a dominating and sagacious man . . . fundamentally a figure of ardor and zeal, with little humor – either about himself or anything else – and with very few doubts."[35]

Although he later became closely identified with other Rockefeller causes, including medicine, Gates's first and most ardent passion was higher education reform. Most notably, he relentlessly sought to systemize and strengthen promising American colleges and universities, while reserving special scorn for weak institutions in isolated locations.

His contemporary Sigmund Freud would have had some psychoanalytical fun with this obsession, given Gates' personal background in higher education. His first *alma mater* was Highland University in rural Kansas, a very modest institution. In his memoirs, Gates reports that it was just a single building,

> two stories, of fifty by eighty feet. . . . We had no great and splendid groups of buildings, no long line of distinguished alumni, presidents, professors, and trustees. We had none of the pride of age or wealth. But we were there for mental work, not play, or amusement, or institutional prestige.[36]

He spent eight years at the institution.

At age 22, he entered the University of Rochester, which only held slightly more claim to the moniker of "university," with less than 200 students and no real graduate training. Gates remembered it as "then a small college under Baptist auspices."[37] Fosdick is blunter, calling it "a Baptist institution whose search for candidates was not handicapped by considerations of academic standards."[38] Gates was blasé about his experience, writing "My college course simply confirmed me in habits of study, reading, and reflection. I can truthfully say little else for it." He also echoed Carnegie's brand of book-based autodidactism, based on his experience of teaching himself classics: "The solitary work on Greek confirmed in me the belief that with modern textbooks a man with reasonable independence and self-reliance need not be dependent on a college classroom."[39] He did not earn a bachelor's degree, and instead transferred his studies to the affiliated Rochester Theological Seminary.

Gates next spent eight years as a minister in Minneapolis, and then in 1888 was chosen as the first executive secretary of the newly founded American Baptist Education Society, largely on his reputation as a tireless fundraiser for Minnesota schools and churches. The organization had oversight of hundreds of loosely connected institutions serving all ages, but Gates immediately fixed his reformist eyes on the "higher" part of the jumbled educational pyramid. Within months he had thrust himself forcefully into the cause of establishing a flagship Baptist institution, as described earlier, issuing a report called "The Need for a Baptist University in Chicago, as Illustrated by a Study of Baptist College Education in the West."

The document is perhaps the ur-text of academic engineering. Gates argued for far more than the endowment of a new institution. Brimming with hastily gathered statistics, charts, and maps, the report laid out a scathing criticism of existing Baptist higher education, which existed in "a state of destitution" and desperately needed top-down reformation. The primary function of a new university would be a normative one, Gates explained: "Before its walls were reared, before its foundations could be laid, the mere assurance of such an enterprise made certainly by means provided would lift up the heads of our colleges and clothe them with renewed vigor and larger influence."[40] His 1888 vision of a dynamic hierarchical system set the tone for much of the academic engineering project of the next three decades. So did his goal of using that ethos to yield philanthropic dollars, as he revealed in a letter to a colleague that same year: "A scheme so vast, so continental, so orderly, so comprehensive, so detailed, will in my view capture a mind so constituted as Mr. Rockefeller's is."[41]

Rockefeller was soon signed up for the project of forming what Chernow calls "an educational trust of Western colleges."[42] More importantly, the industrialist's pocketbook was open to the cause of academic engineering, and the fingers in that pocketbook were Gates's.

The utmost expressions of that relationship took place in the workings of the GEB. Gates was on its board from the beginning and served as its chairman from 1907–1917. Curiously, he devoted just six pages of his memoirs to the organization that he ran. Still, he took care to gloat about its Congressional charter, a first for a philanthropic foundation, which allowed the board "authority to hold limitless capital and to do anything whatever which could be construed to be directly or even remotely educational."[43] He also admitted to ghostwriting Rockefeller's gift letter for his 1905 pledge, which earmarked $10 million for efforts to "promote a comprehensive system of higher education in the United States."[44]

Gates wielded his self-given mandate with vigor, always insisting that the GEB's grants be made with an eye to fostering a balanced national system of colleges and universities. He was especially obsessed with the geography of this hoped-for system. In an obituary in the official GEB bulletin after his death in 1929, the board wrote:

> The great map of the United States which hung on the walls of the General Education Board Room and to which he frequently turned to make graphic his thought and expression symbolized the large way in which his mind worked. Thus he would mark the great fortresses and the outposts of higher education in this country.[45]

The GEB's first public report, published in 1916, contained 31 maps, including oddities like "Map showing the percentage of students coming from within 50 and 100 miles and enrolled in the four regular college classes of Williams College."[46] A 1910 memo from Gates to John D. Rockefeller, Jr., explained his obsession, mixed with a different metaphor:

> I want to see a hundred colleges in this country so planted as to cover the whole land and leave no part destitute, each of them planted in a fruitful soil, each so planted that it shall not be overshadowed by others, each conducted under such auspices as will take care of it,

see that it is watered, particularly in its earlier years, see that it is properly fertilized, see that the forces of destruction which always fasten themselves on institutions shall be pruned away.[47]

This vision, of course, did not come to be, but in his memoirs, Gates flatly credited the GEB with the successful wholesale reform of American colleges and universities. In 1905, he recalled, "I had a reasonably clear bird's-eye view of the whole field and, while there was much to encourage, there was much also to regret. The picture was one of chaos." In 1926, after two decades of the academic engineering project, he could say of the US: "Clearly we have the most efficient system of higher education in the world."[48]

Henry S. Pritchett

Of all the academic engineers, Henry Pritchett experienced perhaps the most dramatic fall from fame to obscurity. We have only three significant explorations of the life and work of the man who served for twenty-five years as the CFAT's founding president: a 1943 biography by Flexner, and two histories of the CFAT, in 1953 and 1983.[49] These were not impromptu scholarly inquiries; all three were commissioned by the Carnegie Corporation. And yet, Pritchett was well-known and highly influential in his day, especially in the key years from 1905–1915. As the foundation's leader, he authored book-length annual reports, gave countless speeches, and published constantly in popular news magazines. Ellen Lagemann, in her 1983 CFAT history, writes: "His rhetoric, embroidered with facts and statistics, was often stirring and earnestly moral. His opinions derived from principle and were tenaciously argued and adhered to."[50] Flexner is even more generous but still hints at his dogmatic streak: "He had a consciousness of what was right which never deserted him. He had 'the prepared mind,' upon the importance of which Pasteur had insisted, but how it was prepared is not known."[51]

On that note, Pritchett's higher education was decidedly haphazard. Whether or not he held a bachelor's degree is in dispute: Flexner claims he did, Lagemann says he did not, and his own unpublished memoir does not mention one.[52] Most of his education took place in rural Missouri at an institution variously known as Pritchett School Institute or Pritchett College, operated by his father. He left at age 18 for training in astronomy at the Naval Observatory in Washington, before returning to Missouri four years later to take a job as the director of an observatory in his hometown. He parlayed this opportunity into an observatory job at Washington University in St. Louis, and eventually a professorship there. Finally, at age 37, he rounded off his education with a PhD, earned at the University of Munich. According to Flexner, he completed the degree in just eight months, during which time he also toured extensively across Europe with his teenage sons.[53]

At 43, Pritchett found himself the president of an urban technical college commonly called "Boston Tech." Its full name was the Massachusetts Institute of Technology, but it was years from being MIT, in terms of both nomenclature and prestige.[54] It was in this capacity that Pritchett first got to know Andrew Carnegie, who had a strong interest in technical education. The industrialist consulted with him often on matters related to the Carnegie Institution of Washington (which counted astronomy as one of its chief foci) and in fact lobbied for him to become the institution's president upon Daniel Coit Gilman's retirement in 1904. In that year, Carnegie wrote to a trustee that "I was very favorably impressed with my friend Pritchett. . . . He seems one of the men who can do things."[55] Pritchett actively pursued this opportunity, but the trustees ultimately passed him over in favor of Robert Woodward, whose candidacy another trustee predicted "would meet with the general approval of the Scientific men of the Country to a much greater extent than would that of Dr. Pritchett."[56] Still, Carnegie continued trying finding a leadership role for this budding reformer.

The two men also saw eye-to-eye on the vision of a bifurcated system of higher education. When Pritchett took the reins at MIT, it was located in cramped quarters in the city of Boston and served commuter students who came to study applied technical fields. This was a situation most unbefitting the research university the young president aspired to lead. Working with the Boston philanthropist Henry Lee Higginson, in 1904 he convinced Carnegie to contribute $400,000 to establish a new technical school in Boston. Pritchett's brilliant apparatus was to convince the industrialist to match a century-old bequest left to the city of Boston by Benjamin Franklin. The association with the most famous American autodidact proved too great to resist, and Carnegie put up the cash to establish the Franklin Institute of Technology in the city's working-class South End. Thus divested from the burden of training Boston's industrial workers, Pritchett was free to pursue his plan of relocating the institute to Cambridge and the academic halo of Harvard.[57]

The next collaboration came quickly, with the establishment of the CFAT. In 1904, Pritchett was seeking contributions to MIT's pension fund, which had already been endowed with $100,000 by another donor.[58] Other, more robust, universities had better-endowed pension plans, including Columbia, Yale, Harvard, and Cornell; German universities also had a long history of professorial pensions.[59] Carnegie declined to contribute to the MIT fund, but proposed a much farther-reaching plan to extend pensions to dozens of institutions as a step toward systematizing the higher education sector. Writing in February of 1905, Pritchett jumped on board with Carnegie's proposal: "Since I talked with you I have been thinking over your idea of a large plan for dealing with the problem of retired pay or insurance for the principal American institutions of learning, and the more I think of it the more feasible the plan seems."[60]

He agreed to run the numbers on what such a scheme would entail, working with Frank Vanderlip, a bank president and Carnegie confidant, as actuarial advisor. Two months later, the research was done, and Carnegie donated $10,000,000 to the still-unnamed foundation, with the clear expectation that professorial pensions would be used as coercive "carrots" spurring reform in colleges and universities.

Pritchett would spend the rest of his professional life wielding the CFAT presidency as a cudgel for the academic engineering agenda. He was immediately cognizant of this power, writing in 1906: "The idea of the scope of the Carnegie Foundation for the Advancement of Teaching as a centralizing and standardizing influence in American education promises to outweigh in importance the primary purpose of the fund, great as that primary purpose is."[61] Like Gates, he held a special, perverse antipathy toward humble colleges like the one he had attended himself, writing in 1908:

> We have founded many more colleges under this system than we can possibly maintain, colleges which are colleges in name only and which will for many years continue to demoralize our standards of education and to place before our people false ideas of what education is. Ultimately, perhaps, the weaker and more objectionable of these colleges will disappear.[62]

Frank Vanderlip

Pritchett's partner in the actuarial framing of the CFAT also started out as an outsider. Frank Vanderlip, vice president and soon-to-be president of the enormous National City Bank in New York, was born in rural Illinois. He was immensely proud of his rustic roots, titling his 1935 memoir, *From Farm Boy to Financier*. He is best remembered as a member of the secretive "Jekyll Island group" that formulated the Federal Reserve System in 1911, but he took plenty of time along the way for the cause of academic engineering.

Like Pritchett, whom he called "my closest friend," Vanderlip had a spotty higher education.[63] It took place at the University of Illinois, his second choice of institution after an initial dream of studying electrical engineering at Cornell. He lasted just one year before returning to his adopted hometown of Aurora, taking a correspondence course in shorthand, and landing a job as an editor at a local newspaper. This turned into years as a business reporter for the *Chicago Tribune*, a position in the Treasury Department (where he first met Pritchett, who was also working in Washington at the time), and eventually bank leadership in Manhattan. The banker went beyond autodidactism into plain anti-intellectualism. Carnegie revered libraries as hubs of self-directed learning, but Vanderlip described even their limits in a 1905 speech: "Book covers contain much knowledge, but may also shut out from a too close student much wisdom, – much of that sort of wisdom which is gained by experience in the world."

Vanderlip was blunt, the kind of bank president who could tell a gathering of bank clerks:

> Certainly you cannot all be bank presidents. We need many privates, and comparatively few generals. Not a few of you, filled with ambition though you may be to-day, will go on year after year in faithful regularity . . . never advancing to the highest positions.[64]

He was equally blunt when it came to a favorite topic, education reform. The cause of many higher education controversies, he claimed in May 1905, was that "the solution of the problem has been left too largely in the hands of educators."[65]

Instead, he suggested that he and his outsider peers had the knowledge to whip the nation's colleges and universities into shape. They also had the money to do it. In the same speech, he predicted the beneficent influence of

> a great central fund, the object of which should be so to distribute the income as to give effective force to an impulse toward co-ordination of our whole system of higher education. If such a fund were in the hands of the wisest body of men that could be brought together for that purpose, it could be so used that it would stimulate the educational system to a symmetrical growth.[66]

That fund, of course, was the CFAT, which he had helped establish the previous month; the "wisest body of men" comprised himself, Pritchett, Carnegie, and their fellow academic engineers on the foundation's board. Vanderlip frankly explained the first goal of the endowment as "the useful purpose of retiring faculty members who have passed their day of usefulness and who, in the interest of highest efficiency, had best make way for others." But he went on to explain that their work would go far beyond that, into organizing a rational system of higher education along the lines of an ideally engineered machine, which included his echo of Gates in calling for "symmetrical growth." "The highest possible success," he declared, "for an institution of learning is to become a perfectly efficient unit in a perfectly co-ordinated scheme."[67]

Vanderlip's interest in education reform ebbed and flowed. He served on the CFAT board for years and established the first Montessori school in the United States, but became consumed by financial matters and a feud with John D. Rockefeller, Sr.'s brother William, who eventually forced him out as president of the National City Bank. Nevertheless, he is emblematic of the interlocking directorate of the Progressive Era. A muckraking author calculated in 1914 that he sat on twenty-one corporate boards, in addition to the boards of the CFAT and New York University; on these he overlapped with many fellow CFAT and GEB trustees.[68] Despite his feud with William and his association with Carnegie, he was also enmeshed in the Rockefeller circle. His close collaborator on the Federal Reserve plan was Sen. Nelson Aldrich, John D. Rockefeller Jr.'s father-in-law and the force behind the Congressional charter for the GEB. This type of social capital underlay the concentrated power of the academic engineering movement.

Abraham Flexner

Many of the academic engineers can be simply described; Abraham Flexner cannot. More than anyone, he managed to be both a relentless gadfly criticizing higher education and a moth drawn continually to its flame. We can certainly classify him as an outsider. He hailed from Kentucky, the son of Jewish immigrants from Germany. He and his siblings, however, were secular, as he recalled in his memoir: "For us Herbert Spencer and Huxley, then at the height of their fame and influence, replaced the Bible and the prayer book."[69] Flexner's worship of Spencer, a former civil engineer who went on to become the father of "social Darwinism," echoed Cooke's and Carnegie's.[70] All three thrilled at Spencer's assurance that human society could become continually more robust through the attrition of its weaker links. This theory would be foremost in Flexner's mind when he turned it to the study of educational institutions.

Flexner's own higher education took place at the cutting edge, in flames of effort that often burned out quickly. At age 17, he enrolled at Johns Hopkins, then just eight years old and branded as the only "true" university in North America. Daniel Coit Gilman's hard-headed empiricism was always a touchstone for Flexner:

> There was no froth in the Johns Hopkins University of my time. . . . I never heard President Gilman or any member of the academic staff urge that the supreme end of a college education is "citizenship" or "character," the slogans under which much modern inefficiency is cloaked.[71]

He certainly took the efficiency ethos to heart as an undergraduate, earning his bachelor's degree in two frenzied years and returning to Louisville before he could even receive his diploma. By his own admission, he had made just one friend among his classmates.[72]

Flexner embarked on a high school teaching career in his hometown, eventually opening his own private college prep school, heavily influenced by Deweyan pedagogy.[73] He married well; his wife wrote a hugely successful play that debuted in New York in 1904. *Mrs. Wiggs of the Cabbage Patch* brought in enough money for Flexner to shut down his school and resume his own higher education. He went first to Harvard, studying under Hugo Münsterberg, an experimental psychologist; Flexner quit his lab after a few months, and Harvard itself after one year.[74] The next stop was Europe, where he toured Oxford and Cambridge and attended classes at the prestigious universities of Berlin and Heidelberg. He never earnestly pursued a degree, however. Instead, he pursued a job.

In Heidelberg, when he should have been writing a dissertation, Flexner instead wrote a slim volume called *The American College: A Criticism*. Published stateside in 1908, it was a scathing indictment of undergraduate education. Some of his comments were simply cruel: "our college students are, and for the most part, emerge, flighty, superficial and immature, lacking, as a class, concentration, seriousness and thoroughness."[75] But elsewhere, he appeared to be plainly appealing to Carnegie's self-made man ideal. He wrote of the graduate: "The college leaves him 'soft'; he has had no such discipline, no such biting realization of consequences as one gets out in the rough and tumble of the world. . . . Practical life with its intense, narrow urgencies binds up the shattered personality, focuses the dispersed energies."[76] Other passages appealed to the broad ethos of academic engineering. The in-vogue elective system of undergraduate study, he wrote, "impoverishes and isolates by excessive and premature specialism where it does not waste by aimless dispersion."[77] In its place, he called for "a more intelligent, systematic and fearless experiment" in college education.[78]

In his memoir, Flexner noted that a copy of *The American College* "fell into the hands of" Henry Pritchett. In reality, it appears to have been written directly for him, citing him extensively and plainly appealing to his sense of educational efficiency. The plan worked; within months, Flexner was on the CFAT payroll, heading a major reform project and working on "an unlimited expense account."[79]

His assigned target for this first project was not undergraduate education, the subject of his book. In the spirit of outsider reform, Pritchett tasked him with a study of medical education, a field in which he had no experience.[80] As with the Cooke report, the academic engineers considered a neophyte's perspective superior to that of a sympathetic insider. Armed with cash and a cause, in less than two years he personally inspected every medical school in the United States and Canada. His research methods were cursory at best; he wrote in his memoir "In the course of a few hours a reliable estimate could be made respecting the possibilities of teaching modern medicine in almost any one of the 155 schools I visited."[81] His final report, published in 1910 as the CFAT's

"Bulletin Number Four" was a virulent attack on most medical schools, finding low standards and shoddy instruction at all but a handful of institutions. His prose was cutting, but it slashed with wit rather than stridency. Of the prospective student, he wrote:

> Her choice is free and varied. She will find schools of every grade accessible: the Johns Hopkins, if she has an academic degree; Cornell, if she has three-fourths of one; Rush and the state universities, if she prefers the combined six years' course; Toronto on the basis of a high school education; Meridian, Mississippi, if she has had no definable education at all.[82]

The "Flexner Report" propelled its author to sudden, lasting fame. It had other major effects, as well. The report is generally credited with the wholesale reform of medical education; within two years of its publication, 30 percent of medical schools in the United States had shut their doors, and the others were frantically taking steps to modernize their curricula and facilities.[83] Carnegie was delighted with the results, writing to Eliot that he welcomed the uproar: "I am quite prepared for the wrath of all the quacks. . . . The bogus 'Colleges' and even 'Universities,' so cald [sic], will soon be things of the past."[84] The report also put the potential of academic engineering on full display, not just for educators and the public, but for funders as well (in 1913, Carnegie donated another $1.25 million to the CFAT to fund a "Division of Educational Enquiry" that would produce similar reports).

Flexner's career as an academic engineer was just beginning. After authoring two more reports for the CFAT he was poached by Gates in 1912, to join the staff of the GEB. He produced voluminous work there on higher education reform for nearly two decades, before leaving for other pursuits including the founding of the Institute of Advanced Studies at Princeton. By that point he was increasingly focused on promoting basic research, which he called "the usefulness of useless knowledge."[85] He never lost his zeal, however, reinserting himself into the higher education debate at age 64 with a book, *Universities: American, English, German*, that reprised many of his themes from *The American College*. Like its predecessor, it brought recognition to its author but had nothing of the impact of his report on medical education. In 1994, Clark Kerr memorably described it as important, but "so wrong":

> Flexner was too addicted to all-out criticism as a mechanism of change. This led him to look mostly for items to criticize in American universities. This led him to unbalanced views. This led him to unbalanced judgements about needed reforms – too drastic.[86]

An assessment of one man, but also an assessment of an entire movement.

John G. Bowman

Flexner was not the only young man who turned academic engineering into a lifelong career. John Gabbert Bowman matched him for that, as well as for zeal and imperiousness. As his peers described earlier, he was born far from the metropole, in Iowa. Unlike them, he had a normal undergraduate education: four years at the University of Iowa leading to a BA, which he followed up with a master's degree at the same institution in 1904. Shortly after, he made his way to New York and a job at Columbia University. The few historiographical references to Bowman describe him as a faculty member there,[87] but the 1906–1907 Columbia catalogue lists him as a tutor in the English department.[88] Regardless, teaching was not in the cards for Bowman. He seems to have caught the eye of Nicholas Murray Butler, and by mid-1907, he was on the Carnegie Foundation's staff, serving as secretary.

The CFAT archives indicate that the bulk of Bowman's duties there were undertaken as Pritchett's enforcer. When professors or college presidents wrote to the foundation to protest its policies (typically in relation to their status on its list of schools approved for pensions), Bowman conducted the back-and-forth. He had a knack for extreme stubbornness and a fondness for rules, many of which he appears to have made himself on an ad hoc basis. He could even be a stickler on the topic of Classics, which Carnegie despised and Pritchett spent little thought on. A series of increasingly distressed letters from the Registrar of Bowdoin College reveal a typical scenario. In yet another demand for higher admission standards, Bowman wrote conciliatorily: "I do not wish to insist upon any dogmatic method of stating requirements." But he quickly went on to insist on very specific curricula:

If it is evidenced then that your standard for Book II of Xenophon is distinctly higher than the standard required, let us say, at Columbia University where four books are required in satisfaction of the Elementary Greek, there will be no further difficulty in the matter.[89]

After four years of this type of nit-picking, Bowman was ready for a new job. He found one at his alma mater – as its president. The Iowa Board of Education had forced out the university's president and needed a new one. According to Stow Persons, it took them just a month to offer the job to the 33-year-old Bowman, based a bit on his Iowa pedigree but mostly on the weight of his CFAT affiliation: "Clearly, no very extensive search had been deemed necessary. President Pritchett's recommendation of Bowman had been sufficient to secure the appointment."[90] He did not last long. Persons calls Bowman's three-year tenure at the University of Iowa "brief and unhappy." The faculty hated him, finding him to be "an exceedingly tough, ruthless individual, 'a little Napoleon.' "[91]

After being forced out of office in 1914, Bowman temporarily left the world of higher education reform. His successor at the CFAT wrote after his dismissal from Iowa that there was "no thought either on Mr. Bowman's part or that of the Foundation of his returning to our work."[92] He spent six years running the American College of Surgeons before reemerging as a university leader.

His new job was as the chancellor of the University of Pittsburgh, in Carnegie's adopted hometown. Surely, Bowman's CFAT pedigree helped him land the job, as did his reputation as a hard-headed reformer. Pittsburgh had low status and massive debt, and it needed a savior. One of Bowman's conditions for taking the job was the end of academic tenure, which he replaced with one-year contracts for all professors. The move was emblematic of his autocratic administration. Christian Anderson writes that students saw him as "a tyrannical patriarch," while the American Association of University Professors repeatedly censured him for repressing academic freedom. However, he remained on good terms with the university's trustees and the Pittsburgh business community. These groups (which overlapped, of course) enthusiastically supported his signature project: the building of the 42-story "Cathedral of Learning," whose construction occupied more than a decade of his tenure.[93] Bowman conceived of the tower as a symbol of the lofty status of the research university, a constant obsession in the academic engineering movement.

In many ways, Bowman was the last academic engineer, as well as a transition figure to the generation that followed. His chancellorship at Pitt lasted until 1945, three decades after the movement had peaked. His final years, however, were spent in isolation. The trustees' patience had been tested in 1939, when he suddenly instituted a series of restrictions designed to cripple the university's storied athletics program, including ending athletic scholarships and defunding the football recruiting program.[94] Killing off the extracurriculum was another recurrent goal of academic engineering, and one that outlived other reform efforts.[95] But by 1939, Bowman's assault was too much, too late; the trustees transferred almost all of his duties to the university provost, leaving Bowman marginalized and ignored.[96] The last of the reformers, who had cut his teeth in the heart of the movement, was finished.

Booker T. Washington

The final academic engineer I profile here is likely the most unexpected. Booker T. Washington is also the only one of the group who remains a household name. Today, he is remembered as a leading voice on turn-of-the-century race relations, but he had a day job, as a higher education leader. And he was firmly in the academic engineering camp, a place that fitted him well.

Washington routinely comes under fire for being a "two-faced"[97] "accommodationist"[98] due to his ability to quickly switch between the worlds of poor African Americans in the South and wealthy White businessmen and philanthropists in the North. But he was hardly unique in that type of switching; Carnegie famously played the role of the genial, simple-minded Scot when it suited him, and the other academic engineers described here routinely invoked their rural or backwater roots, especially when they were in the field, visiting backwater institutions.

That said, even among the outsiders Washington had no equal. He was not born on the family farm like Vanderlip; he was born on James Burroughs' farm in Virginia, as his slave. The Civil War ended when Washington was nine years old. As his hugely popular autobiography, *Up From Slavery*,[99] explained, after emancipation he found work as a child laborer in a West Virginia coal mine before making his way to the Hampton Normal and Agricultural Institute, founded by a Union Army general to educate freed slaves. (Washington called him "superhuman" and "Christlike.")[100] We cannot call the Hampton Washington attended a college, or even a postsecondary institution, since almost none of its students had attended high school. It did not offer the bachelor's degree. But like the colleges of its day, it served young adults starting at age sixteen and looked like a college, with recitation halls, debating societies, intermural athletics, and an active alumni association. James Anderson emphasizes that in terms of academics it largely served as a normal school, training its students to go teach in the segregated Black public schools of the South.[101]

Washington did exactly that for two years before returning to his alma mater for an administrative position. Then, at age 25, he was tapped to serve as the first leader of a new institution in Alabama, designed in the Hampton model. Washington would spend the rest of his life at the helm of Tuskegee Institute, steering its growth and leading the way for a much broader program of education for African Americans across the South.

It may seem inappropriate to group Washington with the academic engineers, since he often appears in the historical record not as their peer, but as a sycophant asking for their money. Indeed, much of his correspondence with the philanthropists concerned appropriations for Tuskegee; Carnegie even funded a personal pension for Washington and his wife.[102] But he also fits the description of an academic engineer: an outsider pulled to Manhattan (where he fundraised relentlessly and where he convened most Tuskegee board meetings) and obsessed with efficiency and control. He shared their ideology prizing practical study over a traditional curriculum, declaring in a commencement address that there was "just as much to be learned that is edifying, broadening and refining in a cabbage as there is in a page of Latin."[103]

He also shared their commitment to systemization. W. E. B. Du Bois famously criticized the "Tuskegee Machine," which was not a lightly chosen phrase, with its vivid imagery of interlocking parts and ruthless efficiency. Washington's most important biographer, Louis Harlan, extends and mixes the metaphor with language borrowed from contemporary critics of the great industrial trusts: "the octopus-like Tuskegee Machine."[104] This apparatus relied upon Tuskegee graduates who maintained their loyalty to Washington and his ethos. Some of these were active in politics or journalism (an area of special concern for Du Bois), but many went on to run sub-baccalaureate colleges for African Americans across the South, looking to Tuskegee for leadership in much the same way that Gates and Harper envisioned Midwestern colleges lining up behind the University of Chicago. Arnold Cooper offers a vivid picture of the Machine at work in his case study of the Utica Normal and Industrial Institute in Mississippi. As he explains, deference to Tuskegee on matters of curriculum and growth hinged on Washington's position as the "sole arbiter" of philanthropic largesse, which meant life or death for the subordinate schools.[105]

Washington was also fully on board with the academic engineers in their goal of choking off support for weak institutions. Harlan writes that he "had dreamed for decades" about conducting a systematic survey of higher education institutions serving African Americans. Washington's words echoed Gates' and Flexner's, collaborating with Anson Phelps Stokes on plans for a

> "study of the entire field with a view for selecting schools that are physically located in the right place." But Washington warned that "to kill out a poor school" was the hardest task, saying: "The killing out of the poorer schools would have to be done very gradually and through a process of placing emphasis upon the efficient ones."[106]

It is important to include Washington here as evidence that the powerful social capital at the heart of the academic engineering movement traded on ideology, not class. Washington, an emancipated slave, was very much a part of the interlocking directorate of academic engineers, chairing Tuskegee board meetings that included many wealthy White reformers and sitting alongside them on the boards of Fisk University and Howard University. The color of his skin always mattered, but it did so less than his ideas and tactics: the curious mix of outsider agitation and top-down control that set the academic engineers apart from other generations of reformers.

The Legacy of Academic Engineering

The academic engineers' best year was arguably 1905, with the massive gifts (collectively, nearly half a billion 2019 dollars) to the two foundations tasked with reforming the American higher education sector. Aside from the resounding triumph of the Flexner report and the establishment of the junior college, it is hard to point to specific changes wrought by this powerful and well-funded movement. By 1915, a major backlash was in place, much of it led by educators and leaders within low-status institutions. That year saw the establishment of both the American Association of University Professors, created to protect faculty members, and the American Association of Colleges, intended as the small college rebuttal to the Association of American Universities (whose 1900 founding was another early hallmark of the academic engineers). The coming of the First World War, too, hastened the end of academic engineering, by delegitimizing the exemplar of German universities. The CFAT pension program was dissolved in 1918, spun off as TIAA, depriving the foundation of its primary "carrot." The GEB's gifts to higher education continued into the 1920s, but its leaders then shifted their focus to secondary education in the South before spending down their endowment in the 1940s.

Despite their decline and fall, the academic engineers established a reform trope in higher education that is still very much with us. They legitimized the idea that outsiders with money had as much to say about the form and function of higher education as did the people who lived their lives within colleges and universities. Bill Gates, a college dropout, does not need apologize for throwing himself into higher education reform. Predictably, the Gates Foundation's postsecondary initiatives are overwhelmingly focused on the lower tiers of the higher education pyramid, including on sub-baccalaureate certificate programs.

They also established the logic that on a systemic level, low-tier institutions are the fundamental problem. Clayton Christensen, a Harvard professor, routinely makes headlines with his assertions that 50 percent of American colleges and universities will close their doors within a decade.[107] Others, including non-academics like Kevin Carey, claim that innovations in information technology will kill off an even higher percentage of institutions in short order.[108] These claims are not new; William Rainey Harper and his fellow academic engineers made similar ones more than a century ago. Today's reformers, though, place less faith in the normative control of elite research universities, redirecting their hopes to the relentless power of the free market, especially its Silicon Valley variant.

But thinking about the academic engineers as a definable, strategically aligned cohort also reminds us that theirs is not the only way. Reform is a constant presence in the American higher education sector, but it comes in many flavors. The academic engineers crafted a specific reform ethos: one focused on efficiency, systems, and accountability. Those goals are still salient today. Still, in the eras that preceded and followed academic engineering, reform took a very different tact, with a focus on growth, curriculum, and values. That ethos, too, is still with us. As American higher education and the nation itself become more pluralistic, we can expect this type of ideological coexistence to continue. Those of us in the rank-and-file of academia will be best served by learning to recognize the strands of reform and to pick our battles accordingly.

Notes

1. P. H. Mattingly, *American Academic Cultures: A History of Higher Education* (Chicago, IL: University of Chicago Press, 2017).
2. Ethan W. Ris, "The Origins of Systemic Reform in American Higher Education, 1895–1920," *Teachers College Record* 120, no. 10 (2018): 1–42.
3. H. S. Pritchett, "The Organization of Higher Education," *Atlantic Monthly* (1908, December): 786.
4. A number of scholars have described the efforts of philanthropy-aligned reformers to reshape American higher education in this period. The best known examples focus on reforms targeted at African American-serving institutions, such as the work of James Anderson, Eric Anderson, and Alfred Moss (J.D. Anderson, *The Education of Blacks in the South, 1860–1935* (Chapel Hill, NC: University of North Carolina Press, 1988); E. Anderson, and A.A. Moss, *Dangerous Donations: Northern Philanthropy and Southern Black Education, 1902–1930* (Columbia, MO: University of Missouri Press, 1999). These works dwell extensively on the ideology of the reformers, but do not extend it beyond the specific context of educating African Americans in the South. Ellen Lagemann's important history of the CFAT also focuses on ideology, but narrows that focus primarily on the foundation's leader, Henry Pritchett, to the exclusion of other leaders and other organizations like the GEB (E. C. Lagemann, *Private Power for the Public Good: A History of the Carnegie Foundation for the Advancement of Teaching* (Middletown, CT: Wesleyan University Press, 1983) Surveys of the history of higher education often mention these reformers and their projects. For example, Roger Geiger's 2015 survey includes a section on the roles of philanthropists in "the standardization of higher education;" following Lagemann's lead, he attributes most of the ideas to one man, with "Pritchett's drive to impose order and efficiency" as the wellspring of pre-1920 reform (R. L. Geiger, *The History of American Higher Education: Learning and Culture from the Founding to World War II* (Princeton, NJ: Princeton University Press, 2015), 479–91; see also R. L. Geiger, *To Advance Knowledge: The Growth of American Research Universities, 1900–1940* (New Brunswick, NJ: Transaction Publishers, 2004), 45–47; and J. R. Thelin, *A History of American Higher Education* (Baltimore, MD: Johns Hopkins University Press, 2004), 122–125.
5. Ethan W. Ris, "The Education of Andrew Carnegie: Strategic Philanthropy in Higher Education, 1880–1919," *Journal of Higher Education* 88, no. 3 (2017): 411–412.
6. Gates explicitly spelled this out to his fellow GEB trustees shortly after the gift: "[Rockefeller's] letter holds our aim strictly to the higher education, that is, to colleges and to universities or to schools having similar educational compass and rank. Other people may give us other funds for other objects. This fund is for higher education exclusively," (F. T. Gates, "The Purpose of the Rockefeller Foundation with Suggestions as to the Policy of Administration," (1906) Box 19, Folder 19, Office of Messrs. Rockefeller Papers, Rockefeller Archive Center, Sleepy Hollow, NY. [OMRP]).
7. Gates, "The Purpose of the Rockefeller Foundation."
8. Ris, "The Education of Andrew Carnegie," 416.
9. A. Carnegie, "Copy of Letter from Mr. Andrew Carnegie," in *Library of Congress Manuscripts Division* (typescript), Box 114 (Washington, DC: Andrew Carnegie Papers, 1905a).

10. F. T. Gates, "Memo. by Mr. Gates," Box 19, Folder 198, OMRP, 1910.
11. A. Carnegie, "Letter to Charles W. Eliot," Box 119 (ACP, August 22, 1905b).
12. H. S. Pritchett, "Mr. Carnegie's Gift to the Teachers," *The Outlook*, May 1906.
13. C. Furst, "The Problem of the Financial Support of Higher Education," *Education* 36, no. 5 (1916): 277.
14. F. W. Taylor, *The Principles of Scientific Management* (New York, NY: Harper & Brothers, 1911).
15. J. Christie, *Morris Llewellyn Cooke: Progressive Engineer* (Taylor & Francis, 1983).
16. Henry S. Pritchett, "Preface," in *Academic and Industrial Efficiency*, ed. Morris L. Cooke (New York, NY: Carnegie Foundation for the Advancement of Teaching, 1910), iv.
17. M. L. Cooke, *Academic and Industrial Efficiency: A Report to the Carnegie Foundation for the Advancement of Teaching (Bulletin Number Five)* (New York: Carnegie Foundation for the Advancement of Teaching, 1910), 5.
18. Ibid., 6–7.
19. C. F. Birdseye, "Analyzing the College Business," *The American College* 1, no. 1 (1909): 85–102.
20. W. Kent, "Academic Efficiency," in *A Symposium on Scientific Management and Efficiency in College* (Lancaster, PA: New Era, 1913), 147.
21. G. H. Shephard, "Efficiency in Engineering Education," in *A Symposium on Scientific Management and Efficiency in College* (Lancaster, PA: New Era, 1913), 190.
22. H. S. Pritchett, "Some Tendencies of the College of Technology," (1906) (Transcript of speech delivered at Clarkson School of Technology), Henry Smith Pritchett Papers, Library of Congress Manuscript Division, Box 11 (HSPP).
23. Cooke, *Academic and Industrial Efficiency*, 8.
24. W. H. G. Armytage, *A Social History of Engineering* (MIT Press, 1961/2003).
25. In his historiographical essay on the Progressive Era, Daniel Rodgers explains: "it was the merger of the prestige of science with the prestige of the well-organized business firm and factory that gave the metaphor of system its tremendous twentieth-century potency – and it was presumably for this reason that that metaphor flourished more exuberantly in the United States, along with industrial capitalism itself, than anywhere else," (D.T. Rodgers, "In Search of Progressivism," *Reviews in American History* 10, no. 4 (1982): 126.
26. L. R. Veysey, *The Emergence of the American University* (University of Chicago Press, 1965), 338.
27. W. R. Harper, *The Prospects of the Small College* (Chicago, IL: University of Chicago Press, 1900).
28. R. J. Storr, *Harper's University: The Beginnings* (Chicago, IL: University of Chicago Press, 1966), 217–222.
29. U. Sinclair, *The Goose-Step, a Study of American Education* (Pasadena, CA: Self-Published, 1923), 115.
30. A. Flexner, *I Remember: The Autobiography of Abraham Flexner* (New York, NY: New York: Simon and Schuster, 1940), 111.
31. N. M. Butler, "True and False Democracy," *Educational Review* 33, no. 4 (1907): 325–343.
32. C. Furst, "Tests of College Efficiency," *The School Review* 20, no. 5 (1912): 320–334.
33. J. Sealander, "Curing Evils at Their Source: The Arrival of Scientific Giving," in *Charity, Philanthropy, and Civility in American History*, eds. L. J. Friedman and M. D. McGarvie (New York, NY: Cambridge University Press, 2003), 217.
34. J. W. Boyer, *The University of Chicago: A History* (University of Chicago Press, 2015), 42.
35. R. B. Fosdick, *Adventure in Giving: The Story of the General Education Board* (New York, NY: Harper & Row, 1962), 6–16.

36. F. T. Gates, *Chapters in My Life* (New York, NY: The Free Press, 1977), 46–53.
37. Ibid., 55.
38. Fosdick, *Adventure in Giving*, 14.
39. Gates, *Chapters in My Life*, 58.
40. Boyer, *The University of Chicago*, 44.
41. R. Chernow, *Titan: The Life of John D. Rockefeller* (New York, NY: Random House, 1998), 310.
42. Ibid., 311.
43. Gates, *Chapters in My Life*, 215. The charter was secured by Senator Nelson Aldrich of Rhode Island, a powerful Republican whose daughter had recently married John D. Rockefeller, Jr.
44. Gates, *Chapters in My Life*, 217.
45. T. Arnett and W. W. Brierly, "Introductory Letter," in *Annual Report of the General Education Board, 1928–1929* (Self-published, 1930).
46. General Education Board, *The General Education Board: An Account of its Activities, 1902–1914*. General Education Board (Self-published, 1915).
47. Gates, "Memo. by Mr. Gates," 7.
48. Gates, *Chapters in My Life*, 217–218.
49. A. Flexner, *Henry S. Pritchett: A Biography* (New York, NY: Columbia University Press, 1943); H. J. Savage, *Fruit of an Impulse: Forty-five Years of the Carnegie Foundation, 1905–1950* (New York, NY: Harcourt, Brace and Company, 1953); Lagemann, *Private Power for the Public Good*.
50. Lagemann, *Private Power for the Public Good*, 22.
51. Flexner, *Henry S. Pritchett*, 198.
52. Ibid., 20; Lagemann, *Private Power for the Public Good*, 23; H. S. Pritchett, "The Chronicles of Henry Smith," (unpublished memoir, n.d.). Box 1, Henry Smith Pritchett Papers, Library of Congress Manuscripts Division, Washington, DC. (HSPP).
53. Flexner, *Henry S. Pritchett*, 29–49.
54. For more on MIT's early, low-status days, see S.C. Prescott, *When M.I.T. Was 'Boston Tech,' 1861–1916* (Cambridge, MA: Technology Press, 1954).
55. A. Carnegie, Letter to Henry L. Higginson, November 26, 1904, Box 109, ACP.
56. W. Frew, Letter to AC, November 29, 1904, Box 109, ACP.
57. H. S. Pritchett, Letter to AC, July 19, 1905, Box 118, ACP. Bruce Sinclair, "Mergers and Acquisitions," in *Becoming MIT: Moments of Decision*, ed. David Kaiser (Cambridge, MA: MIT Press, 2010).
58. H. S. Pritchett, *Massachusetts Institute of Technology Annual Report of the President and Treasurer, December 9, 1903* (Boston: n.p., 1904).
59. C. F. Thwing, "A Pension Fund for College Professors," *The North American Review* 181, no. 588 (1905): 722–730; H.S. Pritchett, Letter to AC, February 6, 1905, Box 111, ACP.
60. Ibid.
61. H. S. Pritchett, "Mr. Carnegie's Gift to the Teachers," *The Outlook* 83 (May 1906): 123.
62. H. S. Pritchett, "A National System of Education," (Typescript, extended version of "The Organization of Higher Education" [*Atlantic Monthly*, December 1908]). Box 7, HSPP.
63. F. A. Vanderlip and B. Sparkes, *From Farm Boy to Financier* (D. Appleton-Century Company, 1935), 77.
64. F. A. Vanderlip, "The Young Man's Future: An Address Delivered Before the American Institute of Bank Clerks, St. Paul, 1906," in *Business and Education* (New York, NY: Duffield and Company, 1907a), 51.
65. F. A. Vanderlip, "The Co-ordination of Higher Education," in *Business and Education* (New York, NY: Duffield and Company, 1907b), 3.

66. Ibid., 10.
67. Ibid., 10–12.
68. Henry H. Klein, *Standard Oil or the People: The End of Corporate Control in America* (New York, NY: Self-published, 1914), 31–32.
69. Flexner, *I Remember*, 13. Thomas Henry Huxley was an English biologist who championed Darwin and coined the word "agnostic."
70. For more on Carnegie and Spencer, see J. White, "Andrew Carnegie and Herbert Spencer: A Special Relationship," *Journal of American Studies* 13, no. 1 (1979): 57–71.
71. Flexner, *I Remember*, 56.
72. Ibid., 62.
73. T. N. Bonner, *Iconoclast: Abraham Flexner and a Life in Learning* (Baltimore, MD: Johns Hopkins University Press, 2002), 32–47.
74. Flexner, *I Remember*, 88–101.
75. A. Flexner, *The American College: A Criticism* (New York, NY: The Century Co., 1908), 11.
76. Ibid., 15.
77. Ibid., 145.
78. Ibid., 12.
79. Flexner, *I Remember*, 111.
80. Flexner proudly had little experience with medical education, but he certainly was familiar with the medical world – and with the world of Manhattan-based strategic philanthropy. His older brother, Simon, was the president of the Rockefeller Institute for Medical Research (which became Rockefeller University in 1965).
81. Flexner, *I Remember*, 121.
82. A. Flexner, *Medical Education in the United States and Canada: A Report to the Carnegie Foundation for the Advancement of Teaching*, CFAT Bulletin No. 4 (Boston, MA: Merrymount Press, 1910), 178. In the course of his study, Flexner got into considerable hot water. Pritchett had to apologize to a member of the Harvard Medical School faculty for "friction" that occurred during his visit there. (HSP to William T. Councilman, 1/22/1909, Box 8, HSPP.) The same day, Pritchett wrote to a mutual friend, expressing concern that "a good many criticisms have come to me concerning him, somewhat to the effect that he is erratic and hard to get along with and somewhat uncertain in his judgment," (HSP to Cyrus Adler, 1/22/1909, Box 8, HSPP).
83. Thelin, *A History of American Higher*, 149. See also Geiger, *The History of American Higher Education*, 387–389. The medical education community continues to see the report's publication as the seminal moment in its history, for better or for worse; see, for example, the 27 articles on Flexner published in a special edition of *Academic Medicine* (85[2]) celebrating the report's centenary in 2010.
84. A. Carnegie, Letter to Charles W. Eliot, June 16, 1910. Box 32. Carnegie Foundation for the Advancement of Teaching Records, Columbia University Rare Books and Manuscripts, New York, NY. (CFATR).
85. Abraham Flexner, "The Usefulness of Useless Knowledge," *Harper's* 179 (October 1939): 544–552.
86. Clark Kerr, "Introduction to the Transaction Edition: Remembering Flexner," in *Universities: American, English, German*, ed. Abraham Flexner (New Brunswick, NJ: Transaction, 1994/1930), ix–xxxii.
87. Christian Anderson, "Building an Icon: The Rise and Fall of John G. Bowman, Chancellor of the University of Pittsburgh, 1921–1945," *Perspectives on the History of Higher Education* 28, no. 1 (2011): 137–159.
88. *Columbia University in the City of New York Catalogue and General Announcement* (1906), 15. https://babel.hathitrust.org/cgi/pt?id=hvd.hnw3yl;view=1up;seq=41.

89. John G. Bowman, Letter to Charles T. Burnett, November 4, 1907. Box 45, CFATR.
90. S. Persons, *The University of Iowa in the Twentieth Century: An Institutional History* (Iowa City, IA: University of Iowa Press, 1990), 57.
91. Ibid.
92. C. Furst, Letter to William Learned, April 28, 1914. Box 38, CFATR.
93. Anderson, "Building an Icon," 141–150.
94. "Boot for Bowman," *Time Magazine*, October 2, 1939. http://content.time.com/time/magazine/article/0,9171,789020,00.html?promoid=googlep.
95. See the CFAT's "Bulletin 23," a book-length attack on intercollegiate sports: H. J. Savage, et al., *American College Athletics* (New York, NY: Carnegie Foundation for the Advancement of Teaching, 1929).
96. Anderson, "Building an Icon," 150–154.
97. M. Bay, *To Tell the Truth Freely: The Life of Ida B. Wells* (Macmillan, 2009), 245.
98. L. R. Harlan, *Booker T. Washington, Volume 2: The Wizard of Tuskegee, 1901–1915* (New York, NY: Oxford University Press, 1983), 322.
99. *Up From Slavery* was only partially an autobiography; it was also a running advertisement for donations to Tuskegee. The text was first serialized in *The Outlook*, a middlebrow New York newsmagazine that served as an outlet for many academic engineers.
100. B. T. Washington, *Up From Slavery: An Autobiography* (New York, NY: Burt Company, 1901), 55–57.
101. Anderson, *The Education of Blacks in the South, 1860–1935*, 34–35.
102. Ris, "The Education of Andrew Carnegie," 414.
103. A. P. Stokes, *A Brief Biography of Booker Washington* (Hampton, VA: Hampton Institute Press, 1936), 21.
104. Harlan, *Booker T. Washington, Volume 2*, viii. The octopus was a metaphor commonly employed by contemporary critics of Gilded Age industrial conglomerates; see R. Solnit, "The Octopus and its Grandchildren," *Harper's*, August 2014, 5–7.
105. Arnold Cooper, "The Tuskegee Machine in Action: Booker T. Washington's Influence on Utica Institute, 1903–1915," *Journal of Mississippi History* 48 (November 1986): 283–295.
106. Harlan, *Booker T. Washington, Volume 2*, 199–200.
107. M. Horn, "Will Half of All Colleges Really Close in The Next Decade?" *Forbes*, December 13, 2018, www.forbes.com/sites/michaelhorn/2018/12/13/will-half-of-all-colleges-really-close-in-the-next-decade/.
108. K. Carey, *The End of College: Creating the Future of Learning and the University of Everywhere* (New York, NY: Penguin, 2015).

3 An "Administrativ" Approach to Innovation

Two Teachers-College Presidents and Simplified Spelling in the Progressive Era

Christine A. Ogren

As the first president of Reed College, William T. Foster sought to reform higher education in the United States by example. The Portland, Oregon, institution that he inaugurated in 1911 focused on rigorous undergraduate academics – Reed required qualifying examinations, theses, and orals, while eschewing intercollegiate athletics and Greek life – as well as improving the larger community. In *The Distinctive College*, Burton Clark explained that these innovations were not exactly popular with the citizens of Portland, who wanted spectator sports rather than condescending "do-goodism." Another annoyance was Foster's insistence on adhering to simplified spelling, a controversial innovation aimed at increasing efficiency in writing and printing. Clark wrote, "To read Reed prose was to be constantly brought up short by words with missing letters ('confirmd'), the letter *c* replaced by *s* ('offises'), and *ph* by *f* ('alfabetical')."[1] Reed presented public lectures on "the Tercentenary of Shakspere's Deth" in 1915, and "War and Foren policy" and "How Geografy Determins History" in 1917.[2] Foster's refusal to use traditional spelling was not the least among the reasons for the trustees' and the local community's easy acceptance of his resignation in 1919. With his departure, Clark explained, "the special irritant of Simplified Spelling was removed from the emerging character of Reed."[3]

Foster was far from alone in supporting spelling reform during the Progressive Era, when efficiency was veritable gospel. Beginning in the late 1870s, many trumpeted the savings of time and money that streamlined spelling would bring to the printing industry and the nation's schools. Editors, publishers, popular writers, school superintendents, professors, and higher-education administrators demonstrated a high level of intellectual commitment to the movement as they voiced their support for shorter, phonetic word forms in the interest of saving ink and effort as well as shortening elementary schooling by as much as two years.[4] Also during the Progressive Era, growth and increased visibility of US higher education required its leaders to focus on public relations to an unprecedented extent. Historian Laurence Veysey argued that, after the turn of the twentieth century, administrators were "establishmentarian" in their "concern for the distinguished appearance of the university as it faced the world"; there was no room for "disturbing iconoclasm," even if rooted in intellectual concerns.[5] When innovation in spelling in the 1900s attracted heightened attention – and ridicule – due to the involvement of industrialist Andrew Carnegie and President Theodore Roosevelt, supporting the reform became increasingly iconoclastic. Foster dug in his heels; he later explained that his use of simplified spelling symbolized Reed College's mission "to stand staunchly – and if necessary, stand alone – for whatever was right."[6] But other leaders allowed public opinion to temper their support for spelling reform – and, likely, for other innovations as well.

This chapter considers how two presidents navigated the controversy over innovation in spelling. Like Foster, Iowa State Teachers College (ISTC) President Homer H. Seerley and Illinois State Normal University (ISNU) President David Felmley faced criticism for their support of simplified spelling. Seerley's use of streamlined word forms in college publications provoked heated debate in the Iowa state legislature in 1911. Regarding a bill establishing a special committee to investigate the practice, Seerley wrote to a fellow spelling reformer: "The fiasco at the Legislature concerning Simplified Spelling is not going to amount to anything. I spent three days there recently and the advertisement given to the cause is remarkably helpful."[7] Nevertheless, after the Board of Education looked into the issue the following year, ISTC publications reverted to traditional spelling. Meanwhile, Felmley had also begun to use simplified spelling in publications, which by law were printed at the Illinois state prison, often with delays and mistakes. In one egregious case, some convicts parodied reformed spelling by typesetting an ISNU catalog with all sorts of errors in spelling as well as in verb forms and punctuation. The galleys were late and the ISNU staff did not have time to proofread, so the catalog appeared with the convicts' edits. When ISNU board member Ella Flagg Young received a scathing critique, she passed it along to Felmley, who replied: "If the use of simplified spelling is everywhere equally successful in drawing attention to our publications our advertising will not be in vain even if attention of the reader is largely dawn from the matter to the form." Before long, however, ISNU publications reverted to traditional spelling.[8]

As leaders of public teacher-education institutions, Seerley and Felmley arguably faced more public scrutiny than presidents of private colleges and research universities.[9] And yet, unlike Foster, each had a long and celebrated presidential career. In the 1930s, ISNU faculty member and historian of teacher education Charles A. Harper wrote that Felmley "was without question, the most outstanding force for an entire generation in formulating and securing the enactment of progressive educational legislation in this State." Beyond their state's borders, both helped to smooth the transition of normal schools into teachers colleges and were among the handful of leaders whom Harper credited with saving the teachers colleges by securing their right to prepare high-school teachers.[10] In 1925, the national *Journal of Education* devoted several pages to a celebration of Seerley's career under the heading "Dean of Educational Common Sense: What Some of Our Foremost Educators Say of Homer H. Seerley."[11]

How did Seerley and Felmley earn such accolades while also receiving public criticism – from legislators, convicts, and others – for their support of a controversial innovation? This chapter explains that the key was their measured approach, which, Seerley explained in 1910, meant treating simplified spelling "from the administrativ point of view rather than from a promoter's point of view."[12] After outlining Seerley's and Felmley's early careers and spelling reform in the late nineteenth century, this chapter explores the two presidents' approaches to supporting this innovation at the national, state, and campus levels in the early twentieth century, when both remained intellectually committed to simplified spelling yet mindful of the practical need to maintain support for their institution. While historians acknowledge that Progressive-Era leaders in higher education found it necessary to cultivate a positive institutional image, they have written little about how presidents actually navigated the perils that public relations posed for innovation.[13] This examination of Seerley's and Felmley's "administrativ" approach to innovation illustrates the ins and outs of higher-education leaders' work in different arenas to reconcile unpopular undertakings with establishmentarian pressures, demonstrating how successful administrators variously push forward and pull back. The experiences of the two teachers-college presidents with simplified spelling in the Progressive Era also suggest that concern over public opinion can work to impede innovation and change in higher education.

Seerley, Felmley, and Spelling Reform in the Late Nineteenth Century

Homer Seerley and David Felmley learned about spelling reform as they were establishing their careers in the late nineteenth century. Born in 1848, Seerley graduated from the University of Iowa and was a teacher and then superintendent of schools in Oskaloosa, Iowa, before becoming president of the Iowa State Normal School (later ISTC) in Cedar Falls in 1886. Nine years younger than Seerley, Felmley graduated from the University of Michigan, taught in rural schools, and served as superintendent of schools in Carrollton, Illinois, before joining the faculty of ISNU in Normal, Illinois, in 1890 as a mathematics instructor; he became president of the institution in 1900.[14] As they focused on teaching, administrating, and then settling into their leadership roles in teacher education, Seerley and Felmley were increasingly active in the

National Education Association (NEA) and its satellite State Teachers' Association (STA) and related education journals in their state. Seerley enrolled in the Iowa STA in 1873, attended every annual meeting thereafter, and was elected president for 1884. As Iowa STA president, Seerley represented the state at the 1884 NEA meeting in Madison, Wisconsin, and was an active participant in the NEA from then on.[15] A little later, Felmley followed a similar trajectory. He was a fixture in the Illinois STA by the 1890s, serving on its Executive Committee in 1899 and as its president in 1901. Like the Iowa STA, the Illinois STA was closely linked to the NEA, and Felmley would have followed the NEA's proceedings and likely attended the annual meeting at least when it was nearby, such as in St. Paul in 1890, Chicago in 1893, and Milwaukee in 1897.[16] The NEA – which from its founding in 1857 into the early twentieth century was a professional organization for school administrators, professors, and higher-education leaders who were interested in educational issues – basically functioned for three decades as the institutional home of the spelling reform movement in the US.[17] Involvement in the NEA and their STA would have familiarized Seerley and Felmley with the movement for spelling reform.

In an effort to build on the pioneering work of Benjamin Franklin and Noah Webster, US advocates of innovation in English spelling formed the Spelling Reform Association (SRA) in 1876. At the NEA meeting the same year, a speaker advocated spelling words more phonetically.[18] Under the leadership of Lafayette College professor of English and philology Francis A. March and former NEA president and superintendent of schools in St. Louis William T. Harris, the SRA met as a department of the NEA in 1879, 1880, and 1881. At the 1880 meeting, Oberlin College professor W. G. Ballantine read a paper on "The Duti ov Our Colejez Toward the Speling Reform" and journal editor E. O. Vaile spoke on "Speling Reform and the Pres." Seerley's predecessor as leader of the Iowa State Normal School, J. C. Gilchrist participated in the "liveli" discussion that followed the two presentations; the SRA secretary noted that Gilchrist and others were "practicali in revolt" against traditional spelling. At the SRA gathering at the 1881 NEA meeting, Gilchrist presented an "Adres" and was elected as a vice president of the SRA, along with Columbia University President F. A. P. Barnard and several others.[19] The general NEA meetings also included addresses on spelling reform by SRA members. March argued in "The Relation of Educators to Spelling Reform" in 1880 that writing and spelling should be "recognized everywhere as machinery of communication, like the telegraf and printing press," and T. R. Vickroy, a journal editor in St. Louis, argued in "The Necessity for Spelling Reform" in 1881 that 25 percent "of all the money used in teaching the common branches is wasted upon and on account of our bad system of spelling."[20] By the time Seerley began attending the NEA in the mid-1880s, spelling reform was a common theme at the annual meeting.

Seerley and Felmley were likely present in St. Paul in 1890 when the NEA passed a resolution by the Minnesota STA supporting spelling reform and appointing a committee to investigate further. Read at the following year's meeting, the committee's reports summarized the progress of reform in Europe and in the US, where, one committee member promised,

> Simplified English spelling and inflection would reduce the cost of books and newspapers one-sixth, would lessen the school taxes many millions of money annually, would develop better reasoning power in the growing mind, would shorten the work of learning to read and write by half, and would greatly lessen the number of illiterates.

In the discussion that followed, one participant mentioned his advocacy of spelling reform decades earlier and quipped, "I was called in those days a fanatic, while I was simply phonetic."[21] The NEA's Department of Superintendence in 1897 appointed a committee – chaired by Harris, who by then was US Commissioner of Education – to decide upon specific "amended spellings" for use in the NEA *Proceedings*, and the Board of Directors in 1898 passed a resolution adopting twelve reformed words: *program* (to replace programme), *tho* (though), *altho* (although), *thoro* (through), *thorofare* (thoroughfare), *thru* (through), *thruout* (throughout), *catalog* (catalogue), *prolog* (prologue), *decalog* (decalogue), *demagog* (demagogue), and *pedagog* (pedagogue). The Board then ordered the use of the twelve words in all NEA publications – with the exception, added the following year, that individual authors could direct that their work be published with "standard spelling."[22] While Seerley was present at the 1899 Department of Superintendence meeting (to present a committee report on normal schools), he and Felmley probably did not attend the 1897 and 1898 Department and Board meetings.[23] As active NEA and STA members, however, they were most certainly aware of these efforts to streamline spelling.

In Iowa, the "official journal" of the State Department of Education and the STA, *The Iowa Normal Monthly*, reported on the 1897 and 1898 actions of the Department of Superintendence and Board of Directors.[24] In fact, spelling reform was a prominent topic during the last quarter of the nineteenth century in STAs in Iowa, Illinois, and other states. As early as 1876 at the Iowa STA meeting, with Seerley as well as Gilchrist of the state normal school in attendance, Superintendent J. K. Pickett of Sigourney presented a paper on spelling reform and the group passed a resolution "That we cordially approve of Spelling Reform, in the English language, in the direction of phonetic simplification, and we will most heartily cooperate with any feasible plans and efforts, for securing said result; also, that a committee of three be appointed" to consider the question further. Pickett was appointed chair of the committee – while Seerley was appointed to a different committee (on nominations).[25] During the next decade and a half, annual meetings of the Iowa STA included papers and a few successful resolutions on spelling reform. Just after Seerley's Iowa STA presidency and appointment to head the state normal school, a professor from Iowa's Cornell College addressed the "Present Status of the Spelling Reform" at the 1886 meeting. In the following years, Seerley was present as the Iowa STA passed resolutions including one of appreciation for a Cedar Rapids newspaper's use of "amended spellings" in 1888 and "That we renew our hearty endorsement of the principles of spelling reform" in 1890.[26] Seerley was also a regular contributor to and, likely, reader of *The Iowa Normal Monthly*. After his piece entitled "Child Study Nonsense" appeared in the August 1896 issue, James Lawry wrote to the editor, "As long as such a man is at the head of our State Normal School we need not fear of any fads creeping into its work." And during the 1897–1898 academic year, Seerley contributed a regular column called "A Few Brief Chapters From Experience." Along with such articles by Seerley, the journal published more than a half-dozen pieces on spelling reform during the last quarter of the nineteenth century. Notwithstanding one that called reform "a remedy worse than the disease," most of these articles favored streamlined spelling.[27]

In Iowa's neighboring state, the Illinois STA similarly embraced the topic of spelling reform, even issuing a *program* rather than a *programme* as early as 1882.[28] Felmley was on the Executive Committee in 1899 when the association expressed appreciation for the NEA's recent adoption of the twelve reformed words and, in the interest of "the educational advantage and comfort of the children now in school as well as of the generations yet to come," passed a resolution directing "the National Educational Association and its Board of Directors to appropriate one thousand dollars each year for the next five years to be expended in promoting the cause of simplifying our English spelling."[29] As he established his career, Felmley likely also read education journals, especially those published in his state. *The Illinois Schoolmaster* included an article on "phonetic type" as early as 1875, and, two decades later, several articles on spelling reform appeared in *The Intelligence: A Journal of Education*, published in Oak Park by Vaile. In the April 1, 1899 issue, I. K. Funk reported on the NEA's twelve words and on William T. Harris's claim that reformed spelling "would save two years of the school life of American children." In other issues, short, unsigned blurbs probably written by Vaile provided updates on reform and suggestions for further action; "A Hint to Those Who Want to Help" described the presentation of a petition requesting that teachers use reformed spelling to the Oak Park Board of Education in "the hope that many of our readers will start similar movements in their communities."[30] Felmley, like Seerley, gained exposure to spelling reform through journals and involvement in his STA and the NEA. Neither educator took a public stand on this innovation as the movement spread in the late nineteenth century, but that would soon change.

Seerley's and Felmley's "Administrativ" Approach to Simplified Spelling in the Early Twentieth Century

At the beginning of the twentieth century, criticism of spelling reform grew louder just as presidents of higher-education institutions became increasingly concerned about public opinion. A 1905 letter to the editor of *The Iowa Normal Monthly* demonstrated the new level of vitriol – not to mention sarcasm – surrounding innovation in spelling:

> We suggest to our friends the spelling reformers that a discussion of the following question might lead to results: "Resolved, That the course of the Gulf Stream be changed so as to bring the current into harmony with the complex demands of our modern civilization." Possibly, the Board of Directors of the N. E. A. might be persuaded to give $2,000 a year for five years to a committee of experts, whose duty it should be to sit on this proposition.[31]

A decade and a half later, a contributor to *The Atlantic Monthly* wrote in a similar tone of the advantages of simplified spelling:

> The idea seems to be that every time you write *thru* instead of *through* you save a second; and if you write it often enough, you might in the course of some years accumulate enough time for a vacation in Italy or an appendicitis operation.[32]

In this climate, even longtime supporter William T. Harris argued that the current movement was "ill-timed and worse than useless as an aid or help to spelling reform" because of its propensity to "produce reaction and stir up feelings." In 1905, the NEA Department of Superintendence's Committee on the Simplification of Spelling advocated only "a discreet, systematic, quiet, and thoroughgoing effort, on a business basis, to disseminate accurate knowledge in regard to English spelling and to promote its simplification."[33] Hamstrung by opposition and an abundance of caution, the NEA took no further action to streamline spelling. The association continued to use the twelve words adopted in 1898 in its publications, to appoint committees, and to occasionally discuss reform, but it passed no further resolutions on the subject. STAs in various states passed a few resolutions supporting reform, but they provoked hostility and did not amount to anything.[34]

Beyond the field of education, Andrew Carnegie's and Theodore Roosevelt's actions on behalf of spelling reform heightened the movement's notoriety. As Carnegie advocated, in 1906 the remnants of the SRA became the Simplified Spelling Board (SSB) and received $250,000 from Carnegie over the course of the next twelve years. The new institutional home of the spelling reform movement, the SSB maintained an office in New York and issued a series of circulars and bulletins. The first circular, issued in March, 1906, listed simplified versions of three hundred common words and invited the reader to sign and return an enclosed postcard which pledged the "use the simpler form as far as may be practically possible." The list of three hundred words included many word forms that were already fairly common, such as those ending in – *or* rather than – *our* or – *er* rather than – *re*. Other simplified spellings on the list were words without phonetically unnecessary letters, such as *dulness* and *thoroly*, and words with more phonetically accurate letters, such as *fantom* and *rime*. One-fourth of the three hundred words were past-tense verbs in which – *ed* became – *t*, such as *dropt* and *strest*. Roosevelt soon adopted simplified spelling and, in August, ordered the Public Printer to use the three hundred words in all federal documents. The President's action unleashed a torrent of criticism and heated debate in Congress; bowing to pressure, he withdrew it in December 1906.[35] Two years later, James Lawry railed in *The Iowa Normal Monthly* against the SSB: "The death of the whole board would not be missed as far as knowledge is concerned . . . it would be such a good thing for the English-speaking race if the Board should be stricken with some deadly disease that would take them off as soon as possible so as to leave the English spelling to regulate itself as it has been doing the past thousand years."[36]

It was in the negatively charged atmosphere of the 1900s that Homer Seerley and David Felmley began to openly advocate innovation in spelling, and that their measured approach allowed them to maintain public favor. Seerley began to articulate this tack in a response to a 1908 letter from Superintendent William Aldrich of Keokuk, Iowa, who wrote because a member of his school board was pushing hard for the adoption of spelling reform with the attitude that "all that is necessary is just to say we will spell by the simplified method and presto change!" Aldrich supported reform, but wanted Seerley's advice on what "would be a safely conservative but at the same time a desirably progressive attitude on the matter." Seerley's reply is not in the archives, but it must have satisfied Aldrich, who wrote back, "I am very much obliged for your letter." It was a couple of years later that Seerley explained, "I look at the [simplified-spelling] question from the administrativ point of view rather than from a promoter's point of view."[37] During the first two decades of the twentieth century, Seerley and Felmley were active members of the SSB, voiced their support in the NEA and their STAs as well as in published articles, used simplified spelling in their personal correspondence and school publications, and taught their students about the cause. In these activities on behalf of spelling reform at the national level, in their respective states, and on campus, Seerley and Felmley adhered consistently to their "safely conservative but at the same time desirably progressive" stance as they balanced their intellectual convictions against practical concerns to take an "administrativ" approach to this innovation.

The National Level

Lawry, who wanted the SSB to be "stricken with some deadly disease," was the Iowa educator who had praised Seerley in 1896 for keeping "fads" from "creeping into" the state normal school. His diatribe against the SSB did not acknowledge whether he knew that Seerley was a charter member of this national, highly visible organization. That other charter members – including William T. Harris, Yale professor Thomas R. Lounsbury, Harvard philosopher William James, University of Nebraska chancellor E. Benjamin Andrews, Stanford University president David Starr Jordan, Columbia University president Nicholas Murray Butler, Supreme Court justice David J. Brewer, publisher Henry Holt, activist and author Thomas Wentworth Higginson, and writer Samuel L. Clemens (Mark Twain)[38] – were better known may have provided Seerley with some cover as he participated actively in the SSB annual meeting every spring in New York City. In 1908, the national journal *Educational Review* published a paper he read at the second annual meeting. "The Attitude of the Leaders of Public Education Toward Simplified Spelling" opened with an "administrativ point of view" on school leadership:

> The men and the women who are leaders in public education . . . are responsible for their opinions and their practice to those who employ them and they are unable to be charlatans or faddists because they continually give an account for their stewardship . . . their influence and efficiency depend entirely upon their personal acceptability, their reasonable requirements, and their humane fitness to conduct such an extensive work for the people.

"Public opinion," he emphasized, "is a potent factor." Seerley reported that these leaders desired simplified spelling in the interest of efficiency, or "a chance to teach English to the foreign and native alike without so much loss of time and effort to pupil and teacher." But he quickly added,

> these men and women are not able to count largely in advancing reform. They are servants of the public, not the dictators of policies to be followed; they are guides controlled by authority and custom rather than the originators of plans and the creators of changes.

Conservative and careful yet also progressive, Seerley then argued that it was up to publishers to incorporate "the simplified forms . . . in order to enable the public school teacher to adopt them without controversy."[39]

At the SSB's third annual meeting in April 1909, Seerley's presentation on "The propaganda in the middle West" followed "The spelling of college students as reveald in ten thousand themes" by William T. Foster, then a professor at Bowdoin College. Felmley joined the SSB in May 1909 after Seerley had recommended him as a candidate to SSB secretary Charles P. G. Scott "on account of his particular interest in this work and because of his earnestness in putting the work into service in his own school."[40] Felmley was present at the following year's meeting, when Seerley was elected as one of nine vice presidents. The announcement of his election in the *Simplified Spelling Bulletin* emphasized Seerley's deliberate nature, stating that "in simplified spelling and all other matters of educational progress" he was "an advocate and prompt practitioner of common sense, under the control of conscience and reason."[41] Felmley was still on the SSB and Seerley was still a vice president in 1913 when Foster, who by then was President of Reed College, joined the Board.[42]

In his *Educational Review* article, Seerley also argued that the state normal school/ teachers college would be "a natural center for the propagation of the ideas of progress and improvement" in spelling. The SSB Executiv Committee in 1909 appointed Seerley and Felmley, along with President Charles McKenny of the Milwaukee State Normal School, to "a committee upon the promotion of simplified spelling in the normal schools of the middle West." All three were prominent in the North Central Council of Normal School Presidents, which had tentatively endorsed spelling reform several years earlier, and they soon began to recruit other presidents to the SSB committee. In December 1909, Seerley, Felmley, and McKenny sent a joint letter "To Presidents and Faculties of State Normal Schools, United States of America," in which they suggested that the addressees "go farther than nominal acceptance, and . . . show their faith by actual practis" through using simplified spelling in all publications and in personal correspondence, encouraging students and their local press to use it, and presenting lectures on spelling reform at teachers institutes and other meetings. The following month, Seerley reported to SSB secretary Scott that they had received "cordial responses" from a few presidents, and that he had received "a very pleasant letter from Mr. Carnegie who seems to think that the whole effort on our part deserved his cordial endorsement." The committee soon morphed into the North Central Branch Simplified Spelling Board, with Seerley as chair. In addition, several normal-school presidents joined the national SSB in the early 1910s after charter members including James, Brewer, and Clemens passed away and Jordan and Butler resigned from the Board due to pressure from the public and their university's trustees.[43]

Seerley's and Felmley's "safely conservative but at the same time desirably progressive" approach to North Central Branch activities was clear in their voluminous correspondence with and regarding Branch secretary and member of the national SSB E. O. Vaile, who was anything but conservative on spelling reform. By all accounts, Vaile was a zealot with a difficult personality. He pushed constantly for the Branch – as well as the SSB and the NEA – to take more radical action, and Seerley and Felmley tried both to reason with him and to temper his impact on others. In a 1909 letter to Felmley, Scott complained about Vaile's "goading," but added that he took "great comfort" that the North Central group as a whole was "engaged in the solid work of investigation, consideration, reporting and publishing results, all in the serene and stedy way in which scientific work should be done."[44] It was in a letter to Vaile that Seerley articulated his "administrativ point of view." As Vaile lobbied in the spring of 1910 for the Branch to promote its work more forcefully, Seerley responded, "I would not be willing to press the matter any more . . . I hope you will not be disappointed in me too much because I look at the question from an administrativ point of view rather than from a promoter's point of view." Vaile was disappointed, and the situation deteriorated. By fall, Seerley offered to resign from his position as chair, writing to Vaile, "I am entirely lacking in interest in getting into controversies, and I have had more controversy with you personally than any man I have had to do with."[45] Felmley served as a reluctant go-between, and Seerley stayed on. By 1913, though, he suggested pragmatically that the Branch be disbanded because it had not been "effectiv." What happened instead was that Vaile withdrew and began to form his own organization through the Illinois STA. Felmley was caught in the middle, but did all he could to maintain a balance between practical considerations and his intellectual convictions: "altho I hav receivd from Mr. Vaile the most acrimonious letters and the most vicious attacks that I have ever experienst," he explained, "I do not propose to let personalities weigh with me in a cause of this magnitude."[46]

Felmley and Seerley also had to deal with Vaile in the NEA, where they also held fast to their "administrativ" approach to reform. The presidents' names first appeared in the NEA *Proceedings* regarding spelling reform in the early 1900s. Felmley was one of 29 signers of a 1901 letter requesting permission from the Board of Directors to form a Simplified Spelling Department in the NEA. Their argument that "the simplifying of our spelling is an educational question" did not hold sway, and their request was unsuccessful; it was in this discussion that Harris called the movement "ill-timed." But Felmley continued to support the cause, skillfully pushing forward while leaving room to pull back when necessary. In 1903, he cosigned a measured resolution that the Department of Superintendence "respectfully suggest" that "other educational, literary, scientific, or philanthropic organizations" join the NEA in advocating spelling reform; instead of passing the resolution, the department formed a committee to consider it further. And when Felmley accepted an invitation to speak at a "round table conference on simplified spelling" organized as part of the 1906 Department of Superintendence meeting in Louisville, he was careful to explain, "my qualifications for speaking upon this are from the standpoint of the practical man closely associated with the public school work."[47]

Although the NEA did not have a department devoted to spelling reform, the Department of Superintendence supported a Committee on Simplification of Spelling in the 1900s. When the committee invited Seerley in 1904 to join a new ad hoc committee to advise the larger group, Seerley wrote to fellow nominee Superintendent Charles M. Jordan of Minneapolis, "I do not feel that our committee could decide the method of making this progress or doing this work though we may have some ideas upon the same." A few months later, he outlined his cautious approach for committee chair Superintendent William H. Maxwell of New York, stating that reform would "best be accomplished by accepting the theory of the revisionists and not rejecting the views of the conservatives. . . . In my judgment the N.E.A. can do this work and can secure results gradually." After the ad hoc committee made little progress, Vaile wrote to Seerley, "You have given the measures proposed no help whatever" with a "middle-of-the-road answer committing you to nothing." Seerley replied, "I am sorry to see you show your temper . . . you forget that other people have rights and have reasons for consideration." His reasons undoubtedly resulted from weighing his intellectual commitments against practical considerations.[48]

By 1908, Seerley argued, "I am not a very good hand to press revolutions because I think the day is past" for passing a resolution on spelling reform in the NEA general assembly, and he and Felmley focused their efforts on the various departments. Before the 1910 meeting in Boston, Seerley wrote to Vaile, "I do not regard the next meeting of the National Educational Association as a desirable one to undertake to raise the question of additional [simplified] words [from the SSB list] to be adopted by said Association." Instead, at the Boston meeting, Seerley, Felmley, and McKenny reported to the Department of Normal Schools on "the Progress of Simplified Spelling in America." In this more sheltered setting, they celebrated advances including the appearance of shorter word forms in dictionaries and the use of simplified spelling in the publications of teacher-education institutions such as ISTC and ISNU. They also called on administrators at normal schools to help "in developing public sentiment," arguing that the institutions "are not bound by traditions that interdict the adoption of sensible reforms. They occupy the key to the position, and their managers should be patriotic enough to cooperate in helping forward a change that means everything for educational progress."[49]

Also outside the spotlight of the general NEA assembly, Seerley delivered an address entitled "Simplified Spelling With Reference to the Masses" at the 1911 meeting of the Secondary Department. In a tone that was less "safely conservative" than usual, he argued that spelling reform

> should not be postponed for a generation. . . . The National Education Association is assumed to be specially interested in the education of the masses. . . . Reforms and progress of every kind that pertain to public education should be its province and its purpose.

In the discussion that followed Seerley's address, Felmley observed that phonetic spelling would improve pronunciation and Foster declared, "anything which is logically defensible will triumph, and simplified spelling is logically defensible."[50] Allied with Foster within the confines of this NEA department, Seerley and Felmley were more measured in other settings. Two years later, Felmley "respectfully" petitioned the Department of Superintendence to adopt additional simplified words recommended by the SSB and then accepted the body's decision to table the resolution.[51] Felmley was careful not to push further; when operating at the national level, he and Seerley did not tie themselves too zealously to a cause with little support.

The State Level

Spelling reform also created contention in educational politics at the state level, where both Seerley and Felmley gained a degree of notoriety for their support of this innovation. The bill introduced early in 1911 by Iowa Representative E. R. Zeller to establish a committee to investigate spelling in ISTC publications put Seerley on the defensive. In carefully worded letters, he explained to legislators and members of the State Board of Education that the shorter word forms were widely accepted, that ISTC did not require students to use them, and that "the whole matter is greatly misunderstood." He traveled to Des Moines and made himself available for meetings, but they were not necessary as the Zeller resolution did not advance. Although Seerley brushed off the negative attention as "remarkably helpful" in advertising the cause, when he realized in the spring of 1912 that there was some opposition on the Board of Education to simplified spelling in ISTC publications, he discontinued its use.[52] The convicts' parody of simplified spelling in the ISNU catalog similarly put Felmley on the defensive. Although he quipped that the attention had helped to advertise the institution and he had often expressed frustration with the Board of Prison Industries' failure to follow instructions, Felmley's "administrativ" sense told him to take this incident seriously and return to traditional spelling in catalogs.[53]

Seerley's and Felmley's sense of when to pull back on spelling reform helped them to navigate sensitive state terrain.

Both presidents continued after the turn of the century to speak and write on a multitude of education-related subjects, which meant that – even after the Zeller resolution and convicts' catalog – their support for simplified spelling shaped only a small part of their reputation in their state. Felmley spoke on "The School and the Industrial World" and "The Educational Value of Manual Training," among other topics, at Illinois STA assemblies, while Seerley wrote on seemingly every educational topic from "Professional Etiquette" to "Mothers' Circles and the Public Schools" in *The Iowa Normal Monthly.* At the 1918 Iowa STA meeting, Seerley delivered a eulogy for a former state superintendent of education and presented a speech on how the NEA and the Iowa STAs worked together on legislation.[54]

When the two presidents publicly supported reform in spelling, they were relatively quiet voices in their state's conversation. During Felmley's term as Illinois STA president, a resolution in support of simplified spelling at the 1901 meeting "aroused much opposition from all sections of the hall," according to the STA *Proceedings.* Felmley did not speak on the record regarding the resolution, which he referred to the Committee on Resolutions after passage of a motion to do so. When the next STA president appointed a Committee on Amelioration of Our Spelling with Felmley as chair, it was after Superintendent J. H. Collins of Springfield, Superintendent J. M. Cox of Moline, and E. O. Vaile had spoken out enthusiastically for reform. John Dewey of the University of Chicago was also a member of the committee. As chair, Felmley reported at the 1903 meeting that resolutions introduced by the committee were also being considered in other states, at the 1904 meeting that the State Printer had agreed to use amended spellings in STA materials, and at the 1905 meeting that the NEA was not making much progress on spelling reform. While Felmley's statements were rather bureaucratic, Collins, Cox, and two others presented papers on spelling reform at the 1902 meeting and Collins offered a resolution on simplified spelling at the 1903 meeting.[55] Felmley served again as chair of what had become the Committee on Simplified Spelling in 1908 and 1909, and remained on the committee into the next decade. But in the 1910s, Vaile was the state's most visible and vocal supporter of simplified spelling by far. He chaired the committee and presented long reports to the association, while Felmley also served on the Legislative Committee. A short article in a 1913 issue of *The Illinois Teacher* noted a new column "devoted to the cause of simplified spelling" in a Chicago newspaper and remarked, "The contributor to these columns one can readily guess is the veteran fighter for the cause, E. O. Vaile." When in 1914 STA secretary and education dean at the University of Illinois Lotus D. Coffman opposed simplified spelling at the STA meeting and in the pages of *The Illinois Teacher*, Vaile – not Felmley – defended the practice in both forums.[56]

Similar to Felmley in Illinois, when Seerley's name appeared on the membership list of the Iowa STA's committee on simplified spelling in 1903, it was alongside other well-known educators in the state, including superintendents Adam Pickett of Mt. Ayr and F. T. Oldt of Dubuque. The Iowa STA passed a few resolutions on spelling reform in the mid-1900s without much public discussion, and then was quiet on the subject. This apparently did not concern Seerley, as he wrote to SSB secretary Scott in 1912, "The passing of a resolution has its effect at one time but after that has been done, as was done some years ago by the State Teachers Association of Iowa, it seems needless to me to have a repetition regularly." He remained intellectually committed to simplified spelling, however, explaining further, "I am working away quietly and moderately to develop a permanent interest in the state. My method may not be the most public, but I hope that it will bring the results."[57]

After writing dozens of articles on other topics for *The Iowa Normal Monthly*, in 1906 Seerley published "The Simplification of the Spelling of the English Language," in which he reported to Iowa educators on the formation of the SSB. He argued that "the commission as organized is neither radical nor revolutionary" and elaborated on "The Need of Simplification," but maintained, "Abuse and Recklessness Must be Avoided." Each spring for the next several years, Seerley reported in *The Iowa Normal Monthly* on the annual SSB meeting and the progress of spelling reform. His 1907 report combined an account of events with reassurance that the people behind the movement were "not a class of cranks or fools" and "There is to be no rash procedure for an attempt is to be made to secure co-operation of all English speaking peoples." Seerley's 1909 report described the speeches at the third annual SSB meeting and ended with the uncharacteristically immoderate statement, "on the outcome of such efforts depends after all the prosperity, the success and the power of the English speaking people." The many articles on other topics that Seerley continued to publish in *The Iowa Normal Monthly* – including "Why Iowa Is Great" in October 1910 – counterbalanced the rare instances in which he wrote stridently about spelling reform.[58] The journal also included articles by other supporters – and opponents – of simplified spelling. For example, Seerley's faculty colleague at ISTC David S. Wright in a 1906 article strongly supported the SSB and President Roosevelt's adoption of simplified spelling, and argued in a 1909 article that if SSB had "erd at all," it was in being too conservative.[59] In the pages of their state education journals and in the activities of their STAs, Seerley and Felmley were not the only or the most zealous supporters of spelling reform; other educators would have been unlikely to associate them primarily with that cause.

Felmley's and Seerley's "safely conservative but at the same time desirably progressive" approach to spelling reform often involved reaching out to their state's schoolteachers. In his report on the work of the Committee on Amelioration of Our Spelling at the 1905 Illinois STA meeting, Felmley said, "we urge the teachers of the state to aid in this work by personal use of all authorized simplified forms, by encouraging pupils to use them."[60] Seerley reported in a 1908 letter to Columbia University professor and SSB member Calvin Thomas that he had helped to see to it that "all the public school teachers" in a particular Iowa county were "furnisht thru the county superintendent with a copy of this list" of SSB simplified words.[61] And for several years, he and Felmley sent SSB secretary Scott lists of teachers in their state who had pledged to support simplified spelling and/or desired copies of various SSB bulletins and lists.[62] At the same time, though, Seerley acknowledged in his 1908 address and article on "The Attitude of Leaders of Public Education" that teachers were also "servants of the public . . . compelled to teach civilization's practices and principles as they find them and as they are assigned by the expert and the scholar."[63] As they encouraged their state's teachers to support simplified spelling, Seerley and Felmley remained mindful of the pressures that teachers faced.

On Campus

The two presidents were especially cautious in introducing teachers-to-be – specifically, the students at their institutions – to simplified spelling. Although Seerley stated in his 1908 address and article that normal-school "students should be mustered into the ranks of an aggressive army that will gladly carry the light of intelligence and reform into the most remote school districts," he wrote to Scott in April 1910, "I will present the matter much more forcefully in the summer session when the [current] teachers are here than I will do now" with normal-school students. In October he clarified,

> I presume you know that these teachers and signatures that I sent you were not students at this college but were teachers and people residing in Hancock County, Iowa. I have been more interested in getting the attention of localities in this direction than in getting the students that are in attendance at the school and would be prospectiv teachers.[64]

On campus, the presidents' "administrativ" approach balanced neutrality on students' spelling with measured promotion by example.

As ISNU and ISTC introduced students to the movement for simplified spelling, they also offered teacher preparation in traditional spelling and did not require that students use the new word forms. Both presidents provided SSB literature to their students, and campus newspapers covered developments in the SSB and NEA. *The Normal Eyte* at ISTC reported in 1906 that Iowa's Drake University would accept "short route spelling" in student papers while Simpson College's student newspaper had denounced simplified spelling. Seerley contributed several short articles on the movement to *The Normal Eyte*, including a report in 1909 of "progress . . . along certain definite lines."[65] In a 1912 issue of the ISNU alumni magazine, Felmley published "A Defense of Simplified Spelling," in which he argued, "English spelling is so irrational that it is the greatest obstacle in bringing children to the conviction that law, order, reason prevail in the world that God has made."[66] Yet the professor on Felmley's faculty who taught spelling methods, Elmer Cavins, continued to base lessons on conventional spelling. Seerley explained ISTC's policies at some length in letters to the legislators who questioned the institution's practices in 1911, writing: "We teach spelling in our elementary classes the same as we always have done, following the spelling books that are commonly prepared for schools." He continued, "There is no special attempt made to instruct students in these shorter forms. . . . There is no claim made that the simpler spelling is more correct than the longer spelling." Simplified forms, he further clarified, "are not required of our students, neither are students supposed to be deserving of censure because they happen to prefer to use the shorter spellings."[67]

While students were free to make their own decisions on how to spell, they and others affiliated with the institutions gained much exposure to simplified spelling through Felmley and Seerley's use of it as administrators. From the early 1900s onward, both presidents used reformed spelling in their personal correspondence, and the letterhead of the ISNU president's office stated, "The spellings recommended by the Simplified Spelling Board are used in the correspondence of this office." Felmley also saw to it that signs in at least one campus building used simplified spelling; even after his death, doors leading to faculty space in the Felmley Hall of Science were labeled "offis." Still, the two presidents exercised a degree of their characteristic caution regarding official college publications. When Felmley asked Seerley in 1909 for advice on official institutional reports, Seerley explained that he had "controlled the original form" of the biennial Board of Trustees report

> when it went to the hands of the Governor . . . I said to our secretaries not to be too severe in regard to the simplified spellings, as the state printer would probably object, and as a consequence we have got a mixture rather than have any controversy with the state printer. I think it is better to use some of these forms in such reports if you cannot get them all in.

It was the use of simplified spelling in school catalogs that sparked the Zeller resolution in 1911, and Seerley was sure to point out to the legislators that the trustees had approved the practice in 1908 and that all catalogs acknowledged it on the title page. Under Felmley, ISNU catalogs noted, "Whenever two spellings of a work are authorized by the New International or by the New Standard Dictionary, it is the practice of the State Normal University to use the shorter form in its publications."[68]

The presidents' measured approach seems to have won over at least some students, even if legislators and the general public remained skeptical. The editors of *The Normal Eyte* commended "the good judgment of the President of the United States" after Roosevelt adopted simplified spelling in 1906, and defended Seerley in the face of the legislators' 1911 inquisition, stating, "The use of this revised spelling in our catalog is only a part of a national movement, backed by the leading educators, to make it the spelling of the masses. It is certainly a wise move and is only another evidence of the progressive element in our noted president."[69] ISNU historian Helen Marshall observed that, for alumni who graduated between the 1900s and the 1920s, the label "offis" in Felmley Hall evoked "nostalgic memories."[70] As students, they had demonstrated their affection for Felmley's simplified spelling by teasing him in the ISNU yearbook. A drawing of "Mr. Felmley's Ghost" in *The Index* for 1901 asked about "vacazhion," and a cartoon depicting "The Simplified Spelling Board Hospital" in the 1909 yearbook showed Felmley holding a saw over the *e* in the word *burned,* while spelling instructor Cavins placed an ether mask over the *b.* In the background, assistants carried a shortened word toward a door marked "Dictionary" and a list of other reformed words appeared on the wall. As late as 1924, a satirical article on "President Phelmleigh" in *The Index* reported that he had swallowed a spelling book as a child.[71] Students' expressions of affection and support for Felmley and Seerley demonstrate the success of the presidents' "administrativ" approach to spelling reform in helping them to maintain good favor on campus, as well as at the state and national levels, even as they embraced a controversial innovation.

Conclusion

As ISTC students praised Homer Seerley's progressivism, he and David Felmley maintained a "desirably progressive" and yet also "safely conservative" – or "administrativ" – approach to promoting spelling reform. After they established their career and the movement gained steam in the late nineteenth century, the two presidents used simplified spelling in their administrative work but did not require it of their students in the early twentieth century, when they also offered measured support for the reform in their STAs, the NEA, and the SSB. Unlike President William T. Foster at Reed College, they balanced their intellectual commitment with practical considerations for the welfare of their institution. Seerley and Felmley variously pushed forward and pulled back as they navigated the perils of supporting a controversial innovation with a sense that they were, as Seerley stated, "responsible for their opinions and their practice to those who employ them and . . . unable to be charlatans or faddists."[72] The approach of the two presidents to simplified spelling is an object lesson on how to maintain support while managing the ins and outs of reform efforts.

Seerley's and Felmley's careers flourished well beyond the demise of the movement for simplified spelling. Seerley retired from ISTC in 1928 with much acclamation and a lifetime membership in the Iowa STA, and Felmley died in "offis" in 1930, soon after learning that ISNU's science building would be named in his honor.[73] Although the two presidents continued to use streamlined word forms in their personal correspondence, the SSB dissolved within a year of Andrew Carnegie's death in 1919, and the NEA stopped supporting spelling reform long before it officially withdrew its endorsement in 1921.[74] As presidents of teachers colleges, Seerley and Felmley worked at the intersection of K–12 and higher education during a time when leaders in both areas faced unprecedented public scrutiny. Historian Raymond Callahan argued in *Education and the Cult of Efficiency* that the vulnerability of Progressive Era leaders in K-12 education "to public criticism and pressure" was detrimental to the development of public education, and Laurence Veysey suggested that concern about external relations often dictated the actions of leaders in higher education as well.[75] Seerley's and Felmley's "administrativ" approach to spelling reform enabled their personal success, but at the expense of full-scale adoption of change, they viewed as beneficial. While this particular innovation invited parody and lacked the potential to transform fundamental aspects of higher education, the story of the two teachers-college presidents and simplified spelling encourages historians and other higher-education researchers to further consider the role of leaders' concern over public opinion in thwarting innovation and change in higher education.

Notes

1. Burton R. Clark, *The Distinctive College: Antioch, Reed, and Swarthmore* (Chicago: Aldine Publishing Company, 1970), chapter 5, quotation on 104.
2. *Reed College Record* (Portland, OR: Reed College) no. 20 (September 1915): 8; no. 26 (October 1917): 9, 12.
3. Clark, *The Distinctive College*, 118. See also Richard E. Ritz, *A History of the Reed College Campus and Its Buildings* (Portland, OR: The Trustees of the Reed Institute, 1990), 31.
4. Jonathan Zimmerman, "Simplified Spelling and the Cult of Efficiency in the 'Progressiv' Era," *Journal of the Gilded Age and the Progressive Era* 9, no. 3 (July 2010): 365–394; Christine A. Ogren, "Complexities of Efficiency

Reform: The Case of Simplified Spelling, 1876–1921," *History of Education Quarterly* 57, no. 3 (August 2017): 333–368; Robert L Hampel, *Fast and Curious: A History of Shortcuts in American Education* (Lanham, MD: Rowman & Littlefield, 2017), 127–132. Until recently, historical scholarship on the spelling reform movement appeared mainly in the areas of linguistics, speech, and journalism. See, for example, Dennis E. Baron, *Grammar and Good Taste: Reforming the American Language* (New Haven, CT: Yale University Press, 1982), 68–98; John H. Vivian, "Spelling an End to Orthographical Reforms: Newspaper Response to the 1906 Roosevelt Simplifications," *American Speech* 54, no. 3 (October 1979): 163–174; Clyde H. Dornbusch, "American Spelling Simplified by Presidential Edict," *American Speech* 36, no. 3 (October 1961): 236–238; and George R. Ranow, "Simplified Spelling in Government Publications," *American Speech* 29, no. 1 (February 1954): 36–44. See also Paula Mitchell Marks, "The Three-Hundred Words," *American History Illustrated* 20, no. 1 (March 1985): 30–35; and Edgar B. Wesley, *NEA: The First Hundred Years: The Building of the Teaching Profession* (New York: Harper & Brothers, 1957), chapter 19. For examples of publications discussing spelling reform during this time period, see T.W. Hunt, "How to Reform English Spelling," *The North American Review* 140 (April 1885): 357–368; F.A. March, et al., "Simplified Spelling," *The American Anthropologist* 6, no. 2 (April 1893): 137–206; Edwin W. Bowen, "A Question of Preference in English Spelling," *Popular Science Monthly* 65 (May–October 1904): 38–44; Brander Matthews, "The Spelling of Yesterday and of To-Morrow," *The Outlook* 82 (April 14, 1906): 848–853; and Thomas R. Lounsbury, *English Spelling and Spelling Reform* (Westport, CT: Greenwood Press, [1909] 1970).

5. Laurence R. Veysey, *The Emergence of the American University* (Chicago: The University of Chicago Press, 1965), chapters 5–7, quotations on 381, 382. Geiger adds, "A president's external relations became more crucial as universities grew dependent on different constituencies for the resources on which they depended," Roger L. Geiger, *A History of American Higher Education: Learning and Culture from the Founding to World War II* (Princeton, NJ: Princeton University Press, 2015), chapter 8, quotation on 363. See also John R. Thelin, *A History of American Higher Education* (Baltimore: The Johns Hopkins University Press, 2004), chapter 4; and Frederick Rudolph, *The American College and University: A History* (Athens: The University of Georgia Press, [1962] 1990), chapter 20. Concern about appearances and public opinion also shaped K-12 school leadership during the Progressive Era. See Raymond Callahan, *Education and the Cult of Efficiency* (Chicago: University of Chicago Press, 1962); Barbara Berman, "Business Efficiency, American Schooling, and the Public School Superintendency: A Reconsideration of the Callahan Thesis," *History of Education Quarterly* 23, no. 3 (Autumn 1983): 297–321.

6. Foster quoted in Clark, *The Distinctive College*, 96.

7. Homer H. Seerley to Charles P.G. Scott, January 23, 1911, Correspondence, Homer H. Seerley Papers, Special Collections and University Archives, Rod Library, University of Northern Iowa, Cedar Falls, IA (hereafter cited as Seerley Papers); William C. Lang, *A Century of Leadership and Service: A Centennial History of the University of Northern Iowa, Volume I, 1876–1928* (Cedar Falls: University of Northern Iowa, 1990), 274.

8. Helen E. Marshall, "Simplified Spelling – and David Felmley," *The Alumni Quarterly of the Illinois State Normal University* (May 1954): 9; Board of Prison Industries, Folder: 1904–1908, Box 5, President David Felmley Papers, Dr. Jo Ann Rayfield Archives at Illinois State University, Milner Library, Normal, IL (hereafter cited as Felmley Papers).

9. State normal schools faced a great deal of opposition from state legislatures and taxpayers when they were first established in the mid-nineteenth century, and legislators continued to debate state financial support into the early twentieth century. Christine A. Ogren, *The American State Normal School: "An Instrument of Great Good"* (New York: Palgrave Macmillan, 2005), chapters 1–2. And state normal schools and teachers colleges were tied to the K-12 system, which faced great public scrutiny. Callahan, *Education and the Cult of Efficiency*.

10. Charles A. Harper, *Development of the Teachers College with Special Reference to the Illinois State Normal University* (Bloomington, IL: McKnight & McKnight, 1935), 295; Charles A. Harper, *A Century of Public Teacher Education: The Story of the State Teachers Colleges as They Evolved from the Normal Schools* (Washington, DC: American Association of Teachers Colleges, 1939), 141. See also Helen E. Marshall, *Grandest of Enterprises: Illinois State Normal University, 1857–1957* (Normal, IL: Illinois State Normal University, 1956), chapters 10–11; and David Sands Wright, *Fifty Years at the Teachers College: Historical and Personal Reminiscences* (Cedar Falls, IA: Iowa State Teachers College, 1926).

11. "Dean of Educational Common Sense: What Some of Our Foremost Educators Say of Homer H. Seerley, President, State Teachers College, Cedar Falls, Iowa," *Journal of Education* 101 (June 25, 1925): 718–730. See also "Rejoicing with Seerley," "Honoring Homer H. Seerley," and A. E. Winship, "English River Township, Iowa," *Journal of Education* 101 (June 25, 1925): 715–718.

12. Homer H. Seerley to E.O. Vaile, April 22, 1910, Seerley Papers.

13. Veysey explains that University of California President Benjamin Ide Wheeler "took moderate, 'sensible' stands on nearly every current issue, political as well as educational," and Geiger adds that Wheeler's leadership "was facilitated by a dignified, yet affable, personality. . . . He was especially adept at charming legislators into generous appropriations." Rudolph quotes Ohio State Board member Rutherford B. Hayes as saying in the early 1890s, "We are looking for a man of fine appearance, of commanding presence, one who will impress the public . . . he must have tact so that he can get along with and govern the faculty; he must be popular with the students; he must also be . . . a great administrator. . . . Gentlemen, there is no such man." Veysey, *The Emergence of the American University*, chapters 5–7, quotation on 364; Geiger, *A History of American Higher Education*, chapter 8, quotation on 361; Rudolph, *The American College and University*, chapter 20, quotation on 419. See also Thelin, *A History of American Higher Education*, chapter 4. Also absent from the discussion of higher-education leaders and public relations are presidents of teacher-education institutions. For background on state normal schools and teachers colleges during this period, see Ogren, *The American State Normal School.*

14. Lang, *A Century of Leadership and Service*, 90–91; Wright, *Fifty Years at the Teachers College*, 104; Marshall, *Grandest of Enterprises*, 228–229.

15. Wright, *Fifty Years at the Teachers College*, 242–243.

16. *Journal of the Proceedings of the 46th Annual Meeting of the Illinois State Teachers' Association and Sections, Held at Springfield, Illinois, December 26–29, 1899*, 27 (Illinois STA proceedings hereafter cited as *Journal of Proceedings . . . Illinois . . . [year].*); *Journal of Proceedings . . . Illinois . . . 1901*, 17; Wesley, *NEA: The First Hundred Years*, 392–393.

17. Ogren, "Complexities of Efficiency Reform," 338–344. On the NEA as a professional organization, see David Tyack and Elisabeth Hansot, *Managers of Virtue: Public School Leadership in America, 1920–1980* (New York: Basic Books, 1982), 98; and Wesley, *NEA: The First Hundred Years*, 3.

18. H.L. Mencken, *The American Language: An Inquiry Into the Development of English in the United States*, 4th ed (New York: Alfred A. Knopf, 1941), 399; W.C. Sawyer, "Report on Orthoepy," *The Addresses and Journal of Proceedings of the National Educational Association* (National Educational Association, 1876): 134–40. Hereafter, *NEA Proceedings* refers to *The Addresses and Journal of Proceedings of the National Educational Association* (National Educational Association, 1876–1891), *Journal of Proceedings and Addresses of the National Educational Association* (National Educational Association, 1897–1906), or the *Journal of Proceedings and Addresses of the National Education Association* (National Education Association, 1907–1920).

19. *NEA Proceedings*, 1879–1881; W.G. Ballantine, "The Duti ov Our Colejez Toward the Speling Reform," *NEA Proceedings*, 1880, 262–267; SRA meeting minutes, *NEA Proceedings*, 1880, 267; SRA proceedings, *NEA Proceedings*, 1881, 274–275, 277.

20. F. A. March, "The Relation of Educators to Spelling-Reform," *NEA Proceedings*, 1880, 146–51, quotation on 151; T.R. Vickroy, "The Necessity for Spelling Reform," *NEA Proceedings*, 1881, 88–93, quotation on 93.

21. *NEA Proceedings*, 1890, 38; H. W. Brewster, "Spelling Reform," *NEA Proceedings*, 1891, 148–156, quotation on 149; *NEA Proceedings*, 1891, 158. See also "T. R. Vickroy, "Spelling Reform," *NEA Proceedings*, 1891, 156–158.

22. Department of Superintendence, *NEA Proceedings*, 1897, 196–197; Board of Directors minutes, *NEA Proceedings*, 1898, 37; Board of Directors minutes, *NEA Proceedings*, 1899, 43.

23. "State News and Notes," *The Iowa Normal Monthly* 22, no. 7 (February 1899): 330 (hereafter cited as *INM*).

24. *INM* 10, no. 1 (August 1886): 1; "Amended Spellings Recommended," *INM* 22, no. 2 (September 1898): 77–78.

25. J. K. Pickett, "The Spelling Reform," *Proceedings of the State Teachers' Association of Iowa, At Its Annual Meeting, Held at Grinnell, December 26, 27, and 28, 1876* (Davenport, IA, 1877), 23–29; *Proceedings of the STA of Iowa . . . 1877*, 68–69, 17.

26. *Proceedings of the Iowa State Teachers' Association, Thirty-First Annual Meeting Held at Des Moines, Iowa, December 28–31, 1886* (Dubuque: Iowa Normal Monthly, 1887), 21, 41–48, 218–225; *Proceedings of the . . . Iowa State Teachers' Association . . . December 22–29, 1888*, 19; *Proceedings of the . . . Iowa State Teachers' Association . . . December 30, 31, 1890, Jan. 1, 2, 1891*, 90–91. See also "Third Day's Proceedings [of Iowa STA]," *INM* 2, no. 7 (February 1879): 233.

27. H. H. Seerley, "Child Study Nonsense," *INM* 20, no. 1 (August 1896): 22–24; Letter by James Lawry, *INM* 20, no. 2 (September 1896): 51; *INM* 21, no. 1 (August 1897): 3–5; *INM*, 21, nos. 2–9; "The Spelling Book – Shall We Discard It," *INM* 8, no. 10–11 (June–July 1885): 448–451, quotation on 451; Mrs. T.F.M. Curry, "Spelling Reform," *INM* 2, no. 10 (May 1897): 322–326; J. S. Huey, "Spelling Reform," *INM* 2, no. 12 (July 1879): 401–403; "Spelling Reform," *INM* 11, no. 6 (January 1888): 238; Fisk P. Brewer, "Thirteen Amended Spellings," *INM* 11, no. 9 (April 1888): 368–369; D. S. Wright, "Spelling," *INM* 19, no. 3 (October 1895): 96–98; "Amended Spelling Recommended," *INM* 22, no. 2 (September 1898): 77–78; "Deformed Spelling," *INM* 23, no. 1 (August 1899): 41–42.

28. *Program of the Twenty-Ninth Annual Session: Illinois State Teachers' Association . . . 1882*, Abraham Lincoln Presidential Library and Museum, Springfield, IL.

29. *Journal of Proceedings . . . Illinois . . . 1899*, 34.

30. E. A. Gastman, "Leigh's Phonic Type," *The Illinois Schoolmaster* 8 (1875): 50; I.K. Funk, "Progress in Spelling Reform," *The Intelligence: A Journal of*

Education 19, no. 7 (April 1, 1899): 247–248, quotation on 248; "A Hint to Those Who Want to Help," *The Intelligence* 19, no. 12 (June 15, 1899): 450–451, quotation on 450.

31. *INM* 28, no. 11–12 (June–July 1905): 549.

32. "The Contributors' Club: The Simple Spellers," *The Atlantic Monthly* 128 (October 1921): n.p.

33. Harris in "Discussion – Subject: Simplified Spelling," *NEA Proceedings*, 1901, 224; W. H. Elson, et al., "Report of the Committee on the Simplification of Spelling," *NEA Proceedings*, 1905, 157.

34. Ogren, "Complexities of Efficiency Reform."

35. "Simplified Spelling Board, Circular No. 1, March 21, 1906," and "Circular No. 2, March 21, 1906," in *Simplified Spelling for the Use of Government Departments* (Washington, DC: Office of the Public Printer, 1906), 7–23; Vivian, "Spelling an End to Orthographical Reforms," 165; Dornbusch, "American Spelling Simplified by Presidential Edict"; Marks, "The Three-Hundred Words"; Wesley, *NEA: The First Hundred Years*, chapter 19. Roosevelt and Carnegie would continue to use simplified spelling for the rest of their lives.

36. James Lawry, "Takes a Rap at Simplified Spelling Board," *INM* 31, no. 9 (April 1908): 503.

37. William Aldrich to Homer H. Seerley, February 1, 1908 and February 5, 1908, Seerley Papers; Homer H. Seerley to E.O. Vaile, April 22, 1910, Seerley Papers.

38. "Simplified Spelling Board, Circular No. 1, March 21, 1906," 9.

39. Homer H. Seerley, "The Attitude of the Leaders of Public Education Toward Simplified Spelling," *Educational Review* 36 (September 1908): 180–189.

40. "Third Annual Meeting," *Simplified Spelling Bulletin* 1, no. 1 (June 1909): 2; Homer H. Seerley to Charles P. G. Scott, March 13, 1907, Seerley Papers.

41. "Items of Interest," *Simplified Spelling Bulletin* 1, no. 1 (June 1909): 8; "Fourth Annual Meeting," *Simplified Spelling Bulletin* 2, no. 1 (June 1910): 1; "Vice Presidents," *Simplified Spelling Bulletin* 2, no. 1 (June 1910): 4.

42. "Seventh Annual Meeting," *Simplified Spelling Bulletin* 5, no. 1 (June 1913): 1–2; "Five New Members," *Simplified Spelling Bulletin* 5, no. 3 (December 1913): 28.

43. Seerley, "The Attitude of the Leaders," 186; Simplified Spelling Board Resolution, April 14, 1909, Felmley Papers; Homer H. Seerley to Geo. W. Jones, October 11, 1905, Seerley Papers; Homer H. Seerley, David Felmley, and Charles McKenny to Presidents and Faculties of the State Normal Schools, United States of America, December 20, 1909, Felmley Papers; Homer H. Seerley to C. P. G. Scott, January 3, 1910, Seerley Papers. Zimmerman points out that Jordan and Butler were pressured to resign, and suggests that lack of open support from prestigious institutions hurt the cause of spelling reform. Zimmerman, "Simplified Spelling and the Cult of Efficiency," 375. See also Ogren, "Complexities of Efficiency Reform," 348.

44. Charles C. P. Scott to David Felmley, July 24, 1909, Folder: Simplified Spelling Board 1906–1910, Box 5, Felmley Papers.

45. Homer H. Seerley to E.O. Vaile, April 22, 1910, Seerley Papers; Homer H. Seerley to E.O. Vaile, October 15, 1910, Seerley Papers.

46. Seerley to members of the North Central Branch, February 17, 1913, Seerley Papers; David Felmley to Edmund James, February 9, 1914, Folder: Simplified Spelling Board, 1911–1918, Box 5, Felmley Papers.

47. "Proceedings of the Board of Directors," *NEA Proceedings*, 1901, 36; Department of Superintendence minutes, *NEA Proceedings*, 1903, 140; W. H. Elson to David Felmley, December 18, 1905, and David Felmley to W. H. Elson,

December 20, 1905, Folder: Miscellaneous Correspondence, A–F, Box 4, Felmley Papers.

48. Elson, et al., "Report of the Committee on the Simplification of Spelling," 157; Homer H. Seerley to Chas M. Jordan, November 10, 1904, Seerley Papers; Homer H. Seerley to W.H. Maxwell, January 14, 1905, Seerley Papers; E.O. Vaile to Homer H. Seerley, April 17, 1905, Seerley Papers; Homer H. Seerley to E.O. Vaile, April 18, 1905, Seerley Papers.

49. Homer H. Seerley to C. P. G. Scott, June 1, 1908, Seerley Papers; Homer H. Seerley to E.O. Vaile, May 7, 1910, Seerley Papers; *NEA Proceedings*, 1910, 589–590; Homer H. Seerley, David Felmley, and Charles McKenny, "Report on the Progress of Simplified Spelling in America, Department of Normal Schools, National Educational Association, Boston, Massachusetts, July 8, 1910, Folder: Simplified Spelling Board, 1906–1910, Box 5, Felmley Papers.

50. Homer H. Seerley, "Simplified Spelling With Reference to the Masses," and "Discussion," *NEA Proceedings*, 1911, 651–657, quotations on 652, 655.

51. "Department of Superintendence, Secretary's Minutes," *NEA Proceedings*, 1912, 332.

52. Homer H. Seerley to Henry Sabin, January 23, 1911, Seerley Papers; Homer H. Seerley to C. P. G. Scott, January 23, 1911, Seerley Papers; Homer H. Seerley to Hon. F. J. Lund, January 25, 1911, Seerley Papers; Homer H. Seerley to Hon. Thomas Lambert, January 25, 1911, Seerley Papers; Homer H. Seerley to C.P.G. Scott, February 4, 1911, Seerley Papers; Homer H. Seerley to J.F. Riggs, February 6, 1911, Seerley Papers; Lang, *A Century of Leadership and Service*, 273–274.

53. Marshall, "Simplified Spelling – and David Felmley"; Board of Prison Industries, Folder: 1904–1908, Box 5, Felmley Papers.

54. *Journal of Proceedings . . . Illinois . . . 1907*, 89–99; *Journal of Proceedings . . . Illinois . . . 1909*, 261; Homer H. Seerley, "Professional Etiquette," *INM* 24, no. 1 (August 1900): 26–28; Homer H. Seerley, "Mothers' Circles and the Public Schools," *INM* 31, no. 2 (September 1907): 95–97; *Proceedings of the Sixty-Fourth Annual Session of the Iowa State Teachers' Association, Held at Des Moines, Iowa, December 26, 27, 28, 1918* (Des Moines [1919]), 26, 84–88.

55. *Journal of Proceedings . . . Illinois . . . 1901*, 17–19; *Journal of Proceedings . . . Illinois . . . 1902*, 10, 41–53; *Journal of Proceedings . . . Illinois . . . 1903*, 20; *Journal of Proceedings . . . Illinois . . . 1904*, 17; *Journal of Proceedings . . . Illinois . . . 1905*, 18.

56. *Journal of Proceedings . . . Illinois . . . 1908*, 6; *Journal of Proceedings . . . Illinois . . . 1909*, 6–7; *Journal of Proceedings . . . Illinois . . . 1910*, 5; *Journal of Proceedings . . . Illinois . . . 1911*, 7–8, 29–35; *Journal of Proceedings . . . Illinois . . . 1912*, 7; *Journal of Proceedings . . . Illinois . . . 1914*, 5, 16, 25–32; "News Items," *The Illinois Teacher* 1, no. 5 (September 1, 1913): 6; L.D. Coffman, "Reformed Spelling in the State," *The Illinois Teacher* 3, no. 1 (September 1, 1914): 3–4.

57. *Proceedings of the Forty-Ninth Annual Session of the Iowa State Teachers' Association, Held at Des Moines, Iowa, December 28, 29, 30 and 31, 1903* (Des Moines, 1904), 7–8; *Proceedings . . . Iowa State Teachers Association . . . 1904–1922*; Homer H. Seerley to C. P. G. Scott, January 13, 1912, Seerley Papers.

58. Homer H. Seerley, "The Simplification of the English Language," *INM* 29, no 9 (April 1906): 442–444; Homer H. Seerley, "Simplified Spelling," *INM* 30, no. 10 (May 1907): 508–509; Homer H. Seerley, "The Third Year of the Simplified Spelling Board," *INM* 32, no. 10 (May 1909): 563–565; Homer H. Seerley, "The Progress in Simpler Spelling," *INM* 33, no. 10 (May 1910): 447–448; Homer H. Seerley, "Simplified Spelling in 1911," *INM* 34, no. 10

(May 1911): 452–453; H.H. Seerley, "Why Iowa Is Great," *INM* 34, no. 3 (October 1910): 104–105.
59. D. S. Wright, "Simplified Spelling," *INM* 30, no. 3 (October 1906): 133–134; D. S. Wright, "Spelling Reform," *INM* 32, nos. 11–12 (June–July 1909): 586–589. See also James Lawrey, "Prof. Lawrey on Simplified Spelling," *INM* 30, no. 4 (November 1906): 166–168; Carl C. Marshall, "Spelling and Pronunciation," *INM* 31, no. 5 (December 1907): 241–245.
60. *Proceedings . . . Illinois . . . 1905*, 18.
61. Homer H. Seerley to Calvin Thomas, February 14, 1908, Seerley Papers.
62. Charles P. G. Scott to David Felmley, July 26, 1906 and September 22, 1906, Folder: Simplified Spelling Board, 1906–1910, Box 5, Felmley Papers; Homer H. Seerley to Charles P. G. Scott, October 7, 1910, Seerley Papers.
63. Seerley, "The Attitude of the Leaders," 182–183.
64. Seerley, "The Attitude of the Leaders," 186; Homer H. Seerley to C. P. G. Scott, April 25, 1910, Seerley Papers; Homer H. Seerley to C.P.G. Scott, October 7, 1910, Seerley Papers.
65. *The Normal Eyte* (Cedar Falls, IA: students of Iowa State Teachers College), October 17, 1906, 82–83; H.H. Seerley, "Simplified Spelling is Popular," *The Normal Eye*, April 21, 1909, 402. See also, for example, *The Normal Eye*, September 26, 1906, 35–36; February 12, 1908, 291; April 8, 1908, 386–388; April 14, 1909, 388–389; and April 13, 1910, 461–462.
66. David Felmley, "A Defense of Simplified Spelling," *The Alumni Quarterly of the Illinois State Normal University* (August 1912): 11–14, quotation on 12.
67. Marshall, *Grandest of Enterprises*, 243; Marshall, "Simplified Spelling – and David Felmley," 9; Homer H. Seerley to Hon F.J. Lund, January 25, 1911, Seerley Papers; Homer H. Seerley to Hon. Thomas Lambert, January 25, 1911, Seerley Papers.
68. Letterhead quoted in Marshall, "Simplified Spelling – and David Felmley," 8; Homer H. Seerley to David Felmley, January 26, 1909, Seerley Papers; Homer H. Seerley to Hon. Thomas Lambert, January 25, 1911, Seerley Papers; ISNU catalog quoted in Harper, *Development of the Teachers College*, 304; *The Normal Eyte*, February 1, 1911, 306.
69. *The Normal Eyte*, October 3, 1906, 50; "Editorial," *The Normal Eyte*, February 1, 1911, 305–306, quotation on 306.
70. Marshall, "Simplified Spelling – and David Felmley," 8.
71. *The Index* (Normal, IL: students of Illinois State Normal University), 1901, 110; 1909, 167; 1924, 281.
72. Seerley, "The Attitude of the Leaders," 180.
73. Lang, *A Century of Leadership and Service*, chapter 6; Marshall, *Grandest of Enterprises*, 278.
74. Ogren, "Complexities of Efficiency Reform," 346, 367–368.
75. Callahan, *Education and the Cult of Efficiency*, vii–viii; Veysey, *The Emergence of the American University*, chapters 5–7.

4 Progressivism, John Dewey, and the University of Chicago Laboratory School

Building Democratic Community

Sam F. Stack Jr.

Innovation implies change or something new, something creative or imaginative. It might bring together ideas from various sources designed to affect society. Innovation typically involves a form of experimentation, testing those new ideas for their workability or effectiveness. This chapter explores the University of Chicago Elementary School, better known as the Dewey lab school, as a form of innovation in American higher education and how it embodied progressive principles of the late 19th century and that those principles are still valid today.

Historians have described the progressive era in countless ways, but generally, it was a reaction to globalization, industrialization, urbanization, massive immigration, and advances in technology.[1] These changes in the post-Civil War era, up to World War I and beyond, elicited concern among many including some Grangers, populists, anti-monopolists, and urban liberals in terms of how to deal with the social, economic, and political transformations taking place. While diverse, these individuals would become known as progressives, and one of the best known was the American intellectual and philosopher John Dewey. Dewey believed that the transformation from rural/agrarian society to industrial society had led to the dissolution of community life and this loss resulted in a form of alienation, where the individual lost the sense of self, place, and one's contribution to society. Dewey thought the school was the one institution that could restore community life, ideally an experimental institution nurturing child interest but guiding that interest into helping children become active agents of inquiry through the use of intelligence, a key concept of the progressive movement.[2] This chapter explores Dewey's attempt to build community through the theory and practice of the University of Chicago's Elementary School, commonly referred to as the Dewey lab school, which grounded its philosophy in the goals of the larger progressive movement. While there are numerous studies of the Dewey lab school, few studies, if any, have attempted to capture the lab school's work within the progressive movement in America during late

19th century. This study reaches beyond the discussion of pedagogical practice of the school and attempts a greater understanding of the philosophy undergirding the curriculum, which was at the heart of Dewey's experimental approach to the curriculum.

Progressivism in the Late 19th Century

Historian Arthur Link asserts that the social, political, and economic changes of the late 19th century created conditions that attracted the attention of reform-minded Americans. These reform-minded Americans, eventually called progressives, were responding to what they perceived as the growing abuses of American capitalism and its nurturing of an individualism that threatened the very nature of democracy and social life. Link writes, "Outpourings of anger at corporate wrongdoing and of hatred of industry's callous pursuit of profit frequently punctuated the cause of reform in the early twentieth century. Indeed, anti-business emotion was a prime mover of progressivism."[3] To the progressives, America was making its fortune at the expense of the working classes and in doing so was "in peril of losing her soul."[4] The American values of meritocracy and equality of opportunity were being undercut by a rampant individualism morally supported by the doctrine of social Darwinism as argued by engineer/sociologist Herbert Spencer. Spencer visited the United States in 1882 and while "lavishly feted by the intellectual and business elite" [such as Andrew Carnegie], his ideas did not find favor among most Americans. Spencer did not support the American common school or public school and held to a Malthusian concept of letting the poor starve-survival of the fittest.[5]

In reaction to social Darwinism, the progressive movement has been described as a type of reform Darwinism. Refusing to accept Spencer's notion of "survival of the fittest," progressives took Darwin's concept and tied it to human intelligence or "intelligence as the method of directing social action."[6] Progressives refused to believe that humankind was not in control of its destiny. This belief challenged the traditional Christian concept of an omnipresent being in control, although progressives did appeal to the empathy and sympathy for humankind associated with the social gospel of the era, which is central to their understanding of community. Progressives also accepted the scientific method as applied through the social sciences and typically saw no contradiction between the Christian ethic and social science. Social science provided the method of inquiry while religion provided the moral justification. Link writes, "The progressives went about methodically to achieve justice through control, first through voluntary associations and then by advocating government intervention."[7] Collective planning was conceived as evolutionary guided by a Christian ethic.

These voluntary associations included "tax clubs, consumer leagues, trade unions, professional societies, and farm and other voluntary associations" attempting to "shape the fast-moving world."[8] Progressives relied on various forms of organization to meet their goals, grounding their methods of inquiry in social science. Link notes that many of the intellectual leaders of the progressives were specialists in the new social science disciplines of "statistics, economics, sociology, and psychology. These social scientists set out to gather data on human behavior as it actually was and to discover the laws that governed it."[9] These methods were undergirded by an optimism in the fact that conditions could be altered if the will and commitment were there. The new values championed efficiency and management, but progressives also championed a faith in democracy "and the exploration of new rights designed to protect American society from the vagaries of the marketplace that resulted in a new assessment of the relationship between the individual and the government."[10] Progressives supposed the state could "be trusted to serve the interests of the people as a whole," and to help individuals "to pursue the good life or to contribute to the life of the community."[11] Indeed, one of the control tenets "of progressivism was the development of state power to deal with the problems of the urban and industrial revolutions, integrating the political and legal theories of historicism, utilitarianism, Darwinism, sociological jurisprudence, and legal realism."[12] The growth of a centralized government during the progressive era was the result of the faith Americans placed in government to lead to the good society, a type of better world community.[13] This belief led to conservation, the development and protection of natural resources, the challenge to monopolies, and tariff reform. "Progressives brought major innovations to almost every facet of public and private life in the United States. The political and governmental systems particularly felt the effects of reform."[14] Yet, the progressive movement was also affecting educational thought and the intellectual climate of the newly formed University of Chicago proved fertile ground for innovative ideas that challenged traditional educational theory and practice.

Pragmatism and the University of Chicago

John Dewey arrived at the University of Chicago in 1894, the university being formed by the philanthropy of John David Rockefeller two years earlier and under the direction of President William Rainey Harper. Upon Dewey's arrival, Colonel Francis Parker of the Cook County Normal School, Jane Addams of Hull House, and Ella Flagg Young, superintendent of the Chicago city schools were actively involved in social, political, and educational reform. In the mid-1890s, Chicago was one of the most diverse cities in America with a population over one million.

Historian Robert Westbrook writes, "All the pathologies and possibilities of urban life were on full display in Chicago in the 1890s, and rapacious entrepreneurs and corrupt politicians struggled with visionary reformers for control of the city's destiny."[15] Dewey considered Chicago as a city of boundless energy, not just one of industrialism and capital growth but of great potential. When Dewey arrived during the summer of 1894, the Pullman strike was at its peak. George Pullman had cut the wages of his Pullman railroad car workers but did not cut their rent in their company owned houses, nor food prices in the company store, and cut other services provided in the Pullman company town. Dewey supported the workers and saw in their actions a clear challenge to wealth and industrial capitalism, particularly the paternalism associated with welfare capitalism. Although the strike was squashed when federal troops were sent to Chicago by President Grover Cleveland, Dewey felt the strikers successful in how the strike had brought a form of solidarity and even community to the labor movement.[16] Chicago and its university provided the perfect forum for Dewey to theorize and practice his ideas. "Turning his own efforts as an activist to the problems of education," notes Westbrook, "he was soon making a distinctive contribution to the social vision of this community and sharing finally in the modest victories and frustrating defeats of democratic radicalism at the term of the century."[17]

Dewey's social and educational "thought grew out of and was influenced by his understanding of pragmatism, a philosophical attempt to clarify ideas and how to think about or inquire into questions regarding knowledge, reality, values, human behavior, and related matters."[18] Education could be educative, but it could also be miseducative. As a philosophical pragmatist, Dewey saw education as a tool, or instrument to help us solve the problems of everyday life, to help us "operate efficiently, effectively, and ethically."[19] Dewey's pragmatism was in constant development, as it should be, and during his life was influenced by many thinkers including Charles Sanders Pierce, William James, Oliver Wendell Holmes, Chauncey Wright, C. S. Schiller, Albion Small, Jane Addams, Ella Flagg Young, Elsie Ripley Clapp, George Herbert Mead, and his wife Alice Chipman Dewey. I will explore the central contributions underlying the theory and practice of the lab school through Ella Flagg Young, Jane Addams, and Alice Chipman Dewey later in the chapter.

The University of Chicago pragmatists, led by Dewey and George Herbert Mead, "saw both science and values arising from human action, and they proceeded to derive an entire philosophy from the analysis of action."[20] Being experimentalists, the Chicago pragmatists challenged the traditional in both thought and scholarship, away from "the more literary tradition of scholarship" to one more aligned with the openness of scientific inquiry and problem solving. This openness to inquiry clearly aligned with the goals of progressive reform and played a central role in designing the curriculum of the Dewey lab school. Louis Menand states,

> Dewey's pragmatism was a consequence of the success of the Laboratory School. The school established for him the validity of his hypothesis that thinking and acting, are just two names for a single process-the process of making our way as best we can in a universe shot through with contingency.[21]

Dewey defied the centering of the individual in the traditional approach to education and envisioned education as a social affair, socializing "the child so that he is better prepared for the intricate world into which he must fit" and not be "merely handed facts and skills in whatever quantity or of whatever sort."[22] Dewey saw education as a form of experience, a social process, a transaction not only between teacher and student, but also a constant transaction as we live and work in the world. Other University of Chicago faculty such as Albion small in sociology concluded with Dewey that traditional education was not meeting the needs of a rapidly changing society and that education needed to help students "see the whole world if they are to make any sense or derive any meaning from the abstractions from the whole that these [traditional-my emphasis] subjects presumably represent."[23]

Influenced by the practice of Colonel Francis Parker of the Chicago Institute or more commonly known as the Cook County Normal School, Dewey, like Parker understood the school as a form of community life, a community being democracy "realizing itself in citizenship" with learning how to live and foster a democracy the "immediate, everlasting and only purpose of the school."[24] As previously mentioned, Dewey like many progressives believed that the transition from rural to urban society had resulted in the dissolution of community, where one's sense of place and identity were formed within the family unit and local community. The industrial revolution had disrupted those entities and resulted in a form of social/psychological alienation, where one no longer understood their place and identity in this brave new world. Dewey believed that the school was the one institution that could restore community life, and this was the

> reason that Dewey tried to make the University Elementary School an extension of family life, designed to lead the child into other, larger social relations. Parker's idea of the connection between home life and school become central in the educational theory of Dewey and Mead.[25]

Within this sense of community and the fostering of democracy, Dewey imagined the school as cooperative rather than competitive and like

Mead, Dewey saw the public school as an instrument for "overcoming the antagonism between labor and management and for bringing about a richer life of the whole community."[26] Dewey wrote in *School and Society*, a book of compiled lectures given to the parents of children in the lab school, "A society is a number of people held together because they are working along common lines, in a common spirit, and with reference to common aims. The common needs and aims demand a growing interchange of thought and growing unity of sympathetic feeling."[27] Dewey is implying that education is fundamentally a moral process where individual aims and goals must be understood in the context of the larger social good. He explained this basic principle underlying the formation of the lab school. "The hypothesis underlying this experiment is that of the school as a social institution. Education outside the school proceeds almost wholly through participation in the social or community life of the groups of which one is a member."[28] So the school for Dewey was society in miniature, and the child was to "leave gradually acquainted with the structure, materials, and modes or operations of the larger community; while, upon the other, it enables him individually to express himself through these lines of conduct, and thus attain control of his own powers."[29]

Dewey never conceived the lab school as a teaching training institute or a blueprint for other schools to follow. He saw the school as a philosophy laboratory to try out and test ideas on a theory of education.[30] This makes the lab school an innovation in American higher education at the time. His philosophy of education is most clearly expressed in his short essay *My Pedagogic Creed*, published shortly after the opening of the lab school in 1896. Writing his philosophy of education in terms of belief statements, Dewey asserts that education should help the child understand "himself from the standpoint of the welfare of the group to which he belongs" and that it is prepare the child for the future and not based in tradition or the past. Traditional education, largely what Dewey terms as teacher and text driven, neglected the school as a form of community life. "I believe that much of present education fails," Dewey wrote,

> because it neglects this fundamental principle of the school as a form of community life. . . . It [the traditional school] conceived the school as a place where certain information is to be given, where certain lessons are to be learned, or where certain habits are to be formed.[31]

Traditional subject matter could and should be taught, but should be grounded in the experiences of the child and driven by the natural interests of the child as motivation. Dewey conceived education as the "continuing reconstruction of experience; that the process and goal of education are one and the same thing."[32] Showing the optimistic nature of the progressive, Dewey contended that education was "the fundamental method of social progress and reform that the school should nurture a social consciousness where the child learns to adjust "individual activity as the basis of this social consciousness" and that education should be a community's "paramount moral duty."[33]

Progressive Education and the Lab School

Dewey's pragmatic philosophy of education, coupled with Francis Parker's practice at the Cook County Normal School (The Chicago Institute) came to be known as the "new education" or better known as progressive education. "At its inception, progressive education was based on the recognition of a need to get away from the traditional system of the three R's which was failing to meet the needs of the growing understanding of child behavior."[34] The child was no longer perceived as a blank slate, learning through passive mental impressions, but bound by action via experience in the environment. George Herbert Mead's social psychology and William James' discussion of the stream of consciousness and active mind influenced progressive education. While the progressive education movement was exceptionally diverse, so diverse that Dewey often criticized many who claimed to practice it, the stage was set at the university elementary school or lab school to integrate theory and practice. Dewey wrote about his experience in education through two primary works, *The Child and the Curriculum* and *School and Society*. These are significant because there were written during the time Dewey directed the lab school and because those who claimed to practice progressive education were familiar with these two works. Subject matter was not to be conceived as something fixed and ready-made, outside the child's experience, but something "fluid and vital."[35] *School and Society* is particularly important because Dewey "draws the most explicit connections between his educational philosophy and his critique of industrial society, there by revealing his attention to the issues of power and the "anti-democratic implications of industrial society."[36] Deron Boyles notes, "In these works Dewey argued that schools should be places where meaning-making occurs through experimentation. Experimentation is based on the interests of children-naturally occurring-but with guidance from teachers."[37] Furthermore, the work is significant because it was a series of lectures given by Dewey to the parents of the children attending the lab school. In a most Marxist sense, Dewey refereed to the worker as an appendage to the machine, the worker with "no opportunity to develop his imagination and his sympathetic insight as to the social and scientific values found in his work."[38] One of the major purposes of the lab school was to help the children develop their imagination, a necessary trait for problem solving but also to learn about the nature of human work and gain a respect for labor. "To do this means to make each one of our schools an embryonic community life, active with types of occupations that reflect the life of the larger society, and permeated throughout with the spirit of art, history, and science."[39] The school was to embody in the child "the spirit of service, and providing him with the instruments of effective self-direction, we shall have the deepest and best guarantee of a larger society which is worthy, lovely, and harmonious."[40] The school environment was to be characterized by free and open communication with the open exchange of ideas. Dewey asserted, "A society is a number of people held together because they are working along common lines, in a common spirit, and with reference to common aims. The common needs and aims demand a growing interchange of thought and growing unity of sympathetic feelings."[41] Like the real world, Dewey sought to have "students engaged in problem solving and experimenting-all the while (unconsciously and consciously) honing the abilities meted out not only to 'get by' in society but to contribute to it as well."[42] The lab school was to be based on cooperation and association over competition, in essence a form of democratic community.[43]

The University of Chicago Elementary School (Dewey Lab School)

William Rainey Harper, a noted scholar in Hebrew, had an interest in pedagogy and wanted the graduate study of education to be an offering at the University of Chicago. Harper "saw it all in Dewey, a teacher and an eminent scholar, in philosophy and psychology, a trainer of discoverers, and above all, an original mind."[44] Harper offered Dewey a position on the faculty and Dewey became head of the philosophy department, which included psychology and education. Dewey had limited practical experience as a teacher in Oil City, Pennsylvania and had been somewhat active in education at the University of Michigan. However, Chicago provided a forum for Dewey to test his philosophy through education, largely shaped by his association with Ella Flagg Young, Jane Addams, and Alice Chipman Dewey.[45] Dewey wrote to future lab schoolteacher Clara Mitchell in 1895 concerning his ideas about a new kind of school.

> This school will be primarily a school of methods, only secondarily a school of practice . . . its primary intention is to attempt a systematic organization of the school curriculum, testing, and developing methods both from the psychological and practical side.[46]

One year later he stated, "The conception underlying the school is that of a laboratory. It bears the same relation to work in pedagogy that a laboratory bears to biology, physics, or chemistry. Like any such laboratory, it has two main purposes: (1) to exhibit, test, verify, and criticize theoretical statements and principles: (2) to add to the sum of facts and principles in its special line."

Dewey believed that in rural/agrarian society, "The entire industrial process stood revealed, from the production on the farm of the raw material till the finished article was actually put to use. Not only this, but practically every member of the household had his own share in the work."[47] Furthermore, he believed this form of sharing gave the individual a sense of identity and a conception of how an individual contributed to the whole. The individual needed to feel part of something and the reason Dewey believed the school should be a miniature community as Herbert Kliebard states, "where the child lived, participated, and contributed-where, in effect, the child's emerging individuality was at one and the same time used to enrich the social community and tested against the dictates of social reality."[48]

Dewey always viewed the formation of the lab school as a modest endeavor and it began "in a small house on Fifty-Seventh Street, with fifteen children."[49] A few years later, school numbers had increased to sixty children in a new location, Rosalie Court, the children ranging in age from four to thirteen. "The educational problem we are at work on," he wrote to Frank Manny,

> is precisely how to start always with expression, and desire the information side from in particular how to get all the early work in reading and writing and number in connection either with the social impulse of communication or else with constructive work that holds the child from its own sake.[50]

Dewey is addressing the need to capture the attention of the children through interest as the first step in beginning to teach subject matter. He believed

> there are no limits to the hold on children's attention when subjects of instruction are presented to them first in terms of their own life experience; as cooking, carpentry; also that such a beginning removes practically completely the school atmosphere, and puts in its place a free social environment.[51]

Dewey referred to activities such as cooking and carpentry as occupations with the goal to have the child begin to "see within his daily work, all there is in it of large and human significance" and "that the child begin to understand "that the worker has had no opportunity to develop his imagination and his sympathetic insight as to the social and scientific value found in his work."[52] Jane Addams was also experimenting with this idea at Hull House through her museum of labor. By modeling occupations, Dewey hoped to engender a respect for labor but also help the child understand their own connection to work of the laborer and how it connected to their own existence through forms of social relations, which the traditional school neglected or ignored. Dewey criticized the traditional school as creating a passive attitude, uniformity and conformity through the curriculum, where the center of gravity was the teacher and the test, not the child.[53] He believed the traditional school through its curriculum stifled growth through what it perceived as intellectual content. Again, this was strictly a mental or psychological approach based on acquisition and not inquiry. "In the long run," notes Kliebard,

> it was intellectual development that Dewey sought to effect through the curriculum, not only because it gave the individual command of his or her environment, but because intelligent social action held out the most promise for a better society. Dewey's rejection of the traditional course of study was not because it emphasized intellectual content; it was precisely because it lacked it.[54]

Intelligent social action was a central theme of the progressive movement at large. One example of this approach to "intelligent action" was how the lab school taught history, not as "a form of acquisition of information," . . . but as "a form of inquiry into humankind's past, how and why they did things in their lives, attentive to their successes and failures."[55]

The role of the teacher was instrumental to the success of the university lab school and necessary for the application of Dewey's theory as a whole as he sought to build community and democracy. Dewey sought a teacher with "a high degree of intelligence, a great deal of skill, and a firm sense of being a teacher and an inquirer rather than the traditional importer of knowledge and trainer for examinations."[56] Dewey envisioned the teacher as a scholar, one interested in learning theory but in the true pragmatist sense the practical application of theory into practice. Due to the traditional training of teachers at the time it was not easy was to locate the teacher inquirer he was seeking. Dewey sought teachers with experience teaching young children, with intelligence and the ability to adjust to a different approach and philosophy of education with "initiative and vivacity."[57] Dewey found the consummate teacher-scholar and colleague in Ella Flagg Young. Dewey and his wife Alice Chipman Dewey had little teaching experience and the addition of Young gave them a better sense of the teaching profession and the everyday life of the teacher. Young was fifty years old when she first met Dewey as a student and had been working in the Chicago city schools for over 30 years. They engaged in "vigorous debates with each other in classes," and Young "deeply admired Dewey's broad philosophy and theoretical understandings."[58] Young and Dewey complemented each other intellectually, providing for the integration of theory and practice grounding the lab school curriculum.

Ella Flagg Young, who supervised the lab school from 1901 to 1904 attempted to create an environment of intellectual freedom for teachers. Flagg Young, educated at the Cook County Normal School and a former teacher in the Chicago trade schools as well as Chicago district superintendent, was a strong teacher advocate.[59] "Teachers at the school were expected and encouraged to be engaged intellectually with understanding the subject matter, discussing the learning capacities and interests of the children and context together through innovative pedagogical methods."[60] Dewey met with the teachers of the lab school at least once a week and the meetings could be described "as a form of cooperation, collaboration, discussion, modification, and reaffirmation of the aims and goals of the school."[61] Lagemann describes Ella Flagg Young as "foremost a teacher advocate and a seasoned politician" skills that served her well as superintendent and supervisor of the lab school. "Deweyan pedagogy," notes historian Robert Westbrook, "called upon teachers to perform the extremely difficult task of reinstating into experience the subject matter of the curriculum." Thus, subject matter, being conceived as human knowledge gained via experience and problem solving served as the foci of the curriculum.[62]

Led by Ella Flagg Young, the intellectual climate of the university lab school fostered a form of democratic community. It allowed for teacher voice and open communication to solve the problems of the school but also to tie learning through subject matter to the real world and life experiences of the children. Teachers were in control of their work, or better their craft, and helped the children develop a character more aligned with a democratic ethic.[63] In her review of Dewey's *Democracy and Education* (1916), Young noted, "In this book the philosophy seeks and points the way that would make education a great instrumentality, helping children and youths to grow into citizenship in a government intended to be of, by, and for all."[64] Young sought freedom and individuality in both students and teachers and

> protested the encroaching movement toward standardization in school. . . . In her classroom, students had voice in how activities unfolded. In her schools, she encouraged teachers to make important decisions together about governance, pedagogy and curriculum-with attention devoted to arts, humanities, and creative expression.[65]

For Young, schools needed to foster freedom and individuality, preparing students for participatory democracy in a democratic institution. This could only be accomplished if teachers were in control over their work.[66]

Intellectualism was coupled with social action via connections to the faculty at the University of Chicago and Hull House, directed by Dewey colleague and friend Jane Addams. The curriculum was focused on common problems and how people work together to solve those problems. The university lab school as a small cooperative society, under wise guidance, allowed children to solve problems at any stage of development and where the "systematic knowledge of adult consciousness is gradually and systematically worked out."[67] John Dewey had lectured at Hull House and knew Jane Addams prior to his arrival in Chicago and was "welcomed into the reform community."[68] Jane Addams, was one of those reformers who

> came to their work convinced that the real course of industrialism lay not so much in its physical blight as in its shattering of historical human association . . . the cry that industrialism had dissolved the fabric of community leaving alienation in its wake, and that this ultimately had cause the deterioration of life in the slum.[69]

As many social scientists and philosophers claimed at the end of the 19th century, including Dewey, that *Gesellschaft* [society] had destroyed *Gemeinshaft* [community]. In the true sense of progressivism, this led reformers to consider education, formal and informal, as a way to rebuild community. Addams envisioned her program at Hull House as a type of socialized education and she challenged those educators whose "narrow view of culture kept them from grasping the rich pedagogical possibilities in the productive life of the city."[70] Addams had challenged traditional education in her work *Democracy and Social Ethics*, critiquing the educator's stress on reading and writing and the view that all knowledge came from books rather than the life about them. The school should "cast itself into the world of affairs, much as the settlement had done, and exert its influence toward the eventual humanizing of the productive system. Industry, she concluded, would have to be seized upon and conquered by the educators."[71] Historian Lawrence Cremin writes, "She [Addams] wanted the school to bathe the surroundings of the ordinary individual with a truly human significance, assuming that unless all mend and all classes contribute to a good, we cannot even be sure that it is worth having."[72] Jane Dewey, John Dewey's daughter and named after Jane Addams, wrote, "Dewey's faith in democracy as a guiding force in education took on both a sharper and a deeper meaning because of Hull House and Jane Addams."[73] It is clear that Dewey was influenced by his association with Addams in crafting his philosophy of education and practices in the lab school and attempting to restoring community even though Dewey never appeared to have Addams' sensitivity to loss of culture experienced by many of the immigrants, which undermined their sense of community.[74]

Alice Chipman Dewey is one of the most important intellectual influences for John Dewey, although she is probably the least understood. Jay Martin notes that "Alice had educated her husband in feminist issues. He was a serious supporter of new feminism, and Alice's influence led him to cultivate important relations with Jane Addams and other activist new feminists."[75] Alan Ryan contends Alice was "chafing at the constraints of domestic life and finding motherhood an inadequate outlet for the energy and the political enthusiasm that had attracted Dewey in the first place."[76] Ryan argues the opening of the Lab School at the University of Chicago gave Alice her opportunity to invest her talent and energy. Part of this investment in energy took place at Hull House, Alice finding philosophical and social justice compatibility with Jane Addams and her attempt to remedy "social inequity." According to Katherine Mayhew and Anna Edwards, Ella Flagg Young and Alice Dewey "introduced intellectual organization without impeding the freedom of the individual teachers."[77] John gave Alice credit for her influence in *How We Think* (1910) stating she had inspired much of the work at the lab school.[78] Like Francis Parker, Alice believed there should be continuity between the home and the school, a bridge "built between the home and the school and that the curriculum and the teaching of a school most consider and relate to both the child's past and the child's future."[79] Teaching is not the mere passing or acquisition of information. Pay attention to the life of the child and do not overestimate or underestimate the intelligence of the child.[80] Alice sought to integrate sensory data with the development of the child's mind, being attentive to subject matter but also interest.

Alice championed her causes in different ways from her husband. She never wrote much but appeared more content to live and act out her convictions. She was prominent voice in the feminist movement of the early 20th century coupled this with concern about equality of opportunity in society and in education and most probably sought full equal rights for women and challenged paternalism. Education was a process of self-identity, but also a social and political awareness, a gospel she preached in Japan and China. She was clearly a suffragist and clearly educated her husband in the concerns and needs of women along with Jane Addams and Ella Flagg Young. Themes that abound in Alice's work include teacher empowerment, student and teacher ownership and accountability, basing curriculum on student interest that includes identity, culture, attachment and experience, not whim. She sought women's rights throughout the world, was attentive to social science research and what it said about child development. She emphasized the reflective practitioners, to know the child and the parent-who they are and where they come from. But, there was another side to Alice, and it was a complicated one. She was no saint, and certainly was not always considerate of the feelings of others, could be biting in her criticism, and not always willing to listen to those who disagreed with her or her husband. Alice was brilliant and compassionate about what she loved and believed in but she also struggled with her own self-identity, could be stubborn, and was often acerbic. Upon her death, Alice was described as a brave and free thinker, an original pioneer for the rights of women, a beloved mother, a wise individual, playful and generous who loved her children.

Despite the philosophical and theoretical foundations of the university lab school and its innovative curriculum, financing the lab school proved difficult from the onset. Dewey felt William Rainey Harper was never fully committed to the lab school and Dewey constantly sought funds from benefactors. Two noted contributors were Nellie B. Linn and Anita McCormick Blaine.[81] Dewey wanted the board of trustees of the University of Chicago to formally recognize the lab school as "an organic part of the university," probably to increase its status but also better elicit financial support. Dewey had moral and some financial support from the University of Chicago Friends of the Elementary School who wrote to Harper to support the lab school's recognition. The "Friends" noted that the influence of Dewey's educational ideas "cannot fail to enhance the reputation of the University of Chicago as a center of original investigation." They further commented on Dewey's educational idea becoming internationally known and that he was a speaker in demand.[82] By the end of the summer of 1899, the lab school was in debt 1200 dollars and Harper did not believe the trustees were willing to commit more funds to the school. Harper contributed 100 dollars to the debt and wrote,

> I am confident that nothing is being done truly from which greater good may be expected for the public school system not only of Chicago and Illinois, but of the entire country that the work of the Elementary School, which is, after all, a pedagogical laboratory.[83]

Dewey believed that university founder John D. Rockefeller matched private gifts given to the university, another reason he wanted the lab school to be formally recognized as an official part of the university.[84]

Resignation from the University of Chicago

When John Dewey resigned his position at the University of Chicago in 1904, the School of Education was running a deficit of 15,000 dollars a year. While he saw some potential relief in the future he realized the School of Education was in financial trouble with a small number of students and thus not enough tuition coming in.[85] Dewey penned his resignation on April 6, 1904, in a letter to President Harper, stepping down as professor and head of the department of philosophy and as director of the School of Education. Harper responded to and implied that he had put forth his "utmost endeavor to support Dewey and the work he had been doing in the philosophy department and lab school."[86] The board of trustees accepted the resignations of both John Dewey and his wife Alice Dewey who was serving at the time as principal of the lab school. Dewey was quite upset with Harper's presentation of the resignations to the Board of trustees. In a letter following the resignations, Dewey wrote to Harper attempting to clarify that his resignation was not because the Board had failed to reappoint Alice Dewey as principal. "Your willingness to embarrass and hamper my work as Director by making use of the fact the Mrs. Dewey was Principal is but one incident in the history of years."[87]

Dewey had no prospects for employment at the time but had been in conversation with James McKeen Cattell at Columbia University in New York for a position. Dewey saw Columbia as "the most attractive proposition" for his future, but also considered an administrative position at the University of Illinois.[88] Dewey quizzed Cattell on teaching load, salary, the connection with Teachers College, and a possible position for Alice Dewey at the Speyer School. Both Alice and John wrote to US Commissioner of Education William Torrey Harris about their resignations, which Dewey attempted to explain. "But the gist of it simply that I found I could not work harmoniously under the conditions which the President's methods of conducting affairs created and imposed."[89] In the letter, Dewey asked Harris for advice about his future and "if the spirit moves you to give any counsel it will be most welcome." Dewey further reiterated his belief in democratic education to Harris.

Dewey accepted a position at Columbia University on April 28, 1904. He never had the opportunity to direct an experimental school after 1904, but due to his experience at the University of Chicago Lab School the theoretical and practical application of his philosophy formed the basis of his continual writing and research on education.[90]

Conclusion: Progressivism and the University of Chicago Lab School

John Dewey contended that traditional education privileges passivity and receptivity in children and this went against the best research in psychology and how children learned. Furthermore, passivity and receptivity are traits that led to conforming to the status quo and are antagonistic to democracy and the development of a social consciousness based on freedom of inquiry. Dewey believed that it was through education the social consciousness came to life.[91] Maintaining the status quo only increased the exploitation and oppression of the working class by the industrial/capitalist complex stressing profit over democracy. The social consciousness was grounded in a social intelligence fostered by the proper school environment, and "the school should examine possibilities of imagination and of life that the surrounding society is unable or unwilling to countenance. It (the school) should be the voice of the future-of alternative futures- within the present, and it should recognize in the child the future worker and citizen, a little prophet."[92] Dewey saw democracy as a fluid concept, a type of ethical association that needed to be discovered and rediscovered, a creation, an evolution.[93] Dewey gave Ella Flagg Young credit for shaping his ideas of democracy in schools along with his wife Alice Chipman Dewey.[94]

As philosophical pragmatists, John Dewey, Jane Addams, Ella Flagg Young, and Alice Dewey believed the process of education itself was evolutionary as it was changed and altered by the social, economic, and political changes in society. The school was to mimic real life

> in miniature, the activities formulated to life as a whole, and thus enable the child, on one side, to become gradually acquainted with the structure, materials, and modes of operation of the larger community; while, upon the other, to enable him individually to express himself through those lines of conduct, and thus attain control of his own powers.[95]

The University of Chicago Elementary School or better known as the Dewey lab school was organized around the concept of the school as a miniature community, with a curriculum based upon the ability and interests of the children. The teachers as experts in their subject matter guided the students during the learning process while the children participated in various activities, with the "social significance of subject matter brought out in instruction."[96] Dewey realized that unless teachers were empowered his ideas could not be implemented.[97] The school was experimental in nature, drew from the expertise of the University of Chicago academic community, and where the children learned the democratic traits of cooperation and service to the community at large "taking advantage of cultural and educational institutions in the community to enrich the curriculum."[98] As addressed in this chapter, Dewey was assisted by many colleagues in his intellectual growth, certainly Ella Flagg Young, Jane Addams, and Alice Chipman Dewey. In a letter to Scudder Klyce, Dewey wrote,

> Only women have ever given [me] really intellectual surprises; I'll be darned if I can see who they do it-but they do. Their observations . . . are more honest than men's-they are much less easily imposed upon. . . [and] more willing to face the unpleasant side of facts. I am not generalizing: I am only reporting what I have seen.[99]

Indeed, education was a moral undertaking where cooperation, responsibility, and respect were nurtured, not through the establishment of rule but by social interaction, essentially through experience. "The true ethical function of the school," Dewey wrote, "is the development of intelligent, self-reliant, socially oriented individuals capable of acting in their own interests, in full awareness of the relation between their individual interests and those of their society."[100] Therefore, the children became

learners "of social responsibility by virtue of the fact that this development is determined by the extent to which their experiences become
increasingly connected to an understanding of their social relations."[101]
In the true sense of progressive pragmatism, the lab school was created
to prepare children for participation in democratic society through the
use of their own intelligence, and then be better prepared to deal with
the problems of the day:

> For Dewey, education was supposed to be both a moralistic renais-
> sance enabling all individual to learn to live together, peacefully as
> well as a practical application of life's everyday experiences to the
> body of common knowledge already acquired. Education was the
> key to social cooperation and peace.[102]

However, the lab school and Dewey's work there are not without its
critics. Historian Robert Westbrook argues that Dewey underestimated

> the degree to which the success of the Dewey School was attributed
> to its insulation from the conflicts, divisions, and inequities besetting
> the larger society, an insulation difficult to replicate. It was, after all,
> a small school comprised of the children of middle-class profession-
> als and staffed by well-trained, dedicated educators with access to the
> intellectual if not the financial resources of one of the nation's great
> universities.[103]

The school never exhibited the diversity of the Chicago community and
the occupations addressed through the curriculum were not those working class children participated in. Thomas Fallace notes that, although
Dewey could not be classed as a racist, the curriculum of the lab school
was ethnocentric, particularly the way it approached the teaching of history. Fallace does assert that Dewey became more of a cultural pluralist
following his international travels although the lab school curriculum
presented Western civilization "as the most advanced, most efficient, and
most evolved culture in the world."[104]

What is the future of progressivism in America? Cornel West claims
that if progressivism is to survive

> it must go beyond the humanization of the inevitable to a better
> state of freedom and possibility, it must hear that message of demo-
> cratic experimentation more clearly and to forward a practical vision
> of the re-energizing of democratic politics and the democratizing of
> the market economy in America.[105]

In more ways than one, this was the hope of Dewey, Flagg Young, Addams,
Alice Dewey and the progressive practitioners of the lab school. "By

questioning the variations of democracy, schooling, and community," writes Deron Boyles, "Dewey set a high standard for conversations about the meaning of life and the ways individuals live those lives."[106] These conversations need to be continued.

Notes

1. Charles Postel, "TR, Wilson, and the Origins of the Progressive Tradition," in *Progressivism in America: Past, Present, and Future*, eds. David Woolner and John Thompson (New York: Oxford University Press, 2016), 4.
2. I am using the term movement in a broad sense. The Progressive movement was diverse in many facets and progressives often had different ideologies and goals, however there were certain traits held in common as discussed in the text. The best-known differentiation of the diverse progressive movement in education is David Tyack, *The One Best System* (Cambridge: Harvard University, 1976).
3. Arthur S. Link and Richard L. McCormick, *Progressivism*, The American History Series (Arlington Heights, IL: Harlan Davidson, Inc., 1983), 21. See also Paul D. Moreno, *The American State from the Civil War to the New Deal: The Twilight of Constitutionalism and the Triumph of Progressivism* (Cambridge, England: Cambridge University Press, 2013), http://catdir.loc.gov/catdir/enhancements/fy1214/2012028189-t.html, 3.
4. Harold Faulkner, *The Quest for Social Justice: 1898–1914* (New York: Macmillan, 1931), 95.
5. Link and McCormick, *Progressivism*, 22.
6. John Dewey, *LW 11:55*. The Collected Works of John Dewey, *1882–1953: The Electronic Edition*, edited by Larry A. Hickman (Charlottesville, Virginia: Intelex Corp., 1996). I am using the recommended citation form for the Collected Dewey works with EW representing the Early Works; MW, the Middle Works; and LW the Later Works followed by the volume and page number. See also Donald Martin Jacobs, Arthur S. Link, and Richard L. McCormick, "Progressivism," *The History Teacher* 17, no. 2 (1984): 304.
7. Link and McCormick, *Progressivism*, 22, 70.
8. Postel, "TR, Wilson, and the Origins of the Progressive Tradition," 6.
9. Link and McCormick, *Progressivism*, 24.
10. William G. Anderson, "Progressivism: An Historiographical Essay," *The History Teacher* 6, no. 3 (1973): 439. See also John J. McDermott and Douglas R. Anderson, *The Drama of Possibility: Experience as Philosophy of Culture*, American Philosophy Series (New York: Fordham University Press, 2007).
11. David Blaazer, "Progressivism: An Idea Whose Time Has Gone?" *Political Studies Review* 12, no. 1 (2014): 8.
12. Moreno, *The American State from the Civil War to the New Deal*, 3.
13. D. Alan Harris and Arthur A. Ekirch, "Progressivism in America: A Study of the Era from Theodore Roosevelt to Woodrow Wilson," *The Journal of Southern History* 41, no. 3 (1975): 424.
14. Link and McCormick, *Progressivism*, 117.
15. Robert B. Westbrook, *John Dewey and American Democracy* (Ithaca, NY: Cornell University Press, 1991), 83. See Susan E. Hirsch, *After the Strike: A Century of Labor Struggle at Pullman*, The Working Class in American History (Urbana: University of Illinois Press, 2003) and David Ray Papke, *The Pullman Case: The Clash of Labor and Capital in Industrial America*, Landmark Law Cases & American Society (Lawrence, KS: University Press of Kansas, 1999).

16. Westbrook, *John Dewey and American Democracy*, 86, 88.
17. Ibid., 85. For other descriptions of Dewey's Pullman strike experience and the early Chicago years see Alan Ryan, *John Dewey and the High Tide of American Liberalism* (New York : W.W. Norton, 1995), 118–123; Douglas J. Simpson and Sam F. Stack, *Teachers, Leaders, and Schools : Essays by John Dewey* (Carbondale, IL: Southern Illinois University Press, 2010), 4–5; Jay Martin, *The Education of John Dewey: A Biography* (New York: Columbia University Press, 2002), 198–201; and George Dykhuisen, *The Life and Mind of John Dewey* (Carbondale, IL: Southern Illinois University Press, 1973), 87–88.
18. Simpson and Stack Jr., *Teachers, Leaders, and Schools: Essays by John Dewey*, 8.
19. Ibid.
20. Darnell Rucker, *The Chicago Pragmatists* (Minneapolis: University of Minnesota, 1969), vi.
21. Louis Menand, *The Metaphysical Club* (New York: Farrar, Straus and Giroux, 2001), 360.
22. Rucker, *The Chicago Pragmatists*, 95.
23. Herbert Kliebard, *The Struggle for the American Curriculum: 1893–1958*, 2nd ed. (New York: Routledge, 1995), 53–54. Small was a follower of Lester Frank Ward and had a keen interest in educational issues. In 1896, the onset of the Dewey lab school, Small gave an address to the National Education Association titled, "Demands of Sociology upon Pedagogy." Like, Dewey Small advocated for a connection of the home to the school, emphasizing those interests serve as the basis for curriculum.
24. Francis Wayland Parker, "The Plan and Purpose of the Chicago Institute," *The Course of Study* 1 (July 1900): 10. For biographical studies on Parker see Ida Heffron, *Francis Wayland Parker: An Interpretive Biography* (Los Angeles: I. Deach, Jr., 1934) and Jack K. Campbell, *Colonel Francis W. Parker: The Children's Crusader* (New York: Teachers College Press, 1967). Dewey respected Parker's work and sent his children to Parker's school, but the relationship between the Dewey lab school and the Chicago Institute became contentious when the university attempted to combine the schools.
25. Rucker, *The Chicago Pragmatists*, 86.
26. Ibid., 102. See also George Herbert Mead, "Editorial Notes," *The Elementary School Teacher* 9, no. 3 (November 1908): 156–57. Mead's view of the individual in a social context, his social psychology, greatly influenced Dewey as he attempted to understand the construction of meaning and identity through social interaction or for Dewey a form of experience. See George Herbert Mead, *Mind, Self, and Society* (Chicago: University of Chicago, 1934).
27. John Dewey, *The School and Society* (Chicago, IL: The University of Chicago Press, 1915), 27–28.
28. Ibid., EW 5:437.
29. Ibid., 438.
30. Menand, *The Metaphysical Club*, 322.
31. Dewey, EW:5.
32. Ibid., 91, 93.
33. Ibid., 94.
34. Sylvia Paulay, "Progressivism and Democracy," *The Elementary School Journal* 42, no. 6 (1942): 420. The literature on progressive education is immense. Some noted works are Lawrence Cremin, *The Transformation of the School: Progressivism in American Education 1876–1957* (New York: Vintage, 1964), Arthur Zilversmit, *Changing Schools: Progressive Education Theory and Practice, 1930–1960* (Chicago: University of Chicago, 1993), Ronald Cohen and Raymond A. Mohl, *The Paradox of Progressive Education: The Gary Plan and Urban*

Schooling (Port Washington and New York: Kennikat, 1979), and Sam F. Stack Jr., *The Arthurdale Community School: Education and Reform in Depression Era Appalachia* (Lexington: University of Kentucky Press, 2016).

35. Dewey, MW 2:278.
36. Alison Kadlec, *Dewey's Critical Pragmatism* (New York: Rowan and Littlefield, 2007), 60. Kadlec challenges Dewey's critics who argue that he had nothing to say about power and politics. See pages 121–124.
37. Deron Boyles, "John Dewey (1859–1952)," in *Dictionary of Literary Biography*, ed. Paul Hansom (Farmington Hills, MI: The Gale Group, 2001), 88.
38. Dewey, MW 1:16.
39. Ibid., 19–20.
40. Ibid.
41. Ibid., 10.
42. Boyles, *John Dewey*, 89.
43. See Dewey, MW 1:11; Westbrook, *John Dewey and American Democracy*, 106; and Laurel Tanner, *Dewey's Laboratory School* (New York: Teachers College Press, 1997), 178.
44. Tanner, *Dewey's Laboratory School*, 16. See also Kliebard, *The Struggle for the American Curriculum*, for Harper's interest in creating relationships with the local schools in Chicago, which at the time was more prevalent among public universities. 52.
45. John Dewey, "The University School," *University Record* 1 (November 6, 1896): 417. Boyles, "John Dewey (1859–1952)," 75–97.
46. John Dewey to Clara Mitchell, November 6, 1895. *The Correspondence of John Dewey, 1871–1952.* Intelex Past Masters. Charlottesville, VA: Intelex Past Masters, 1997. [hereafter cited as John Dewey Correspondence]. Clara Mitchell taught at Francis Parker's Cook County Normal School, which became the Chicago Normal School in 1896 when the Dewey lab school was formed. Mitchell later taught history and literature at the lab school.
47. Dewey, MW 1:7.
48. Kliebard, *The Struggle for the American Curriculum*, 54. Dewey was attempting to resolve the dualism fostered in traditional education by the conflict between the psychological and the social with traditional education emphasizing the mental or psychological. This dualism created a tension for Dewey regarding the role of the individual and that role of the individual in a democratic society. Dewey addressed this concern in Experience *and Education* (New York: Vintage, 1938) and John Dewey, *Individualism Old and New* (New York: Minton and Balch, 1930).
49. Kliebard, *The Struggle for the American Curriculum*, 59. Dewey asked his colleague Julia Bulkley, an associate professor in the Department of Pedagogy to help in the decision to house the lab school but this is apparently the only time he involved her in the lab school although she had extensive experience in teacher education, a Swiss doctorate in philosophy, and knowledge of Pestalozzian theory and practice. Bulkley taught the overwhelming majority of courses in the Department of pedagogy, not Dewey. Politically savvy and seeking to draw Chicago teachers to study at the university, Harper, who had a contentious relationship with Bulkley had been seeking to hire Ella Flagg Young since 1887. Harper was keenly interested in attracting Chicago teachers to the University of Chicago. See Kathleen Cruikshank, "In Dewey's Shadow: Julia Bulkley and the University of Chicago Department of Pedagogy, 1895–1900," *History of Education Quarterly* 38, no. 4 (Winter 1998): 373–406 for a thorough discussion of Bulkley's role at Chicago and her relationship with Harper and Dewey.

50. John Dewey to Frank Manny, 10 May 1896. *John Dewey Correspondence.* Frank Manny (1868–1954) spent 1899–1897 at the lab school as an assistant to Dewey. Manny was an experienced school administrator in 1894 established an extension program to assist factory workers in pursuit of education. He supported Dewey's idea of the classroom as a forum for inquiry and was a critic of standardization, which was the watchword for traditional education in the late 19th century.

51. John Dewey to Frank Manny, 26 May 1896. *John Dewey Correspondence.*

52. Kadlec, *Dewey's Critical Pragmatism*, 61.

53. Dewey, MW 1:23. See Martin Bickman, *Minding American Education: Reclaiming the Tradition of Active Learning* (New York: Teachers College Press, 2003).

54. Kliebard, *The Struggle for the American Curriculum*, 71.

55. Ibid., 65 and John Dewey, "The Aim of History in Elementary Education," *The Elementary School Record* 1 (1900): 199–203.

56. Rucker, *The Chicago Pragmatists*, 165.

57. John Dewey to Frank Manny, 16 March 1896. *John Dewey Correspondence.*

58. Jackie M. Blount, "Ella Flagg Young and the Gender Politics of Democracy and Education," *The Journal of the Gilded Age and Progressive Era* 16 (2017): 412.

59. Ella Flagg Young received her PhD from the University of Chicago in 1900 and worked in the lab school from 1901 to 1904 and left when Dewey resigned his position from the university. She was the first female superintendent of Chicago public school and served as president of the National Education Association in 1910. See Ella Flagg Young to William Rainey Harper, 28 October 1898. *John Dewey Correspondence.*

60. Anne Durst, "The Union of Intellectual Freedom and Cooperation. Learning from the University of Chicago's Laboratory School Community, 1896–1904," *Teachers College Record* 107, no. 5 (May 2005): 970.

61. Ellen Condliffe Lagemann, "Experimenting with Education: John Dewey and Ella Flagg Young at the University of Chicago," *American Journal of Education* 104, no. 3 (1996): 179. Dewey's early meetings with the lab school teachers did not go well until Young began to get involved.

62. Ibid. See also Westbrook, *John Dewey and American Democracy*, 100.

63. Westbrook, *John Dewey and American Democracy*, 107; Tanner, *Dewey's Laboratory School*, 151–152.

64. Ella Flagg Young, "Democracy and Education," *The Journal of Education* 84, no. 1 (July 6, 1916): 6. Dewey has been criticized for not including issues facing teachers in *Democracy and Education*, that he failed to "address teacher freedom, respect, equal pay, classroom autonomy, and intellectually challenging professional training." See Lagemann, "Experimenting with Education," 181. Clearly attuned to the teacher issues of the day, Young does not mention these concerns in her review of Dewey's *Democracy and Education*.

65. Jackie M. Blount, "Individuality, Freedom, and Community: Ella Flagg Young's Quest for Teacher Empowerment," *History of Education Quarterly* 58, no. 2 (May 2018): 197.

66. Blount, "Ella Flagg Young," 416.

67. Dewey, EW 5:171.

68. Westbrook, *John Dewey and American Democracy*, 85.

69. Cremin, *The Transformation of the School*, 60.

70. Ibid., 61–62.

71. Ibid., 62. See Jane Addams, *Democracy and Social Ethics*, The John Harvard Library (Cambridge: Belknap Press of Harvard University Press, 1964), 180–181.

72. Cremin, *The Transformation of the School*, 63; Addams, *Democracy and Social Ethics*, 219.

73. Jane Dewey, "Biography of John Dewey," in *The Philosophy of John Dewey* ed. Paul Arthur Schilpp (New York: Tudor, 1939), 29–30.

74. For a discussion Dewey's nationalism, see Ryan, *John Dewey and the High Tide of American Liberalism*, 153.

75. Martin, *The Education of John Dewey*, 349. George Dykhuizen notes that John Dewey was an attentive father but that traditional gender roles were present in the Dewey home. Alice did "most of the cooking, baking, cleaning, knitting, and sewing for the family, also seeing to it that the children met their appointments on time and that her husband did not forget to meet his scheduled classes." Dykhuizen, *The Life and Mind of John Dewey*, 149. Much of this discussion on Alice Dewey comes from Sam F. Stack Jr., "Alice Chipman Dewey (1858–1927): Still a Mystery?" *Journal of Philosophy and History of Education* 59 (2009): 28–37.

76. Ryan, *John Dewey and the High Tide of American Liberalism*, 122.

77. Ibid.

78. Dewey, MW 6: 179.

79. Ibid., 284.

80. Ibid., 286.

81. Nellie B. Linn was a major benefactor to the University of Chicago, her husband Charles R. Linn a grain merchant and financier. Anita McCormick was the daughter of Cyrus McCormick of McCormick reaper fame. See Nellie Linn to John Dewey, June 11, 1896. *John Dewey Correspondence*; and John Dewey to Mrs. Emmons Blaine, January 8, 1897. *John Dewey Correspondence* and John Dewey to William Rainey Harper, November 8, 1897. *John Dewey Correspondence*.

82. John Dewey to Patrick Geddes, April 13, 1899. *John Dewey Correspondence*.

83. William Rainey Harper to E.A. Turner, August 15, 1899. *John Dewey Correspondence*. Turner was an author of textbooks in math, reading, and teaching.

84. John Dewey to William Rainey Harper, March 6, 1899. *John Dewey Correspondence*.

85. John Dewey to Wilbur Jackman, January 26, 1904. *John Dewey Correspondence*.

86. See William Rainey Harper to John Dewey, April 30, 1904 and John Dewey to William Rainey Harper, 6 April 1904. *John Dewey Correspondence*.

87. John Dewey to William Rainey Harper, May 10, 1904. *John Dewey Correspondence*.

88. John Dewey to James McKeen Cattell, April 21, 1904. *John Dewey Correspondence*.

89. John Dewey to William Torrey Harris, April 25, 1904. *John Dewey Correspondence*.

90. While Dewey never directed another school like the lab school at the University of Chicago, he did have some association with the Lincoln School at Teachers College, Columbia University, and he maintained informal school contacts through his students. See Susan and Sadovnik Semel Alan, ed., *Founding Mothers and Others: Women Educational Leaders During the Progressive Era* (New York: Palgrave, 2002) and Susan and Sadovnik Semel Alan, ed., *Schools of Tomorrow, Schools of Today*, History of Education (New York: Peter Lang, 1999). These books chronicle the work of women progressives and their schools and also institutional history of selected progressive schools.

91. Kadlec, *Dewey's Critical Pragmatism*, 59. See also Boyles, *John Dewey*, 92.

92. Roberto Mangabeira Unger and Cornel West, *The Future of American Progressivism: An Initiative for Political and Economic Reform* (Boston: Beacon Press, 1998), 70.

93. John Narayan, *John Dewey: The Global Public and Its Problems: Theory for a Global Age* (Manchester: Manchester University Press, 2016), 38.

94. See Jane Dewey, "Biography of John Dewey," 29.

95. Dewey, EW 5:438.
96. Tanner, *Dewey's Laboratory School*, 177–78.
97. Kliebard, *The Struggle for the American Curriculum*, 75.
98. Ibid.
99. As quoted in Martin, *The Education of John Dewey*, 349–50. Original source is John Dewey to Scudder Klyce, 5 July 1915. *John Dewey Correspondence.*
100. Rucker, *The Chicago Pragmatists*, 100. Elsie Ripley Clapp, *The Use of Resources in Education* (New York: Harper and Row, 1952).
101. Kadlec, *Dewey's Critical Pragmatism*, 63.
102. Charles F. Howlett and Audrey Cohan, *John Dewey, America's Peace-Minded Educator* (Carbondale: Southern Illinois University Press, 2016), 39.
103. Westbrook, *John Dewey and American Democracy*, 110. Unfortunately, most progressive schools were associated with university lab schools or were private schools and if it had impact it was at the elementary level. Dewey was clearly frustrated at the lack of success of progressive education in the American public school. See Elsie Ripley Clapp, *The Use of Resources in Education* (New York: Harper and Row, 1952), viii. Dewey wrote the Introduction to this book.
104. Thomas Fallace, "Repeating the Race Experience: John Dewey and the History Curriculum at the University of Chicago Laboratory School," *Curriculum Inquiry* 39, no. 3 (June 2008): 401.
105. Unger and West, *The Future of American Progressivism*, 22.
106. Boyles, "John Dewey," 95. Although some disagree, Boyles argues that Dewey saw the "pointed questions and the larger issues of gender, race, and class."

5   The Inner Restoration

Christian Humanists Fighting for the Supernatural Order, 1925–1955

Bryan McAllister-Grande

This study demonstrates that a religious system of thought – Christian humanism – shaped three historic universities and the construction of general education models deep into the twentieth century. Challenging the common historiography of the triumph of science and secularism, this study instead emphasizes the role of religion and ancient truth in the shaping of contemporary American higher education.[1] Indeed, the study presents new evidence that nominally secular universities were sacred in their approach to knowledge in the twentieth century.

Christian humanism is a system of thought with many variations.[2] At its core, Christian humanism involves making linkages between the secular and the religious worlds – in other words, between the natural and the supernatural realms. Historically, Christian humanists – such as the Cambridge Platonists of the University of Cambridge or the Puritans of Harvard, circa the 1680s – attempted to marry the secular with the religious.[3] That marriage produced a conviction in the "unity of truth," or the fundamental unity between the natural and supernatural worlds.[4]

I show that educators at Harvard, Princeton, and Yale, working on the shoulders of their ancestors, infused twentieth-century core curricula, humanities courses, honors programs, admissions, and selectivity with Christian humanist philosophies.[5] Based on 30 separate archival collections, the study tracks classicists, literary critics, university presidents, trustees, historians, and other humanists in a collective fight against secularism.

James Conant, president of Harvard from 1933 to 1953, a prominent writer on American education, and the first US Ambassador to West Germany, is one of the Christian humanists profiled here. This study recasts Conant as a closeted Puritan who hid his larger aims for a restoration of religion behind a scientific guise. I show how Conant drew on Francis Bacon (a common source of Christian humanist wisdom) to formulate policies and curricula at Harvard and beyond.[6]

I call the combined efforts of these Christian humanists an "inner restoration." It was "inner" because these leaders sometimes hid their true intentions from public view. Yet, it was also "inner" because it attempted to re-engineer American intellectual and cultural life. Concerned that the diversity of modern society would destroy Christianity, these educators sought to restructure how Americans think.

"One Small Chapel in the Big Church": The Baltimores of Princeton

In 1932, a group of Princetonians began meeting in a tiny café across from "Old Nassau" (Nassau Hall, a home of the American Revolution and Constitutional Convention). They formed a metaphysical club. They discussed politics, religion, education, and the place of God in an increasingly secular world.[7]

This group at Princeton called themselves the "Baltimores" after the café – the Baltimore Dairy Lunch – that they frequented. The Baltimores hoped to reshape American education and intellectual life. Their enemies were John Dewey, the behavioral psychologists, scientists, social scientists, anthropologists, progressive educators, and cultural relativists. Sometimes the Baltimores had a simple name for their common enemy: the "naturalists."

The Baltimores' inspiration – and a Christ-like figure at the head of the table – was Paul Elmer More. The Princeton adjunct professor was a notable name in American intellectual life as a founder of the new humanism. Along with Harvard's Irving Babbitt, More had made the new humanism into a household name. The movement aimed to infuse religious and classical conservatism into American literature, higher education, and cultural life.[8] Writing in the 1910s, More had prophesized:

> I can foresee no restoration of humane studies to their lost position of leadership until they are felt once more to radiate from some central spiritual truth. I do not believe that the aesthetic charms of literature can supply this want, nor is it clear to me that a purely scientific analysis of the facts of moral experience can furnish the needed motive . . . only through the centralizing force of religious faith or through its equivalent in philosophy can intellectual life regain its meaning and authority for earnest men.[9]

In particular, More felt that Princeton was abdicating its duty to God by deserting its religious authority. He believed that the university was "blindly and contemptibly [lowering] her flag" of religious freedom. More argued that Princeton's recent presidents – John G. Hibben and Woodrow Wilson – were dangerous collectivists and secularists who "should be cut with the executioner's sword," as he put it in a letter to Princeton's Dean, Christian Gauss. In More's view, Hibben and Wilson had sacrificed Princeton's religious mission in favor of scientific exploration and research.[10] More also likely spoke about John Dewey and pragmatism, since More had previously written that Dewey was "striking at the roots of everything that makes life worthwhile" with Dewey's seeming abandonment of traditional religious authority for scientific pragmatism.[11] More lambasted Progressive Education as vacuous, social science as fracturing, and Americans as consumers of vapid and meaningless scientific knowledge. These attacks against Dewey were familiar refrains in the 1920s, but More added more urgency and venom to the movement against pragmatism.[12]

More's and the Baltimores' inner circle included their good friend Gauss, a prominent man of letters and Dean of Princeton College. In the late 1920s and early 1930s, Dean Christian Gauss was forming similar views about the restoration of Christian authority in American intellectual life.[13] Science, Gauss wrote, "cannot tell us what is just and what is beautiful. It should be equally clear that the advance of science alone cannot save democracy."[14] Gauss believed that scientists at Princeton were "running away with civilization's apple-cart," leading to the eventual destruction of "man."[15] Citing Hitler, Gauss wrote in an unpublished essay that, for all of Hitler's faults, at least Hitler understood that leaders must "appeal to emotions," which religion and religious feeling alone could provide. Gauss wrote that, like Hitlerism, democracy and education "can and must influence conduct" rather than put the child or student in control of the curriculum.[16]

The Baltimores and Gauss received additional help in their quest from George Thomas, professor of religion, who arrived at Princeton in the late 1930s. Thomas came to Princeton believing that, "Since the collapse of the unity of medieval Christianity every attempt to make one human interest the basic principle of all culture has failed completely." He continued:

> There have been ages of beauty, of reason, of imagination and feeling, of science and technology, and of material prosperity and comfort. But none of these and no combination of them has proved itself capable for any length of time of drawing all others into its service or even making them its permanent allies.[17]

Thomas believed that the secret to the unity and authority of medieval Christianity was "Idealism" or "Platonism," which he argued drew together all human interests into its service and made them permanent allies. Thomas called this linkage of Idealism and Platonism the belief that, "The world is a divinely created Mind whose purpose is to realize Good in different forms and at different levels."[18]

For Thomas, Idealism and Platonism were synonymous with a theistic and supernatural Christianity. "All Idealism is Platonism, i.e. the view that there are divine principles of order and goodness at work in the world and that man's action should cooperate with it, as well as in spiritual (rather than material) interpretation of nature."[19] For Thomas, Platonism and Idealism were the joint belief in transcendental order – the "Four Transcendentals" or "Cardinal Virtues" of the ancient and Christian world: Wisdom, Temperance, Courage, and Justice. (Thomas, Gauss, and the Baltimores viewed Plato not as a Greek secularist, but rather as a spiritual figure who had designed and mapped the divine order.)[20]

Expressions of Christian humanism went beyond professors of religion, with university leaders and faculty also claiming a Christian humanist philosophy. Calling himself a "philosophy a-typical Christian idealist," Princeton philosophy professor Theodore M. Greene lamented a decline of belief and trust in Western "objective values," which he associated with both Greek classicism and Christian theism. He lauded Plato as the only "pagan" to map out "Reality" in all its dimensions and aspects. He also observed that this Platonic "Reality" was identical to God's kingdom.[21] Writing of the "intrinsic values" of "truth, goodness, and beauty," Greene believed that these "innermost regions of man's personality . . . penetrate beneath mere sensation and ratiocination, mere knowledge of an external world and of social phenomena" to the very contemplation of the divine and universal.[22]

The Baltimores launched two curricular programs, "Man and His Freedom" and the "Special Program in the Humanities," to carry Christian humanist virtues to a new generation of students. "Man and His Freedom" carried, as its official course motto, the words of Paul Elmer More:

> We are born knowing nothing and with much striving we learn but a little; yet all the while we are bound by laws that hearken to no plea of ignorance. . . . In such a state humility is the virtue of men, and their only defense: to walk humbly with God, never doubting, whatever befall, that . . . His Law is right.[23]

The Baltimores set up the course as a "viable alternative to the social sciences and the anthropological view of man," which they believed was corrupting American classrooms and lecture halls. They viewed the course as part of a spiritual war for the "World's Best View of Man."[24] Against the social scientific or anthropological view, the course would teach students the application of God's Law to the natural world.

One of the more interesting aspects of the course was its equation of metaphysics and politics. In setting up on the course design, the Baltimores readily assumed that politics and metaphysics possessed an intrinsic and binary relationship.[25] The group designed the course as both an empirical and spiritual glance into "Three Views of Reality." They identified these three views of reality as liberal humanism, naturalism, and theism. Each carried inherited political meanings.[26]

For the Baltimores, liberal humanism was both the basis of, and the mirror image to, political liberalism.[27] They identified the view with a line of thought running through John Locke, John Stuart Mill, John Dewey, Reinhold Niebuhr, and liberal consensus politics. This was a view that, according to the Baltimores, "discounts divinity, when it doesn't omit God entirely, but at the same time, it regards man as somehow superior to natural processes." The Baltimores saw this "view of reality" as a direct threat to their brand of Christian humanism. Although liberal humanism lauds "reason and intellect" and has "receptiveness to beauty," it erroneously places "Man at the center," a lineage of thought the Baltimores traced back to the 'errors' of Aristotle.[28]

An even more threatening "View of Reality" came from naturalism. According to the Baltimores, naturalism "regards the world as entirely a matter of physical processes and so it regards man as primarily a biological organism." In this view, the Baltimores asserted, "man" is no more than a "high-grade animal."[29] The Baltimores identified "Marxism" with this view; but, in calling it the "dominant one in 20th century intellectual circles," they insinuated that other philosophies and epistemologies, such as varieties of liberal humanism, also fell under the general category of "naturalism."[30] They also described naturalism as an "ideational force" that Plato, early Christian thinkers, and the ancients were in contestation about, and that Aristotle had mistakenly embraced.[31]

Less easy to categorize politically was the third view of reality, theism. In course planning notes, the Baltimores linked theism directly to Catholicism.[32] They described it, more favorably, as "the activity of God in history." Theism, they asserted, balanced humanism and naturalism by drawing them together into a total unity. Proper theism was the view that there is a "super-natural, super-human agency of some sort acting in the world." The Baltimores also called this tradition the "Hebraic" one that drew God, Christ, and Plato together into a unitary historical and religious tradition.[33] Yet, theism, on its own, could also be dangerous, the Baltimores asserted. Theism and naturalism must be linked together in a complete unity of man, nature, and God.

"Man and His Freedom" – known around campus as simply HUM201/202 – was a fixture in the Princeton curriculum of the post-World War II and Cold War eras.[34] Although, on the surface, it appeared like any other of the "Western Tradition" courses in American universities, the course had explicitly sacred aims for a reeducation of American leaders.[35] Aiming to strike into the "anthropological," modern tradition of empirical science, the course drew a reputation for being interdisciplinary: at once historical, empirical, and, ultimately, spiritual.[36] "Man and His Freedom" attempted to show that all activity – especially science and empirical research – was infused with sacred principles.[37]

While the first half of the course covered the unity of the ancient world and Biblical times, the latter half dealt with the Baltimores' views on the disunity caused by modern science. Like previous moral philosophy courses, circa the eighteenth and nineteenth centuries, the course dealt with an inner conflict between "man's" "faculties" of "will" and "intellect." The course positioned the Western mind in fundamental tension – a tension between the will, or God's desires, and the intellect, or man's reason. The essential learning outcome of the course was the lesson that "will" must trump "intellect" in times of crisis and danger. The Baltimores positioned will over intellect as the "Hebraic" tradition enveloping and protecting the "Greek." Among the implications was that research had significant limits on serving human intelligence and betterment.[38]

From this view, the Baltimores developed a theory of knowledge. They asserted that the humanities enveloped and protected the social sciences and sciences from becoming too powerful. Thus, the Baltimores positioned the humanities as the savior of humanity as a necessary check on more scientific or anthropological approaches to humanism. Examples from the course attempted to show that the existence of God and the Cardinal Virtues were both empirical and transcendent; historical and actual. The Baltimores positioned the humanities as lessons that guided human choices and leadership, with science no more than a tool that could either destroy or create technology – but never guide moral action.

To understand this goal of the course, it is important to remember that rival thinkers of the early to mid-twentieth century placed science on a high pedestal as a possible moral replacement for religion and traditional morality. At Columbia University, Dewey, anthropologist Franz Boas, and philosopher Ernst Nagel imagined science and what some called "scientific humanism" as the cosmopolitan mediator of race relations, ethnic conflict, and religious clashes. The scientific method, Columbia's naturalists idealized, would wipe away the idealism of tradition in favor of a new naturalist, cosmopolitan world order.[39] In contrast, Princeton's "Man and His Freedom" course attempted to wipe away such scientific internationalism. "Man and His Freedom" dealt, instead, with "the Problem of Destiny," or "the meaning of history and time." Course instructors asked, "Is there a cosmic scheme? Does man have a meaningful place in it? Is the course of history one of advancing development or of repetitive recurrence? Is human destiny an individual or social matter? Is it a question of this world or the next?"[40] As an answer to the Columbia naturalists, Princeton's Christian humanists asserted that the story of humankind was one of the individual, working in communion with God. It was God as mediator rather than science as a new international order.

The Baltimores attempted to put the idea of supernaturalism in practice through a special training program. In 1936, they launched "The Special Program in the Humanities." SPH, as it was termed, gave elite students a chance to create their own curriculum and thesis.[41] SPH modeled the "human figure . . . man with feet on familiar ground but hands reaching for a wider interdepartmental sky." The chronology of the program "swung down to departmental earth, then up again in search of synthesis."[42] Students began the program with a general topic of wide interest to several of the humanities. Their training took them into the fields of metaphysics and religion. They discussed the relationship between reason and faith, truth and fiction, and the very nature of reality.

Modeled on the long-standing University of Oxford program, "The Greats," SPH offered students a chance to map the contours of reality. Students discussed great intellectual and religious traditions of Western thought, including Rationalism, Empiricism, and Platonic Idealism. They learned that both "science and philosophy suffered" from their lack of communion with God. Because scientists and philosophers were trying to "annex" religion, SPH students learned that true Christian humanists must fight back with aggressive tactics.[43]

"The Kingdom of God is a real social order in which God reigns," George Thomas affirmed to students.[44] Princeton's president, the diplomat Harold Dodds, agreed. The true "ethic" of America, he said, is the "Christian ethic," not the "scientific" one. He told Princetonians that Western history was a "spiritual achievement," for which "science can provide no answer."[45] The Baltimores referred to themselves as "one small chapel in the big church" and they regularly implied that they were saving all of civilization.[46]

"We Must Take the Offensive in the War of Ideas": God and Man at Yale

When William F. Buckley published *God and Man at Yale* (1951), Americans assumed that Buckley's popular book was a scathing critique of Yale secularism.[47] Yet, Yale officials had a close relationship with Buckley. President Charles Seymour and the aging trustee Henry Sloane Coffin – then one of the most famous ministers in America – had followed and even befriended Buckley when he was an undergraduate editor of the *Yale Daily News*. Yale officials exchanged regular letters about Buckley, his religious views, and his experiences at Yale.[48]

God and Man at Yale did scathe Yale, especially its social sciences courses. Buckley thought these courses taught "collectivism." Yet, Buckley and Yale officials shared a deep conviction about Yale's relationship with God. As at Princeton, certain Yale officials and faculty believed that Yale had a supernatural mission, that Yale's scholarship and research properly contributed to a supernatural order, and that Yale's curriculum would teach students Christian values.[49]

Like Princeton, Yale took its Christian mission especially seriously. In 1937, when newly appointed president Charles Seymour delivered his inauguration address, he chose to deliver it in Battell Chapel, the university's Congregational home. In that inaugural speech, Seymour called upon the Yale community to reject secularism, to combat "foreign" ideas, and to return to Yale's "sacred trust" – the "teaching of Christ in our life-and-death struggle against the forces of selfish materialism."[50] Seymour's 1937 speech could have been lifted directly from Buckley's *God and Man at Yale.*

Yale also possessed deep ties to the Christian liberal education tradition. Historically, Yale officials had defended the classical languages and classical teachings as the *sine qua non* of a good and pious mind. *The Yale Report(s)* (1828) on liberal education had earnestly defended the classical mind against the scientific one.[51] Yale officials had historically believed that the classics furnished discipline. The classics did not necessarily teach Christianity specifically (this was the Bible's role), however, in Yale's view they did condition the mind to accept God's teachings.[52]

The hundred years between the publication of the *Yale Reports* (1828) and Seymour's inauguration speech (1937) had not been kind to this educational philosophy. New intellectual traditions – Dewey's pragmatism, empiricism, and Hegelian thought – had disrupted the old order. In the late nineteenth century, the pioneering Yale sociologist William Graham Sumner and other colleagues launched an all-out attack against Yale's traditional, classical-Christian synthesis. The Young Turks of Yale created new social sciences courses and core economics curricula. Facing external pressure, Yale morphed from a small teaching college into a fledgling research university based largely around the new social sciences.[53]

In the 1940s, however, a group of pious professors of philosophy, history, and literature collaborated to revive religion under the banner of the humanities. They created new courses and a general education program to rival Princeton's and Harvard's efforts. Their "Yale Reform" of the 1940s asserted the Christian social order as the goal of the curriculum. "The rise of naturalism in American thought reaching its high point in the decades of the 1930s and 1940s," historian Ralph Gabriel asserted, had led to the "decline of religion and philosophy, of disillusionment and cynicism."[54] According to Gabriel, "Idealism is also a weapon. Let us use it. . . . We must take the offensive in the war of ideas."[55] It was supernaturalism versus naturalism, with Yale taking the lead.

Yale had at least two groups vying for leadership of this new "humanistic idealism," as Gabriel called it. One group, emanating primarily out of the English Department, was ultra-conservative and viewed Western thought and literature as a Christian achievement. These "new aesthetes," as they were dubbed, were the Yale equivalent to the Baltimores at Princeton.[56] The new aesthetes believed that, "Reason" is "simply the name of the universal and permanent," which the poet "shares with angels."[57] The new aesthetes attacked all of the naturalists, "Marxists," "free-thinkers," and cultural relativists, who took a merely "anthropological" view of the world.[58] The new aesthetes believed, instead, in the "ideal community achieved through grace."[59]

Competing with the new aesthetes was a second movement led by the idealist philosopher F. S. C. Northrop. Like Columbia University's Naturalists, this second group took "scientific humanism" to new levels. Science, Northrop and his peers philosophized, was not just natural or social science. It was a way of thinking – an intellectual revolution, even – that could be applied to every aspect of human affairs, from poetry to religion. Northrop joined his fellow scientific humanists around the nation in aiming to revolutionize intellectual life around a symbolic language and a scientific approach to value judgments.[60]

This fight between Yale's humanists had major implications for the university's curricular future. "Western" thought courses competed with a kind of mega-area studies and philosophy curriculum that Northrop hoped to create. Northrop wanted to generate a new symbolic language and philosophy, uniting all disciplines and all areas of the world in common philosophical unity – and united through the scientific method.[61]

Yale officials clamped down on Northrop's scientific humanism. In addition to statements issued by Yale faculty and President Seymour, the Yale Corporation (the Board of Trustees) effectively settled the debate. The Corporation issued a clarifying statement of Yale's mid-twentieth-century mission: Defending historic Christianity against any new-fangled modern interpretations. They titled the statement the "Liberal Arts," and asked, "Of what worth . . . is freedom of religion if we bring a less enlightened faith to the worship of God?"[62] Shortly after that statement, the new aesthetes gained control of the curriculum and issued a general education program that one Yale official called "conservative" and "religious" in tone and content.[63]

The "Moral Order of the Universe": James Conant's Harvard

A similar pattern of supernaturalism versus science occurred at nearby Harvard – and within relatively the same timeline as the two cases presented in the previous sections. Some key figures at Harvard included James Conant, inaugurated president in 1933; John H. Finley, Jr, a classicist, religious devotee, and master of Eliot House; John Nash Douglas Bush, Professor of English Literature; and the journalist Walter Lippmann, a Harvard graduate, architect of neoliberalism, and informal consultant to Conant throughout his presidency.

As a scientist remembered for his pragmatism, James Conant seems an unlikely candidate to be a promoter of Christian humanism. Yet, Conant possessed deep religious convictions and a Puritan lineage that historians have yet to explore.[64] Conant often wrote about his Puritan heritage and love for Puritan literature, theology, and science. In the

1930s, Conant authored a series of strongly worded, almost aggressive, articles. He argued that education is a divine activity, not a secular one. "The understanding of man," Conant wrote in 1936, "is, . . . the candle of the Lord." Conant wrote of the Puritans as attempting to "keep alive a spirit of learning . . . to fight an exhausting rear guard action against the violence and intolerance which reigned in the minds of men." He warned against "insane passions, uncontrolled prejudices, mob violence" that are "familiar spectacles to those of us who man universities today." Conant cautioned, in particular, of following atheists who denied the "divine nature of man's rational faculties," thus inciting "mob violence" against the true, spiritual nature of the university. He highlighted the Puritans as the builders of the city on the hill that shaped the world. "From their citadel of learning they proclaimed the significance of man's power of understanding," Conant wrote. "Have we less need to do the same today?"[65]

Conant also believed that American universities – especially Harvard – had a spiritual mission. Conant described the entire philosophy of Western "civilization" as spiritual. Writing to a Presbyterian church leader in 1936, Conant argued that, "I believe that our colleges in this country are doing quite as much as they ever did to . . . interest [students] in a non-material, otherworldly point of view which is the basis of all our civilization."[66] Quoting the Cambridge Platonists, Conant also spoke of the need for "a profound analysis of values, a penetrating discussion of Truth, Beauty, and Goodness" which would show that "Reason" is a divine activity. He spoke of the need to guide Americans toward divinity. Conant wrote, "The more men *exercise Reason*, the more they *resemble God* himself."[67]

In shaping Harvard's mid-twentieth century curriculum, Conant also relied on a scheme that he borrowed from Francis Bacon. In the seventeenth century, Bacon had divided all truth into several metaphysical divisions. Conant constructed a similar scheme for twentieth century intellectual life. He divided "learning into three parts, two of which are most closely related to each other than either is the third. Thus the division is at the same time into two parts," wrote a colleague of his, describing Conant's 'inner' philosophy of knowledge. These two parts, according to Conant himself, were "accumulative and non-accumulative knowledge." For Conant, "accumulative knowledge" included science but also "more than science."[68] Conant also subdivided "non-accumulative knowledge" into "philosophy and what Bacon called poesy." These terms did not have a strictly contemporary meaning; they had "a somewhat wider meaning than is ordinarily given to them," according to a colleague, the Platonist philosopher Raphael Demos.[69] Here, in non-accumulative knowledge, Conant placed Platonic value judgments of "Truth, Beauty, and Goodness." He wrote that, "When questions of value are involved, when judgments – political, social, or aesthetic – must be made, no law of progress appears valid." Conant warned of taking naturalism too far, since, "If this be true we do no service to the cause of extending Man's rational power by expecting the record of accomplishment in the future to be totally different from the past."[70] Conant defended divine "Man" against those who he perceived to attack divinity and the Cardinal Virtues.

A close confident of Conant's, the classicist John H. Finley, Jr., was the principle author of *General Education in a Free Society* (1945), commonly known as the "Harvard Redbook."[71] *General Education in a Free Society*, written by a committee of Harvard faculty for which Finley served as vice-chair, recommended common principles for American general education programs, curricula, and theory after World War II. *General Education in a Free Society* also recommended pedagogical theories and curricula for American high schools. It is one of the most widely cited books on general education in American history. As part of Harvard's own General Education program, Finley taught Humanities 103 – the Great Age of Athens – to generations of Harvard students.[72]

John Nash Douglas Bush was a Harvard authority on Renaissance English literature. His work on Milton was widely recognized. Yet, it was a teacher that Bush made his mark.[73] Bush taught not only students about the Christian humanism of the Renaissance; he also lectured fellow Harvard faculty and leaders about a need to restore Christian humanism as a central authority. Bush defined Christian humanism as:

> a religious, ethical, rational, and largely unmystical view of God, man, and the world. Its basis was the conception of right reason, that is reason conceived of not as a dry light, an unmoral instrument of inquiry, but as the moral will, the divine faculty in man which allied him with God, which assumed certain absolute values in life and thought and made those values the goal of human effort. It was a fusion of Christian revelation with the highest wisdom of those pagans who had groped their way toward the true light.[74]

In particular, Bush argued that Plato was "a profoundly spiritual philosopher whose vision of the good life for man is illuminated by his vision of the divine Ideas."[75] The spiritualization of Plato gave Bush the belief that, "There is no conflict between reason and faith because both are divine gifts." Echoing Matthew Arnold, he called Christian humanism "a conservative force on the side of moderation and order, sweetness and light," one that was armed to "combat the irreligious and naturalistic implications of science – and also, one might add, such other things as irrational 'enthusiasm' in religion."[76]

During his life, Walter Lippmann was among the most famous journalists and political commentators in America. Trained in philosophy under the Harvard pragmatist William James, Lippmann, like many of his generation, briefly flirted with socialism and scientific utopias before becoming a stout capitalist and religious devotee later in his life.[77] Although born to Jewish parents, Lippmann famously ignored his Jewish upbringing and frequently spoke of Western civilization as Christian or Judeo-Christian. He was a principle founder of the movement and world order known today as neoliberalism.

In 1941, Lippmann entered the educational debates with the publication of an inflammatory piece, "Education vs. Western Civilization," in *American Scholar*.[78] In his essay, Lippmann, echoing the Christian humanists, blasted progressive educators, scientists, and other moderns for effectively "destroying . . . Western civilization."[79] He said that they had "progressively removed from the curriculum of studies the Western culture which produced the modern democratic state."[80] Lippmann claimed that, "The institutions of the Western world were formed by men who learned to regard themselves as inviolable persons because they were rational and free. They meant by rational that they were capable of comprehending the moral order of the universe."[81] Lippmann criticized moderns and progressives for denying "that there is such a thing as Western culture." He called for a restoration of studies that would allow students to comprehend the "religious tradition of the West."[82]

The issue at Harvard, as at Princeton and Yale, was the leadership of former Harvard presidents. Charles Eliot, Harvard's pioneering president of the Gilded Age, had transformed Harvard into a modern university and had embraced the sciences and pragmatism in Cambridge. In the late 1920s and early 1930s, discussions began among certain leadership circles and Gentlemen's Clubs about how to reshape Harvard to reclaim its classical and religious heritage. Some Harvard Corporation members wanted to keep the pragmatism but curtail the role of science, especially in the curriculum.[83]

Around the same time – late 1930s and 1940s America – the *Boston Globe* began printing a series of editorials on education under the authorship of the long-running, mythic editorialist "Uncle Dudley." Uncle Dudley was a moniker for two *Globe* editors and influential Harvard voices: Lucien Price (Harvard 1907) and James Powers. Using the quaint, gentlemanly voice of Uncle Dudley, Price and Powers wrote about the appeal of a Christian "humanism" in education. This "constructive spirit" and "creative power," they wrote, "indoctrinate[s] a boy with the body of thought necessary to carry forward a free civilization."[84] Uncle Dudley quoted Harvard's Puritan founders in arguing for a restoration of the "moral controls of humanism" to teach the "illiterate ministry" of America.[85]

Thus, it was not just advocates of the "Great Books" and conservatives that attacked progressives, but also so-called liberal university officials.[86] These nominal liberals sometimes hid behind official statements of modernity and progress, while occasionally – in the cases of Lippmann and the Uncle Dudley editorials – their statements were more open to the public eye.

Another statement that was in public view – yet also, in its own way, quite subversive – was *General Education in a Free Society*. I reexamine this famous work as a defense of Christian humanism against the rising forces of secularism.

Although, technically, *General Education in a Free Society* was a work-by-committee, the archival records show that Finley exerted a powerful influence if not a stronghold on the committee's deliberations. In this effort, Finely had support from the historian, Harvard Dean of the Faculty, and committee chairman, Paul Buck – Conant's right-hand man. Indeed, Conant was also more involved in the committee deliberations than previously recognized.[87]

Although *General Education in Free Society* rejected an outright religious mission for American schools and colleges, the authors did not reject religion as a basis of American "civilization." Indeed, Finley and his co-authors went to great lengths to reconcile religion and science. The authors based the scheme of the book directly on Conant's Baconian philosophy: some knowledge, the authors say, is "accumulative" or changing, while some knowledge is "non-accumulative" or absolute. This tension between change and tradition is the central feature of the American project, the authors repeatedly state.

In deliberations and early drafts of the book, Finley compared Harvard's efforts (with much seriousness) to the issuance of the Nicene Creed. An early draft of Finley's noted that the aim of education was clearly to "mold students to a received idea of the good." He described this aim as Christian, since "the essence of historical Christianity. . . [is] the pragmatic testing of the love of God."[88] Similarly, the Platonist philosopher Demos, in another early draft, wrote that, "Like an ellipse, an educational institution has two centers, not one." These "two centers," Demos wrote, were "the abstract and impersonal values of truth and beauty on the one hand, and the concrete values of human personality on the other."[89] Demos and Finley identified the former with religious experience, and the latter with secular experience or naturalism. The goal of Christian humanism was to re-unite the two.

Other Harvard faculty protested these proclamations for *General Education in a Free Society*. The English professor Theodore Morrison rejected the aggressive tactics of the Harvard leadership. After reviewing an early draft of the Redbook, Morrison wrote, "I am so afraid from this document someone will feel that we have a plan of humanism up our sleeves . . . I fear . . . the acceptance of an official philosophy." He then identified the Redbook's underlying philosophy as Platonist. Morrison agreed that there can be a "Platonist" on the faculty of a university, someone who tries to "indoctrinate" people. "But I don't believe a university should, and I don't believe that general education should," he wrote in a message to Harvard leadership.[90] Despite these warnings, *General Education in a Free Society* largely escaped public criticism. Its authors tampered the language while keeping many of the central recommendations for more Western, American, and Christian-oriented educational programs in place.

Conclusion: "A New Species"

Although leaders at Harvard, Princeton, and Yale wished to restore supernaturalism as an American ethic, they did not seem particularly interested in teaching the nuances of faith. Indeed, their aims seemed almost matter-of-fact. What seemed to appeal more was an organized attack on progressive education and scientific humanism. Yet, behind these instrumental aims lay a deep conviction in the divine nature of humankind. We, as a society, must "leap into the higher dialectic," Finley claimed, in 1943. Finley described an "emotional coloring . . . which has carried over from a momentary or specific experience where it existed strongly and then continues to pervade one's reaction to a certain class of things."[91] Finley criticized learning and education based purely on intellect – intellect alone, he argued, never made human beings. Instead, Finley championed "emotional coloring" that "transcends America as she exists today."[92]

Perhaps T. S. Eliot put the aims of the Christian humanists best when he wrote to his friend, Princeton's Paul Elmer More, in 1929. Eliot wrote that he and others were trying to create, through education and culture, a "new type of intellectual." This new "man" would be both "intellectual and devotional." It would be "a new species which cannot be created hurriedly . . . the coordination of thought and feeling, without either debauchery or repression . . . seems to me what is needed," Eliot wrote to More.[93]

With theistic Christianity under threat, elites at the big three universities did more than preserve church services on campus and religious studies courses in the curriculum. They sought out to re-engineer rationality. Scientific humanists such as Dewey, Boas, and Northrop were putting together a kind of intellectual revolution – a revolution based on a new, shared rationality organized around science. Putting out the flames of scientific humanism, the supernaturalists not only restored Christianity as a viable national ethic, but engineered a rationality mixed with devotion and emotional fervor. This "new type of species," as Eliot put it, was now poised to lead the country into the future.

Notes

1. The literature on religious and religious classicism in higher education before 1930 is expansive; some representative texts include Theodore Dwight Bozeman, *Protestants in an Age of Science: The Baconian Ideal and AnteBellum*

American Religious Thought (Chapel Hill: University of North Carolina Press, 1977); William C. Ringenberg, *The Christian College: A History of Protestant Higher Education in America* (Grand Rapids: Christian University Press, 1984); Robert Shepard, *God's People in the Ivory Tower: Religion in the Early American University* (Brooklyn: Carlson, 1991); George M. Marsden, *The Soul of the American University: From Protestant Establishment to Established Nonbelief* (New York: Oxford University Press, 1994); Julie A. Reuben, *The Making of the Modern University: Intellectual Transformation and the Marginalization of Morality* (Chicago: University of Chicago Press, 1996); J. David Hoeveler, *Creating the American Mind: Intellect and Politics in the Colonial Colleges* (Lanham, MD: Rowman & Littlefield Publishers, 2002). An exception to the gap in studies of religion in higher education after 1930 is Douglas Sloan, *Faith and Knowledge: Mainline Protestantism and American Higher Education* (Louisville, KY: Westminster/John Knox Press, 1994).

2. For some examples, see Frank M. Turner, *Contesting Cultural Authority: Essays in Victorian Intellectual Life* (Cambridge, UK; New York, NY: Cambridge University Press, 1993).

3. See Frederick J. Powicke, *The Cambridge Platonists: A Study* (Hamden, CT: Archon Books, 1971); Hoeveler, *Creating the American Mind*; Margo Todd, *Christian Humanism and the Puritan Social Order* (New York: Cambridge University Press, 1987).

4. See Reuben, *The Making of the Modern University*, chapter 1, "The Unity of Truth."

5. Bryan McAllister-Grande, "The Inner Restoration: Protestants Fighting for the Unity of Truth, 1930–1960" (EdD Dissertation, Harvard Graduate School of Education, 2017).

6. On Baconianism, see Bozeman, *Protestants in an Age of Science*.

7. Like many metaphysical clubs, this one has many origin stories. Different accounts can be gleaned in Wallace Irwin Jr., "The Legacy of SPH: How a Small Program in the Humanities Changed Princeton's Entire Curriculum," *Princeton Alumni Weekly* (January 14, 1987). A longer version of the Irwin article, "SPH: Special Program in the Humanities at Princeton", is located in Records Concerning the Creation of the Department of Religion; 1935–1969; George F. Thomas Papers, Box 1 Folder 7; Manuscripts Division, Department of Rare Books and Special Collections, Princeton University Library. In addition, elements of the story of the Baltimores are present in Arthur Hazard Dakin, *Paul Elmer More* (Princeton: Princeton University Press, 1960); and in J. Duncan Spaeth, "Conversations with Paul Elmer More," *The Sewanee Review* 51, no. 4 (October–December 1943): 532–545.

8. J. David Hoeveler, *The New Humanism: A Critique of Modern America, 1900–1940* (Charlottesville: University Press of Virginia, 1977); Dakin, *Paul Elmore More*; Stephen L. Tanner, *Paul Elmer More: Literary Criticism as the History of Ideas* (Provo, UT and Albany, NY: Brigham Young University; Distributed by State University of New York Press, 1987).

9. Dakin, *Paul Elmer More*, 171.

10. Paul Elmer More to Christian Gauss, February 23, 1930, Correspondence between More and Gauss; Paul Elmer More Papers, Box 26 Folder 4; Manuscripts Division, Department of Rare Books and Special Collections, Princeton University Library. Cf. Paul Charles Kemeny, *Princeton in the Nation's Service: Religious Ideals and Educational Practice, 1868–1928* (New York: Oxford University Press, 1998).

11. Dakin, *Paul Elmer More*, 185.

12. These early twentieth-century battles are covered in Edward A. Purcell, *The Crisis of Democratic Theory: Scientific Naturalism & the Problem of Value* (Lexington: University Press of Kentucky, 1973); and Andrew Jewett, *Science,*

Democracy, and the American University: From the Civil War to the Cold War (Cambridge: Cambridge University Press, 2012).

13. Christian Gauss, *Democracy Today: An American Interpretation* (Chicago and New York: Scott, Foresman, 1917), *A Primer for Tomorrow; Being an Introduction to Contemporary Civilization* (New York and London: Scribner, 1934).

14. Christian Gauss, "Peace at Gettysburg," undated; Christian Gauss Papers, Box 25 Folder 4; Manuscripts Division, Department of Rare Books and Special Collections, Princeton University Library. See also Christian Gauss, "The Threat of Science," *Scribner's* LXXXVII, no. 5 (May 1930): 467–478. Gauss was also responding directly to an article by physicist Robert Millikan, "Alleged Sins of Science," *Scribner's Magazine* LXXXVII, no. 2 (February 1930): 119–129.

15. Christian Gauss to Edwin Grant Conklin, October 25, 1930, C: Miscellaneous; 1935–1945; Christian Gauss Papers, Box 57 Folder 16; Manuscripts Division, Department of Rare Books and Special Collections, Princeton University Library.

16. Christian Gauss, "Nationalism in the Colleges," Christian Gauss Papers, Box 24 Folder 5; Manuscripts Division, Department of Rare Books and Special Collections, Princeton University Library.

17. George Thomas, "Religion in an Age of Secularism," General; 1935–1941; Office of the Secretary Records, Box 14, Folder 7; Princeton University Archives, Department of Rare Books and Special Collections, Princeton University Library. c.f. Sloan, *Faith and Knowledge*; David A. Hollinger, *After Cloven Tongues of Fire: Protestant Liberalism in Modern American History* (Princeton, NJ: Princeton University Press, 2013).

18. "My Story by George Thomas," My Story TMS; 1977; George F. Thomas Papers, Box 1 Folder 2, Manuscripts Division, Department of Rare Books and Special Collections, Princeton University Library.

19. Thomas, "Notes on Breadloaf Courses," George F. Thomas Papers, Box 1 Folder 7, Manuscripts Division, Department of Rare Books and Special Collections, Princeton University Library.

20. On the importance of the virtues in early American higher education, see Hoeveler, *Creating the American Mind.*

21. Theodore Meyer Greene, *The Meaning of the Humanities* (Princeton and London: Princeton University Press, 1938); Elizabeth Caroline van Horn, "The Philosophy of Theodore M. Greene and Its Significance for Philosophy of Education," (PhD Dissertation, The Ohio State University, 1964); Ethan Schrum, "Establishing a Democratic Religion: Metaphysics and Democracy in the Debates over the President's Commission on Higher Education," *History of Education Quarterly* 47, no. 3 (2007): 277–301.

22. William Dighton, Theodore Meyer Greene, Henry M. Wriston, and Charles C. Fries, *Liberal Education Re-examined: Its Role in a Democracy* (New York and London: Harper & Brothers, 1943), 32–33, 69–70. Greene was the author of these particular sections/chapters of the volume.

23. Humanities 201–202: The Western Tradition: Man and his Freedom; 1948–1955; Robert F. Goheen Papers, Public Policy Papers, Folder 1, Department of Rare Books and Special Collections, Princeton University Library. The quote is from Paul Elmer More, *Pages From an Oxford Diary* (Princeton: Princeton University Press, 1937).

24. Humanities 201–202: The Western Tradition.

25. This was another common feature of Puritan and Christian learning in the early American republic. See Hoeveler, *Creating the American Mind.* On Princeton specifically, see Bozeman, *Protestants in an Age of Science*; J. David

Hoeveler, *James McCosh and the Scottish Intellectual Tradition: From Glasgow to Princeton* (Princeton: Princeton University Press, 1981); Mark A. Noll, *Princeton and the Republic, 1768–1822: The Search for a Christian Enlightenment in the Era of Samuel Stanhope Smith* (Princeton: Princeton University Press, 1989); Scott Philip Segrest, *America and the Political Philosophy of Common Sense* (Columbia, MO: University of Missouri Press, 2010); and Sophia A. Rosenfeld, *Common Sense: A Political History* (Cambridge: Harvard University Press, 2011).

26. Humanities 201–202: The Western Tradition.
27. Charles Hendel to Harold Dodds, November 15, 1949, Humanities; 1934 May – 1957; Office of the President Records: Jonathan Dickinson to Harold W. Dodds Subgroup, Box 117 Folder 1, Princeton University Archives, Department of Rare Books and Special Collections, Princeton University Library.
28. Humanities 201–202: The Western Tradition.
29. Ibid.
30. Charles Hendel to Harold Dodds, November 15, 1949.
31. Humanities 201–202: The Western Tradition.
32. Charles Hendel to Harold Dodds, November 15, 1949.
33. Humanities 201–202: The Western Tradition.
34. HUM201/202 was part of a General Education distribution requirement in the Humanities. Princeton students did not have to take it, but it was one of the few Humanities courses offered within the requirement. It ran from 1942 to the early 1960s, educating around 5,000 students over a twenty-year period.
35. Gilbert Allardyce, "The Rise and Fall of the Western Civilization Course," *The American Historical Review* 87, no. 3 (1982): 695–725.
36. C.F. John S. Gilkeson, *Anthropologists and the Rediscovery of America, 1886–1965* (New York: Cambridge University Press, 2010).
37. For the earlier version of this viewpoint, see Bozeman, *Protestants in an Age of Science*.
38. Humanities 201–202: The Western Tradition.
39. David Hollinger, "The Unity of Knowledge and the Diversity of Knowers: Science as an Agent of Cultural Integration in the United States Between the Two World Wars," *Pacific Historical Review* 80, no. 2 (May 2011): 211–230; Andrew Jewett, "Canonizing Dewey: Naturalism, Logical Empiricism, and the Idea of American Philosophy," *Modern Intellectual History* 8, no. 1 (2011): 91–125; Gilkeson, *Anthropologists and the Rediscovery of America*; Marshall Hyatt, *Franz Boas, Social Activist: The Dynamics of Ethnicity* (New York: Greenwood Press, 1990). On the religious perspective on science and scientific humanism, see Ferenc Morton Szasz, *The Divided Mind of Protestant America, 1880–1930* (University, AL: University of Alabama Press, 1982); Kenneth Cauthen, *The Impact of American Religious Liberalism* (Washington, DC: University Press of America, 1983); and William R. Hutchinson, *The Modernist Impulse in American Protestantism* (Durham: Duke University Press, 1992).
40. Humanities 201–202: The Western Tradition.
41. Irwin Jr., "The Legacy of SPH"; Irwin, "SPH: Special Program in the Humanities at Princeton".
42. Irwin Jr., "The Legacy of SPH."
43. "Philosophy v. History," n.d., 1930–1950; Historical Subject Files Collection, Box 38, Folder 5; Princeton University Archives, Department of Rare Books and Special Collections, Princeton University Library.
44. Humanities 201–202: The Western Tradition.

45. Harold W. Dodds, *Out of This Nettle, Danger* (Princeton: Princeton University Press, 1943).

46. Irwin Jr., "The Legacy of SPH."

47. William F. Buckley, *God and Man at Yale: The Superstitions of Academic Freedom* (Chicago: Regnery, 1951); James Green, "'God and Man at Yale' and Beyond: The Thoughts of William F. Buckley, Jr. on Higher Education, 1949–1955," *American Educational History Journal* 39, no. 1 (2012): 201–216.

48. Charles Seymour, President of Yale University, Records (RU 23), Box 43, Folder 366, Manuscripts and Archives, Yale University Library.

49. For a nineteenth-century perspective on this relationship, see Louise L. Stevenson, *Scholarly Means to Evangelical Ends: The New Haven Scholars and the Transformation of Higher Learning in America, 1830–1890* (Baltimore: Johns Hopkins University Press, 1986); on twentieth-century manifestations, see Bruce Kuklick, "Philosophy at Yale in the Century after Darwin," *History of Philosophy Quarterly* 21, no. 3 (2004): 313–336.

50. Charles Seymour Inauguration Speech, 1937, copy in Charles Seymour, President of Yale University, Records (RU 23), Box 86 Folder 144, Manuscripts and Archives, Yale University Library.

51. Richard Warch, *School of the Prophets: Yale College, 1701–1740* (New Haven: Yale University Press, 1973); David B. Potts, ed., *Liberal Education for a Land of Colleges: Yale's Reports of 1828* (New York: Palgrave Macmillan, 2010); Jurgen Herbst, "The Yale Report of 1828," *International Journal of the Classical Tradition* 11, no. 2 (2004): 213–231.

52. On this point, see Jack C. Lane, "The Yale Report of 1828 and Liberal Education: A Neorepublican Manifesto," *History of Education Quarterly* 27, no. 3 (1987): 325–338.

53. Sumner's reforms and subsequent curricular wars are covered in George Wilson Pierson, *Yale: College and University, 1871–1937* (New Haven: Yale University Press, 1952). Pierson was a member of the 1940s group that sought to restore the Christian-classical synthesis.

54. Ralph Gabriel, "Principles and Policies of the Course of Study Committee of Yale College," May 7, 1943, Eugene Harold Kone Papers (MS 1221), Manuscripts and Archives, Yale University Library.

55. Gabriel quoted in Eugene Kone's unpublished "Yale in WWII" Manuscript, Eugene Harold Kone Papers (MS 1221), Box 1, Manuscripts and Archives, Yale University Library.

56. On the formation of the New Aesthetes, see Pierson, *Yale: College and University*, 310. They also went under the name of the "New Classicists." See Maynard Mack Papers, Yale Collection of American Literature, Beinecke Rare Book and Manuscript Library, letters, as well as Box 101, "Dryden Criticism" folder, lecture notes on "Classicism to Romanticism," folder "Classical Tradition," folder "Essay on Criticism." The New Aesthetes were a group closely related to the New Criticism, a movement for textual analysis and close reading in literature. On the history of the New Criticism, see Murray Krieger, *The New Apologists for Poetry* (Minneapolis: University of Minnesota Press, 1956); John Henry Raleigh, "The New Criticism as a Historical Phenomenon," *Comparative Literature* 11, no. 1 (Winter 1959): 21–28; John Ransom, *The New Criticism* (Westport, CT: Greenwood Press, 1979); Mark Jancovich, *The Cultural Politics of the New Criticism* (Cambridge and New York: Cambridge University Press, 1993); and Donald J. Childs, *The Birth of New Criticism: Conflict and Conciliation in the Early Work of William Empson, I.A. Richards, Laura Riding, and Robert Graves* (Montréal & Kingston: McGill-Queen's University Press, 2013). The New Aesthetes group also overlapped with the progenitors of

Yale's American Studies program; see Sydney E. Ahlstrom, "Studying American Studies at Yale," *American Quarterly*, 22, no. 2 (Summer, 1970): 503–517; Michael Holzman, "The Ideological Origins of American Studies at Yale," 40, no. 2 (Summer, 1999): 71–99; Holzman, *James Jesus Angleton, the CIA, and the Craft of Counterintelligence* (Amherst: University of Massachusetts Press, 2008).

57. Maynard Mack, ed., *The Augustans* (New York: Prentice-Hall, 1950), 27.

58. Maynard Mack, Leonard Dean, and William Frost, eds., *Modern Poetry* (New York: Prentice-Hall, 1950), 2; and Mack, *The Augustans*.

59. Mack, *The Augustans*, 3.

60. On this logic empirical brand of scientific humanism, see Jewett, *Science, Democracy, and the American* University; Purcell, *The Crisis of Democratic Theory*; Hollinger, "The Unity of Knowledge and the Diversity of Knowers"; Friedrich Stadler and Camilla Nielsen, *The Vienna Circle: Studies in the Origins, Development, and Influence of Logical Empiricism* (Wien: Springer, 2001); George A. Reisch, *How the Cold War Transformed Philosophy of Science: To the Icy Slopes of Logic* (Cambridge: Cambridge University Press, 2005); Peter Galison, "The Americanization of Unity," *Daedelus* 127, no. 1 (Winter, 1998): 45–71; Steve J. Heims, *The Cybernetics Group* (Cambridge, MA: MIT Press, 1991). On F. S. C. Northrop and scientific humanism, see Heims, *The Cybernetics Group*; Andrew Reck, *The New American Philosophers: An Exploration of Thought Since World War II* (Baton Rouge: Louisiana State University Press, 1968); Fred Seddon, *An Introduction to the Philosophical Works of F. S. C. Northrop* (Lewiston, NY: Edwin Mellen Press, 1995); Francisco Escobar, "The Logical and Epistemological Foundations of Sociology in the Philosophy of F.S.C. Northrop," (PhD Dissertation, University of Kansas, 1992); Fred W. Beuttler, "Organizing an American Conscience: The Conferences on Science, Philosophy, and Religion, 1940–1948," (PhD Dissertation, University of Chicago, 1995); and Robert Smid, "Comparing Comparisons: An Analysis and Appraisal of Methodologies of Cross-Cultural Comparison from the American Pragmatist and Process Philosophical Traditions," (PhD Dissertation, Boston University, 2007). Northrop's magnum opus was *The Meeting of East and West: An Inquiry Concerning World Understanding* (New York: Macmillan Company, 1946).

61. F.S.C. Northrop, "Education for Intercultural Understanding," *The Journal of Higher Education* 18, no. 4 (1947): 171–181.

62. Yale University, *Statement by the Corporation, 12 December 1942* (New Haven: Yale University Press, 1942).

63. Charles Seymour, "On a Program of Studies in the Liberal Arts, Following the Cessation of Hostilities," December 29, 1942, MS 1221: Eugene H. Kone Papers, Box 2 Folder Liberal Arts, Manuscripts and Archives, Yale University Library; Yale College, *Report of the Committee on the Course of Study* (New Haven: The University, 1945); Charles Hendel, "The Nature and Aims of General Education," March 9, 1943, Richard C. Carroll, Assistant and Associate Dean of Yale College, Records (RU 20), Accession 1971-A003, Box 10, Folder 121, Manuscripts and Archives, Yale University Library.

64. James Hershberg alluded to Conant's Puritan heritage in his *James B. Conant, Harvard to Hiroshima and the Making of the Nuclear Age* (New York: Knopf, 1993), yet the heritage is not fully explored. Other works on Conant's thought include Justin Biddle, "Putting Pragmatism to Work in the Cold War: Science, Technology, and Politics in the Writings of James B. Conant," *Studies in History and Philosophy of Science* 42 (2011): 552–561; and Christopher Hamlin, "The Pedagogical Roots of the History of Science: Revisiting the Vision of James Bryant Conant," *Isis* 107, no. 2 (June 2016). Steve Fuller discusses Conant's Platonist thought and that of his protégés in Thomas Kuhn,

A Philosophical History for Our Times (Chicago: University of Chicago Press, 2000).

65. James Conant, "The Examined Life," *Vital Speeches of the Day* 2, no. 21 (1936): 638; see also Conant, "Friends and Enemies of Learning," *The Yale Review* 25 (Spring 1936): 463–476; James Conant, "Free Inquiry or Dogma?" *Atlantic* 155 (January 1, 1935); James Conant, "The Advancement of Learning During the Puritan Commonwealth," *Proceedings of the Massachusetts Historical Society*, 66 (October 1, 1936): 3–31.

66. Letter from James Bryant Conant to the Reverend William B. Lampe, April 26, 1936, Records of the President of Harvard University, James Bryant Conant, Box 61, Folder Lab-Lat, Harvard University Archives.

67. Conant, "Friends and Enemies of Learning."

68. "Chapter II, partial revision by R. Demos, beginning with section 3 of Chapter II", Harvard Committee on the Objectives of General Education in a Free Society, Material Presented to the Committee, 1943–1945, UAI10.528.10 Box 2 Serial Numbers 118–131, Harvard University Archives. See also James Conant, "The Advancement of Learning in the United States in the Post-War World," *Science* 99, no. 2562 (1944).

69. "Chapter II, partial revision by R. Demos, beginning with section 3 of Chapter II".

70. Conant, "The Examined Life."

71. Harvard University Committee on the Objectives of a General Education in a Free Society, *General Education in a Free Society: Report of the Harvard Committee* (Cambridge: The University, 1945). For previous discussions of the Redbook, see Frederick Rudolph, *Curriculum: A History of the American Undergraduate Course of Study since 1636* (San Francisco: Jossey-Bass Publishers, 1977); Phyllis Keller, *Getting at the Core: Curricular Reform at Harvard* (Cambridge: Harvard University Press, 1982); Gary E. Miller, *The Meaning of General Education: The Emergence of a Curriculum Paradigm* (New York: Teachers College Press, Columbia University, 1988); W.B. Carnochan, *The Battleground of the Curriculum: Liberal Education and the American Experience* (Stanford: Stanford University Press, 1993); Anita Fay Kravitz, "The Harvard Report of 1945: An Historical Ethnography," (PhD Dissertation, University of Pennsylvania, 1994); Morton Keller and Phyllis Keller, *Making Harvard Modern: The Rise of America's University* (Oxford: Oxford University Press, 2001); Nathan M. Sorber and Jordan Humphrey, "The Era of Student Bureaucracy and the Contested Road to the Harvard Redbook, 1925–1945," *Higher Education in Review* 8 (2011): 13–40; Craig Kridel, "The Harvard Redbook and the 1939 Student Council Report," in Craig Kridel ed., *Curriculum History* (Lanham, MD: University Press of America, 1989): 161–170; and Jamie Cohen-Cole, *The Open Mind: Cold War Politics and the Sciences of Human Nature* (Chicago: Chicago University Press, 2014).

72. This information is according to a Harvard biography. See www.nytimes.com/1995/06/14/obituaries/john-h-finley-jr-91-classicist-at-harvard-for-43-years-is-dead.html.

73. Douglas Bush, *Engaged & Disengaged* (Cambridge: Harvard University Press, 1966).

74. Douglas Bush, "Two Roads to Truth: Science and Religion in the Seventeenth Century," *ELH: A Journal of English Literary History* 8, no. 2 (June 1941): 82.

75. Ibid., 83.

76. Ibid.

77. Ronald Steel, *Walter Lippmann and the American Century* (New York: Vintage Books, 2017); and Angus Burgin, *The Great Persuasion: Reinventing Free Markets since the Depression* (Cambridge, MA: Harvard University Press, 2012).

78. Walter Lippmann, "Education vs Western Civilization," *American Scholar* 10 (1941): 184–193.
79. Ibid., 184.
80. Ibid.
81. Ibid., 186.
82. Ibid., 187.
83. See especially Elizabeth Melia, "Science, Values, and Education: The Search for Cultural Unity at Harvard under Charles W. Eliot, A. Lawrence Lowell and James B. Conant," (PhD Dissertation, Johns Hopkins University, 1995). The Eliot presidency and its effects on American higher education are covered in numerous books, including Hugh Hawkins, *Between Harvard and America: The Educational Leadership of Charles W. Eliot* (New York: Oxford University Press, 1972).
84. Uncle Dudley, "Woodman, Spare That Sapling," The Emergency in Education, Reprints of Nine "Uncle Dudley" Editorials Appearing in THE BOSTON GLOBE between October 17, 1942 and January 16, 1943, Global Newspaper Company (1943): 17.
85. Uncle Dudley, The Quarries of Syracuse," The Emergency in Education, Reprints of Nine "Uncle Dudley" Editorials Appearing in THE BOSTON GLOBE between October 17, 1942 and January 16, 1943, Global Newspaper Company (1943): 27.
86. On the attacks against progressive education, see Andrew Hartman, *Education and the Cold War: The Battle for the American School* (New York: Palgrave Macmillan, 2008).
87. McAllister-Grande, "The Inner Restoration."
88. Finley, "Highly Tentative Draft of Chapter II," Committee Files, Box 2 Serial Numbers 118–131.
89. "Chapter II, partial revision by R. Demos, beginning with section 3 of Chapter II", Committee Files, Box 2 Serial Numbers 118–131.
90. Committee on the Objectives of General Education in a Free Society, April 25, 1944 Meeting Minutes, Committee Files, Box 1, Serial Numbers 99–112.
91. Committee on the Objectives of General Education in a Free Society, December 14, 1943 Meeting Minutes, Committee Files, Box 1, Serial Numbers 67–78.
92. Ibid.
93. T. S. Eliot to Paul Elmer More, August 3, 1929, Eliot, Thomas Stearns, 22 letters; Paul Elmer More Papers, C0054, Manuscripts Division, Department of Rare Books and Special Collections, Princeton University Library.

6 "We Felt . . . That We Were Talking to Old Friends"

Catholic and Protestant Colleges and Their Cooperation for Curriculum Reform

Kevin S. Zayed

On November 22, 1940, the *Catherine Wheel*, the newspaper of the College of St. Catherine (CSC), a women's college located in St. Paul Minnesota, reported

> Mrs. S.H. McGuire and Mr. T.A. Barnhart of Muskingum College, New Concord, Ohio, visited St. Catherine's recently to study the Humanities program at the college. They interviewed Sister Maris Stella about the English program and the problems of creative writing, and Sister Mona about techniques and problems of the Humanities course. They are planning on introducing such a course at Muskingum.[1]

Both institutions were members of the Cooperative Study in General Education, a philanthropically funded venture where nearly two dozen institutions of higher learning worked to reform their general education programs, or the portions of their curricula that dealt with competing conceptions of culture and citizenship, between 1938 and 1945.[2] Although the CSC was the sole Catholic college in the study, a variety of Protestant denominations were represented by Allegheny College (Methodist), Antioch College (Unitarian), Bethany College (Disciples of Christ), Centre College (Episcopalian), Fisk College (United Church of Christ), Hiram College (Disciples of Christ), Hendrix College (Methodist), Hope College (Reformed Church in America), Macalester College (Presbyterian), Muskingum College (Presbyterian), Olivet College (United Church of Christ), Park College (Presbyterian), Stephens College (Baptist), Talladega College (Baptist), and the College of Wooster (Presbyterian).

By many accounts, the visit was a positive experience for all involved. "A few days ago," the associate director of the Cooperative Study wrote to CSC professor Sister Annette Walters,

> I had a very glowing report from the representatives of Muskingum College who visited your institution. They were simply rhapsodizing

about the splendid program which you have. They were talking about the exceedingly stimulating humanities course . . . and about many other things too numerous to mention.[3]

Sister Annette responded to this letter in kind:

> Your letter came as a happy reminder of the very pleasant day we spent with your Muskingum faculty members during their recent visit to St. Catherine's. We felt, in visiting with these people that we were talking to old friends, and that we were getting more ideas from them than they were getting from us. At any rate, we enjoyed the day very much and are now more than ever convinced that the ideals of the Muskingum faculty are very similar to our own.[4]

What made this campus visit and its aftermath particularly notable was the religious affiliations of the two institutions. On the one hand, the College of St. Catherine was and is a Catholic institution. Muskingum College, on the other hand, was and is affiliated with the Presbyterian Church. Indeed, this moment in 1940 was an example of interinstitutional cooperation between a Catholic and Protestant institution of higher learning.[5] Yet, this seems out of place when considering that historians of Catholic and Protestant higher education have, for good reason, emphasized the role of conflict and hostility between the two.[6] Historian Kathleen A. Mahoney observed, "for the Roman Catholic minority, the project of higher education has entailed the complex task of contending with Protestantism, wrestling not only with anti-Catholic sentiment but Protestantism's profound influence in society and culture exercised through its educational institutions," while historian George M. Marsden went as far as to call Protestant education's attitude toward Catholic education a "deep irony" because Protestantism itself was based upon a theory of cooperation, but had been represented in practice by instances of exclusion.[7] The CSC and Muskingum's cooperation also seems out of place when considering the documented instances of cooperation among and between Catholic and Protestant institutions of higher learning. In reading the history of Catholic higher education, one comes across little evidence that Catholic colleges cooperated with each other, and the few instances of documented cooperation that exist took place after 1950.[8] While there is a robust literature on cooperation between Protestant colleges, again, there is little documented cooperation before 1950.[9] Examples of cooperation between Catholic and Protestant colleges, before or after 1950, however, are almost nonexistent in the literature.[10]

What does appear in the literature prior to 1950 are a few restrained discussions about the possibility of Protestant and Catholic cooperation. "The question has sometimes been raised as to the possibility and desirability of cooperation between Catholic and non-Catholic institutions of higher education," wrote Roy J. Deferrari, the Secretary General of the Catholic University of America, in 1946. "It is obvious," he continued, "that fundamental differences in basic philosophy constitute a serious obstacle to the development of such cooperation. It is equally obvious that Catholic institutions may not join with non-Catholic groups in any common project in which there might even appear to be any compromise in fundamental doctrine." Exercising discretion Deferrari concluded that "This phase of the question is a very delicate one, but I personally feel that something by way of cooperation between Catholics and non-Catholics can be achieved in a restricted manner."[11]

Another curious factor surrounding the cooperation between the CSC and Muskingum is that, unlike many of the other institutions of higher learning that had de-emphasized their relationship with religion in the late nineteenth and early twentieth centuries, these two institutions remained staunchly committed to providing an educational experience that emanated not only from the Christian faith, but also from their own denomination's understanding of that faith.[12] The CSC's president effectively summed up their strong commitment to Catholicism in a 1939 faculty meeting, arguing that "for years we have based our aims and ideals of a Catholic Women's College on the Pope's Encyclicals."[13] The Synod of Ohio sponsored Muskingum and it maintained a strong connection with the Mansfield and Muskingum Presbyteries. In 1937, the annual meeting of the synod was held on Muskingum's campus, proving to be "the largest attended Synod meeting for many years." One of the "principal addresses" featured a trustee of Muskingum who spoke extensively on the long association between the Synod and the college.[14]

The following year, President Robert N. Montgomery concluded a report to the Board of trustees by suggesting that "We purpose [sic.] to continue to carry forward our program of education with a distinctly Christian emphasis."[15] For the most part, these sentiments were held not only by the presidents, but also by the professors and made their way into the curriculum.[16] At the College of St. Catherine, the faculty consisted almost entirely of Catholic Sisters. The professors at Muskingum began faculty meetings with prayers and other devotional exercises.

This chapter not only catalogs and contextualizes the cooperation between the CSC and Muskingum, but that of several other denominational colleges during the 1930s and 1940s. I argue that a secularizing and chaotic social context as well as trying institutional conditions drove a form of cooperation – that I am calling "cooperation without consensus" – between Catholic and Protestant institutions. By embracing progressive and somewhat scientific methods of curriculum reform to facilitate more traditional religious aims, cooperating institutions ultimately fostered goodwill, stimulated tangible curriculum reform (with particular emphasis placed the religious aspects of each school's program), and thrived in a rapidly modernizing world.

The concept of "cooperation without consensus" may be defined as the willingness of institutions and individuals with different values and objectives to engage in philanthropically funded and experimental interinstitutional cooperation (particularly in joint ventures related to curricular reform), as long the general autonomy of each was respected. Put simply, although institutions and their representatives learned from each other, they only did so out of the belief that they could return to their own campuses and create their own curricula. At the end of the day, each institution's curricula needed to serve *their* constituents and advance *their* worldview. Cooperation without consensus was an innovative approach to reforming curricula secondary and higher education that was developed during the Great Depression to deal with a paradox identified by administrators: increased enrollments required wide scale curriculum reform and institution building, but the pecuniary resources necessary to engage in these tasks were drying up. Cooperation without consensus allowed diverse institutional types to engage in work that was labeled as "experimental," "individualized," "cooperative," and "democratic." It was precisely these methods of working preferred by philanthropic foundations with the resources necessary to finance wide scale reform. This served as one of many motivations for institutions to engage in cooperation without consensus. Good experiences were another. As individuals and institutions engaged in cooperation without consensus, they were occasionally surprised by whom they learned from and what they learned. More surprising still is the reality that Catholics and Protestants worked together to strengthen the core religious foundations of their offerings and found their former foes to be strong allies.

This chapter begins by exploring several factors that contributed to the existence of interinstitutional cooperation between Catholic and Protestant institutions of higher education and examples from the College of St. Catherine and its many Protestant collaborators offer keen insight. These factors included: secularization of the American society and academy, the growth of American and Christian higher education, such issues in secondary education as accreditation and enrollment, and the general education movement. The chapter then uses the lens of the Cooperative Study in General Education to explore cooperation without consensus on a more intensive level. As a study comprising almost two dozen diverse institutions of higher learning – including several Christian institutions of various denominations – this was a key site of cooperation that led to tangible curriculum reform. Finally, the chapter provides some examples of curricular reforms that emerged, including new courses in the humanities and theology, and the creation of inventories to understand the role of religious education in determining student values.

By exploring Catholic and Protestant cooperation, this chapter highlights shared concerns, methods, and contact that previous historians of higher education may have overlooked. It also responds to historian Linda Eisenmann's call to examine Catholic and Protestant institutions in a "comparative" manner.[17]

Common Threats, Common Ground: Secularization, Standardization, and Scarcity

Before analyzing the obstacles that Catholic colleges faced in a Protestant world, Kathleen A. Mahoney noted that many Catholic and Protestant institutions "bore notable similarities: clergyman presidents, largely if not entirely prescribed curricula with heavy emphases on the classics, small student bodies drawn primarily from local youth, and discipline saturated with piety."[18] This point applies particularly well to the smaller Midwestern denominational liberal arts colleges during the 1930s and 1940s.[19] Yet, their similarities were not only limited to common features, like curricula and demographics, but to common intellectual and cultural contexts as well. Their contexts might best be broken down into three perceived threats that emanated from modern American society and the changing landscape of higher education. The first was secularization, or the perception held by progressive reformers, policymakers, and other citizens that the gospel no longer offered people the "Truth" and that the scientific method was the way to understand and impact the course of humankind.[20] The second was standardization, or new (occasionally scientific) requirements created and enforced by educational organizations to operate a credible educational institution.[21] Finally, scarcity, or the sheer lack of financial and other resources needed to experiment, grow, and evolve posed a threat especially in light of the devastating conditions brought on by the Great Depression.[22] Ultimately, one question Catholics and Protestants began to ask was: in the face of secularization, standardization, and scarcity, how might cooperation with religious and non-religious allies allow *our* institutions to continue providing an educational experience consistent with *our* values? Denominational colleges employed new strategies and worked with new partners to answer that pivotal question. The Dean of Muskingum College captured this well in 1937, writing

> For a good many years the American Arts college has been ailing. At least so most thinkers in education believe. Criticisms abound so also do panaceas. The Muskingum faculty became impatient with verbalisms and decided to attempt the solution of the college problems by scientific analysis.[23]

But, why would interinstitutional cooperation become such a crucial strategy among denominational colleges? Although every college faced a similarly threatening landscape during the 1930s and 1940s, the future of denominational colleges was considered especially precarious by many working within them as their very personal and professional identities were being challenged by others eager to see them either modernize or cease to exist.[24] A 1940 commemorative pamphlet produced by Allegheny College illustrates this point: "Education on the elementary and secondary level is now a completely secular process, and more and more on the college level the expansion of state supported schools threatens to remove from education all instruction in religion. Only the Christian college still defends the place of moral training and religious faith." Allegheny College, the pamphlet continued, "insists that spiritual growth and ethical instruction are both normal and necessary."[25]

Indeed, liberal arts colleges – especially those with strong religious affiliations and a desire to maintain them – were seen by some educational reformers and critics as ancient relics when compared to the modern research universities that had renegotiated their relationship to religion and embraced modernity.[26] Moreover, there was a strong push by some government officials and educational policymakers to create a more "efficient" and less "redundant" system of higher education.[27] These views, along with the "constant fear of impending financial disaster" during the Great Depression created a "crisis of confidence" for liberal arts colleges at the beginning of the 1930s.[28]

To combat the argument that liberal arts colleges were outmoded and to reestablish their importance without neglecting their purposes, liberal arts colleges cooperated with one another. For Catholic and Protestant institutions, this meant seeing other Christian institutions with competing doctrinal commitments as allies. A clear illustration of this can be seen by examining the Conference of Liberal Arts College, which was held in Chicago in March 1930 and where representatives from 278 liberal arts colleges convened to discuss the future of their institutions and the liberal arts college concept.[29] President Herbert Hoover, who enrolled in a Quaker academy before attending Stanford University in its inaugural year, lent his support to this conference. "I am glad," he wrote,

> to learn that a movement is being organized to preserve the more vital role of the smaller colleges, which have been suffering from the competition of the great universities. . . . I warmly commend the effort to maintain [liberal arts colleges], which have played and should still play so large a part in the development of leaders of American life.[30]

An implication of Hoover's argument – that interinstitutional cooperation was a key strategy for competing with larger universities – was intimated by each of the twenty-five papers delivered at the conference. The conference proceedings were published and nationally distributed as an edited volume entitled *The Liberal Arts College Movement.*

Interinstitutional cooperation featured heavily in one paper, "The Church and the College," that was given by William S. Bovard, the Secretary of the Board of Education of the Methodist Episcopal Church. After raising and responding to the contemporary feeling that religion should be marginalized in colleges, Bovard turned his attention to the argument that denominationalism should be eradicated from higher education altogether. He rejected the notion that denominational liberal arts colleges "ought to go out of business." Instead, he advocated that

> all Christian bodies ought, with the finest kind of breadth of spirit and the finest sort of catholicity of vision, and with the most splendid fidelity to conscience, to face the question as to whether it may not be possible for many of these institutions . . . to pool their resources, and to correlate their work with respect to their objectives and with respect to the service being rendered to their respective constituency.[31]

Following this call for interinstitutional cooperation, Bovard indicated that most denominational colleges would likely put their religious work over their denominational outlook, if pressed to do so. Focused on the Methodist institutions that he represented, Bovard proclaimed: "I do not know of a single Methodist institution that thinks of itself as an institution existing for the purpose of making a contribution to the definite increase of the prestige of that particular denomination. But every [denominational liberal arts college] thinks of itself as an agency of a great religious movement on behalf of the education and spiritualization of the total life of the community which it serves."[32] Bovard's session, like each one at the conference, opened and closed with a prayer.[33] Present at this conference was at least one representative from each of the denominational colleges that later cooperated in the Cooperative Study in General Education.[34]

Similar examples from other conferences abound. A vigorous conversation about the role of interinstitutional cooperation took place at a session focused on the future of "independent colleges" at the 1938 educational conference sponsored by the Association of American Colleges. J. R. McCain, President of Agnes Scott College, argued that of the existing 1,700 colleges in the United States, only 300–400 were likely to survive the current economic turmoil. Building on the arguments of earlier papers delivered at the conference, McCain reemphasized the importance of denominational colleges. Then, he turned his attention to the issue of interinstitutional cooperation by reflecting on a philanthropically funded program that allowed seventeen college professors (largely from the state of Georgia) to visit Toronto the previous year.

"There" McCain recalled, "we have a Presbyterian Theological Seminary, Catholic institutions, Methodists, the United Church of Canada and the state institutions all working together. They are working harmoniously, so much so that we in Georgia have taken heart and we have gotten six institutions to sign an agreement for cooperation."[35] Such cooperation, McCain and other speakers in this conference's session proposed, would allow religious institutions to elucidate their strengths and survive.

This conclusion echoed at numerous conferences and was marshalled by individual college presidents while fundraising.[36] Indeed, a similar conclusion was made by Muskingum College President Robert N. Montgomery in a 1940 letter to potential donors. In the letter, he cited a recent argument by Francis Keppel of the Carnegie Corporation "to the effect that 'there are far more colleges in the United States than the nation can possibly afford.'" Montgomery then added "I also realize that if Mr. Keppel had his way he would be very glad to blot out colleges such as Muskingum that are trying to give a strong Christian emphasis." Montgomery then pointed the plight of all denominational colleges before suggesting that all Christians must band resources together: "For some reason or other the Christian college has more difficulty in getting money than the college that has no church connections. In spite of what of Mr. Keppel and others say, I still believe in the place of the Christian college, but I do know that we must have larger financial support from our Christian friends if we are going to maintain a strong program."[37]

Calls for Christian institutions of higher learning to cooperate with others that were driven by different denominational concerns fit well in an increasingly secularized period when a number of religious leaders called for greater interfaith cooperation.[38] Some of these calls even resulted in educational projects that were driven by denominational and interfaith cooperation.[39] Another stimulant of these calls to cooperate was a minor and scattered relaxing of decades-long anti-Catholic sentiment that began in the 1930s. Much of this was due to the early twentieth century split of Protestants into a majority liberal, or "mainline" base and a distinguishable minority of fundamentalists.[40]

Prior to this split, Protestants had often saved their ammunition for ideological skirmishes with Catholics. However, mainline Protestants, which included "Methodists, Presbyterians, Congregationalists, Disciplines of Christ, Dutch Reformed, Episcopalians, Northern Baptists, Quakers, several Lutheran Denominations, and a smattering of Anabaptist and Reformed confessions," proved somewhat amenable to working with Catholics.[41] "Though mainline Protestant leaders frequently condemned Catholic authoritarianism," George M. Marsden reminds us, "they also often made special efforts to be tolerant of individual Catholics, especially if they were willing to act like tolerant Protestants."[42] Cooperation was not only a result of the relaxation of anti-Catholic sentiment, but also one of the principles that drove it. "During the early

1930s," historian Anthony Burke Smith explains, "anti-Catholicism receded as the nation's turn to collective solutions gave the traditional Catholic emphasis on the common good over individual interests a new credibility."[43]

Secularization was a key threat that drove denominational colleges to cooperate primarily with one another. However, standardization – with its scientific undertones – was a threat that often required denominational colleges to cooperate with individuals in non-religious organizations, universities, and philanthropic groups.[44] Pressure to standardize came from research universities and other educational organizations, as well as secondary schools, and somewhat ironically, Catholic secondary schools. A brief history of the College of St. Catherine is representative of how much denominational colleges (*both* Catholic and Protestant) stood to gain by cooperating with non-religious entities. It must be noted that the CSC was both representative and unique among Catholic colleges for women in their approaches to curricular reform. Other studies that contextualize Catholic women's colleges include Sister Mary Redempta Prose, *The Liberal Arts Ideal in the Catholic College for Women in the United States* (Washington, DC: The Catholic University of America, 1943); Sister Margaret Loretto Ryan, "General Education in Catholic Colleges for Women" (PhD diss., Fordham University, 1950). Discussions of general education reform in denominational institutions feature heavily in William F. Cunningham, *General Education and the Liberal College* (St. Louis, B. Herder Book Company, 1953).

The CSC was founded in 1905 by the Sisters of St. Joseph of Carondelet (CSJ) as a direct response to the growth and success of Catholic high schools who produced college-bound seniors in then-record numbers.[45] Far less methodologically rigid than some of their male counterparts leading the Catholic school systems, the CSJs had spent several decades navigating Protestant and secular influences on schooling and embracing new methods of teaching and curriculum without compromising the doctrinal integrity or Catholicism of their schools.[46] These students had both the preparation and the desire to attend postsecondary institutions, even if it meant that the college they attended was not Catholic.[47] Naturally, this concerned Catholic educators who were in favor of students continuing their education in a Catholic setting. Catholic colleges were promoted to seniors in both Catholic and public schools located in major metropolitan areas with a high concentration of Catholics.[48] To accommodate these students, existing Catholic colleges expanded and new ones were chartered.[49] The twin cities of St. Paul and Minneapolis were representative of a major Catholic metropolitan area and schools in the cities underwent many of the same shifts in enrollment. In particular, the CSC's enrollment figures grew exponentially. By 1920, the College of St. Catherine's enrollment was just above 200 students. An author in the college's literary magazine, the *Ariston*, remarked that she was impressed by this "decided increase in enrollment."[50] By 1934, this number had tripled.[51] And, three years after that, the *Catherine Wheel* discussed the demographics of the incoming freshman class and noted that "One hundred and five girls came to St. Catherine's from Catholic Schools. . . [and] One hundred and twenty-one attended public schools."[52]

This surge in enrollment brought upon two necessities for CSC: accreditation and growth. Undertaking these projects required CSC to cooperate with non-Catholic colleges, and in some cases, non-Catholic Christian organizations and entities. Indeed, accreditation was a national trend that was in full swing during the early twentieth century, creating an imperative that Catholic high schools could not ignore: gain accreditation by reconciling the tensions between current public school reform movements and scientific measurements and their religious values; or face extinction as Catholic students migrated to the public high schools and colleges.[53] This demand was also placed on Catholic colleges that were, in the words of one Catholic University of America official, "alive to the advantages accruing from an accredited standing for their institutions."[54] Perhaps their greatest ally in this quest was the North Central Association of Colleges and Secondary Schools (NCA), an organization that "welcomed Catholic involvement."[55]

The first Catholic institution accredited by the NCA was the College of St. Catherine. And, this was a source of great pride for the CSC: senior Constance Logue referred to it "a signal distinction" in the 1920 yearbook.[56] Indeed, accreditation was partially a result of cooperation with neighboring Protestant and secular organizations. As Logue also remarked, "from the opening year, members of the faculties of the St. Paul Seminary, the College of St. Thomas, and the University of Minnesota, have offered courses at St. Catherine's thereby broadening considerably the scope of the College program."[57] Not only did accreditation come as a result of interinstitutional cooperation, but it also helped to spur further cooperation.

Working with the NCA required the administrators of the CSC to cooperate with the other member institutions, almost all of which were non-Catholic institutions. An example of this took place in 1935. Mother Antonia McHugh, President of the CSC (1919–1937), and Sister Antonine, a faculty member in the English department, attended the annual meeting of the NCA in Chicago. While there, "Mother Antonia presided over the meeting of the Colleges for Women at the Chicago women's club . . . Sister Antonine spoke on the Guidance program in Colleges for women at the same meeting."[58] The interchange of ideas at these meetings also focused the participating faculty's attention on larger educational movements that sought to improve the quality of the educational experience offered at the College of St. Catherine. Sister (later Mother) Antonia McHugh wrote about the experiences she and other CSC faculty members had at conferences. She also argued that engagement with conferences were crucial for all faculty members committed to improving and evolving their teaching.[59]

As Sister Annette Walters wrote just a few years later, "We are being stimulated from so many directions – General Education, Teacher Education, North Central Association (to mention only a few)."[60] Additionally, "North Central's steadily rising expectations on the amount and quality of graduate training college faculty members should have" was a driving force behind "faculty development."[61] Indeed, *sustaining* accreditation was crucial to administrators and faculty at the CSC. A routine visit by a representative of the NCA in 1933, almost two decades after first receiving accreditation, left the institution "agog with fearsome anticipation."[62] This was a contributing factor to faculty members' decision to earn graduate degrees from the Universities of Chicago, Minnesota, and numerous other institutions.[63] It also may have factored into the launch of a successful campaign to become the first Catholic college to receive a chapter of Phi Beta Kappa in 1934.[64]

Accreditation and growth would require consistent financial commitments, however. Although there were numerous Catholic donors, they alone would not be enough to sustain the institution. Moreover, the Great Depression would put a greater strain on the donors themselves.[65] Increasingly, the College of St. Catherine turned, as many other institutions of higher learning did, to philanthropic foundations. "I went to five different enormously wealthy Catholics," Sister (later Mother) Antonia lamented to the president of the General Education Board (the portion of the of the Rockefeller philanthropies that dealt with schooling issues), "but in each case I could get no consideration. Their whole interest seems to be allotted to church building, orphan asylums and such like institutions."[66] Surveying the landscape of philanthropic organizations willing to donate to higher education in the early twentieth century, there were but a few options. "More than three-fourths of the known [philanthropic foundation] assets," scholar Ernest Victor Hollis noted in 1938, "are still in the group established before 1915 by Andrew Carnegie and John D. Rockefeller, Sr."[67] And while the CSC did receive some funding from the Carnegie Foundation, much of their philanthropic funding came from the General Education Board of the Rockefeller Foundation because of its relationship with the University of Chicago.[68]

It was this university where Mother Antonia did her graduate work and she later used this connection to seek grants from the GEB.[69] In doing so, she inaugurated a tradition that continued during her presidency and beyond. Subsequent grants grew larger and came with greater frequency. On the twenty-fifth anniversary of the college, the GEB awarded the CSC the considerable sum of $300,000 (about $5.5 million in 2020).[70] However, this connection with the General Education Board was not merely symbolized by funding, but also resulted in other exchanges. For example, in 1933, the *Ariston* noted that "An old friend of Mother Antonia's,

Dr. George Vincent, former chairman of the General Education Board of the Rockefeller Foundation and former President of the University of Minnesota, came . . . to visit St. Catherine's and speak."[71] This fact is quite notable given that many Baptists, whose religious affiliation informed their work, staffed the GEB and the broader Rockefeller Foundation.[72] Though the University of Chicago was a secular institution, it was founded with GEB money and influence and a number of historians have explored its early relationship to Christianity.[73] Additionally, the GEB assisted the CSC in obtaining grants from the Carnegie Corporation. "I have often said that I do not know of any college president in America [than Antonia McHugh] more splendidly qualified for high service in the directing of higher learning" GEB officer Wallace Buttrick wrote to Frederick Keppel of the Carnegie Corporation in 1924. "I have visited the College of St. Catherine several times," Buttrick continued, "as have some of my associates. It is perhaps the strongest institution in the country devoted to higher education of Catholic women."[74]

Cooperation with non-Catholic organizations and institutions had transformed the College of St. Catherine during its first three decades of existence. By 1936, an author in the *Ariston* reported that,

> St. Catherine's was the first Catholic women's college to be accredited by the North Central Association, that the library school was the first Catholic library school approved by the American Library Association; that the College has won the recognition of the General Education Board and the Carnegie Corporation; that the members of her faculty have been educated in the great universities and cultural centers of the world.[75]

Written in this fashion, these developments come across as completed accomplishments. However, these developments were not simply one-time events or triumphs, but the foundational beginnings of a self-perpetuating and iterative cycle of cooperation at the CSC. Each of these developments would need to be sustained throughout the 1930s and beyond. Accreditation would need to be renewed, therefore cooperation within that venue could not end. Neither would the professionalization of the faculty. Similarly, constant increases in enrollment necessitated physical growth, which meant that the CSC frequently beseeched philanthropists for donations.

These cyclical factors, however, were also a means to an end. While accreditation and funds were necessary to sustain CSC as an institution, its curriculum and the values it reflected was the very reason why the college existed. Yet, the influx of new students, anxieties about American youth writ large, and the issues related to organizing an increasingly complex college curriculum necessitated constant revision to ensure that the curriculum (particularly the general education curriculum) reflected the institution's values and met student needs. Taking a keen interest in reforming their general education curricula, the CSC found itself as a member of a national movement known at the time as the "general education movement."[76]

Members of this movement had divergent understandings and goals. As historian David R. Russell explains "Before the new century was half over, *general education*, like democracy, had become a god-term; everyone proclaimed it a worthy goal, but few agreed on its meaning."[77] Many institutions did, however, agree on the method of reform. Rather than accepting general education curricula wholesale from elite institutions that drew attention for their work in general education (e.g. Columbia University, the University of Chicago), smaller institutions instead experimented to find curricula that served their own clientele and advanced their own worldviews.[78] "Indubitably," one college president opined in 1939, "the watchword of education today is 'experimentation.' "[79]

But experimentation raised a troubling paradox: Increased enrollments and growth created the necessity for comprehensive curricular reform (particularly in general education), and experimentation was considered the best method to achieve this reform. Yet, experimentation and reform were expensive, and the pecuniary resources necessary to finance these undertakings were especially scarce during the Great Depression.[80] "Many institutions are eager to make a reappraisal of their work [in general education]," one academic lamented in 1939, "but lack financial and human resources adequate to the task."[81] Denominational colleges felt this paradox acutely partially due to the issues discussed earlier, but also because they failed to bring in as much funding from research as universities did.[82] To combat the problem of scarcity, members of the general education movement relied upon philanthropic funding, educational research, and most importantly, interinstitutional cooperation to efficiently utilize available resources.[83] Often, this took the form of "cooperative studies," or a scenario "in which several [institutions], recognizing a common interest project or problem or individual campus problems, unite under some accepted plan to analyze the problem or problems and share their discoveries with all participating institutions."[84] The Cooperative Study in General Education was one such project that also served as a key site of Catholic and Protestant cooperation in curriculum reform.

Resolving the Paradox: Cooperative Studies and Cooperation Without Consensus

The Cooperative Study in General Education originated at the annual meetings of the North Central Association during the mid-1930s. Discussing general education in this forum had always made good sense to secondary school and collegiate educators (especially those affiliated with denominational colleges) because the NCA considered curricula as a key factor in its accrediting standards.[85] However, criticism during the previous decade led the NCA to reemphasize the importance of not only the content of general education but also the necessity of its reform via experimentation during the mid-1930s. Having faced harsh criticism over seemingly "arbitrary" accreditation standards that threatened the "autonomy" of institutions, the NCA recently transformed itself from an organization "solely concerned with assuring the quality of education to one which could serve as a stimulus to the various institutions in their experimentation and improvement."[86]

For its part, the NCA was quick to link its new accrediting standards to experimentation to improve curriculum. The NCA respected the uniqueness and autonomy of individual institutions, noting that it sought "to observe such principles as will preserve whatever desirable individual qualities member institutions may have." "Uniformity in every detail of institutional policies and practices," the NCA stressed "is believed to be not only unnecessary, but undesirable. Well conceived experiments aimed to improve educational processes are considered essential to the growth of higher institutions and will be encouraged."[87] For denominational colleges, this was a desirable shift. They could now feel comfortable experimenting with their general education programs and know that they would still retain accreditation while doing so. The NCA also provided a hospitable space where members could cooperate on general education experimentation with each other.

Around this time, a group of NCA colleges began "inquiring . . . about the possibility of a survey" of their general education programs.[88] A series of "informal discussions" between faculty and administrators at these colleges led to work on a proposal that could be sent to the American Council on Education (ACE). The NCA and its members saw the ACE as an able sponsor of experimental studies because of the success it had with acquiring philanthropic funding for these purposes.[89] In searching for precedents to guide their work, the NCA group of colleges and the ACE looked to secondary schools and institutions of higher learning that were also vexed by the paradox of needing to accomplish wide-scale reform in a period of financial retrenchment.[90] They had many examples to choose from. By 1934, there were over 250 "National Deliberative Committees in Education in operation."[91]

Of greatest interest to all involved was the Eight-Year Study, a joint effort by more than thirty high schools (and a few citywide school systems) to reform their general education programs under the auspices of the Progressive Education Association. This study also secured hundreds of thousands of dollars from the Carnegie and Rockefeller philanthropies, and set a precedent for similar experimental and cooperative studies to receive substantial philanthropic funding for the next several years.[92] Members of the Eight-Year Study frequently gave papers at the annual meetings of the NCA and published widely on their experiences and findings.[93] They had also innovated and refined methods of cooperative experimentation, including workshops, student and teacher assisted reforms, and the creation of shared curricular materials.[94] Assisted by central staffs of educational researchers and financed by major philanthropic foundations, participating high schools in the Eight-Year Study collectively accomplished what they could not do individually in an efficient manner: They were reforming their general education curricula, together. What if, the NCA institutions wondered, they could form a cooperative study to explore their general education programs similar to the Eight-Year Study?

Upon receiving a proposal from the NCA colleges, the administrators of the ACE were open to such a collegiate version of the Eight-Year Study. They selected Ralph W. Tyler (who was by then a major force behind the Eight-Year Study) to be the director of this endeavor. As Tyler would later recall "the ACE asked him 'to follow the procedure that worked so well with the Eight-Year Study.' "[95] This involved a Cooperative Study with four major goals: training and assisting faculty to lead studies of their general education programs, revise curricula, create evaluation instruments, and expand student personnel services.[96] Tyler and his colleagues began by securing philanthropic funding from the General Education Board. Next, they moved to make the Cooperative Study more salient by ensuring that the participating colleges would "constitute almost a complete cross section of American higher education."[97] Given the numerous institutions that wanted to join and the limited resources available, the leaders of the Cooperative Study began a selection process.

Interestingly, the scientific imperative of creating a generalizable sample as one characteristic of sound (educational) research led to a process that brought together a Catholic college and several Protestant colleges.[98] Tyler noted this diversity and emphasized the religious affiliations of schools decades later as he recalled the twenty-two schools that participated many decades later. "It included two state universities, Michigan State and Iowa State;" he explained,

> it included some excellent women's colleges, the College of St. Catherine, a Catholic women's college, in St. Paul, Mills College, and Stephen's College; it included Allegheny College, Methodist, and Bethany College, a Disciples school; it included the Centre College of Kentucky which is, as I recall, Episcopalian; it included the University of Louisville, which was then a municipal university.[99]

In creating a generalizable sample, Tyler and his colleagues had brought the College of St. Catherine to a place where it could cooperate with several Protestant institutions.

The faculty members of the College of St. Catherine were keen to participate in the Cooperative Study in General Education. This not only provided them the resources necessary to reform their general education programs, but also created an opportunity to engage in cooperation.[100] In late 1938, they were invited by the leadership of the Cooperative Study to join. Sister Eucharista Galvin, who had taken over as the second president of CSC one year earlier, reported that she had "made a complete canvass of the faculty and f[ound] a very great deal of interest in the proposed study and hearty approval in regard to our entering into it."[101] Sister Annette Walters recalled that faculty "were allowed to decide whether or not we should cooperate in such a project. This they unanimously decided to do, promising at the same time their wholehearted cooperation." No administrative pressure," she stressed "was brought to bear on anyone."[102] By January of 1939, CSC's administrators required faculty to "submit . . . a written report" that would grapple with the following questions, "1. What specific attitudes and interests should a student acquire before she completes her general education in a Catholic college? 2. What specific knowledge should a student possess before she completes her general education in a Catholic college?"[103] The fact that CSC faculty members (and faculty members from other colleges) agreed to cooperate without being coerced suggested that they were more likely to take cooperation seriously and engage with an open mind.

Protestant colleges were also keen to join the Cooperative Study in General Education. Muskingum College, for instance, applied for GEB funding to revise their general education program in 1937 and was denied.[104] Yet, their strong interest in general education reform was one factor that caused the leadership of the Cooperative Study in General Education to invite them.[105] The faculty at Muskingum College were excited to participate and agreed to block off 3:30 to 5:30 PM each Wednesday solely for work on the Cooperative Study.[106] Though Muskingum faculty members were all invited to participate in the research activity, the dean of the college indicated that "no faculty member should feel under any obligation whatever to undertake some research activity merely because Muskingum has pledged itself to become a cooperating college." "The only valid reason," the dean continued, "why any faculty member should report his desire to study a research problem is that he is personally convinced that the problem is extraordinarily important and worth while [sic] and that he would personally enjoy working on the problem."[107]

Although Catholic and Protestant institutions were among those that joined the Cooperative Study, getting individuals from these colleges to work together required a degree of sensitivity on the part of the "central staff," which was a group of educational researchers who were employed by the Cooperative Study and "function[ed] as consultants, collaborators, and as coordinators among the several colleges."[108] Indeed, the central staff sought to maintain a level of collegiality by imbuing their work, as well as the study with four basic assumptions. The study's associate director, Ralph Ogan, wrote these goals for a national audience. The first assumption, he suggested, was that "because of the differences among colleges, no one plan of general education and no one philosophy of education can be universally appropriate to the colleges." The second recommended that "Each college shall exercise full autonomy" while the third reminded all involved that "Cooperative efforts are mutually helpful." The final assumption maintained that "A continuous program of self-examination in each cooperating college is beneficial."[109] Each institution was also asked to nominate a liaison officer, or a faculty contact that would help coordinate the efforts on their home campus. This philosophy served as the foundation of cooperation without consensus.

The Catholic and Protestant institutions involved in the Cooperative Study in General Education began their work in earnest in late 1938. The central staff began by organizing inter-collegiate committees, or small focus groups attacking "common threads running through many diverse projects" where faculty could work together at the University of Chicago.[110] These "small working committees . . . dealt with problems of student personnel, problems in the sciences, in social sciences, in philosophy and in religion, in the humanities, and in problems for the improvement of evaluation."[111] These were well attended by faculty members at the colleges. Muskingum reported sending twenty-five faculty members to various inter-collegiate committee meetings while the *Catherine Wheel* reported when its faculty members went.[112] Other Protestant colleges in the Study were also well represented.

Summer workshops drew a far larger crowd. Faculty members were told that "One of the important values of the Workshop will be the opportunity for participants to live together, to work together, and to play together."[113] After observing the level of cooperation on display at workshops during the summer of 1939 and 1940, the chairman of the Cooperative Study was quoted in the *New York Times* claiming that the workshops had "toned up the faculty morale and shattered provincialism and localism."[114] Ultimately, committee meetings and workshops in Chicago supplemented the correspondence and individual campus visits of participating faculty members involved in the Cooperative Study in General Education. By exploring the experiences that these institutions had in intercollegiate committees, summer workshops, and through private correspondence and visits, we are able to see cooperation without consensus in action. More important, we are able to see courses emerge in the humanities, sciences, and religion.

Cooperation Without Consensus in Action: Sharing Materials, Reforming Courses, and Producing Inventories

The Cooperative Study in General Education operated from 1939 to 1944. Exploring the experiences of the CSC and its Protestant collaborators during first three years of the study's existence illustrates cooperation without consensus in action. What began as resource sharing turned into more sustained collaboration on the content and structure of courses, and of religious education itself. These early years show an upward trend toward the openness of participants to collaborate across denominational lines, while still maintaining their stalwart commitments to institutional and curricular autonomy.

As the Study commenced, each of the institutions began to cull curricular materials that other participating institutions could avail themselves to and learn from. The central staff at the University of Chicago cataloged these.[115] The central staff also compiled lists of the research interests and contact information of faculty members.[116] Any participating faculty or administrators could request mimeographs of these materials or even travel to Chicago to study them. Though faculty at the participating colleges were eager to learn what their collaborators were doing, the central staff encouraged them to spend time identifying the objectives of their general education programs first. This process involved reflecting, reconsidering, and articulating the objectives (or changes they wished to see in students) undergirding their general education programs. This effectively limited the amount of cooperation that took place in 1939 when compared to later years.

The College of St. Catherine began by devoting its first year "to a review of our unique functions as a Catholic college for women, in the hope that we would thus build up a guiding set of principles against which to evaluate our program" and nominating Sister Annette as liaison officer.[117] Muskingum held three campus wide seminars in 1939 to reevaluate their goals in general education.[118] Although cooperation did occur, little wholesale revision of courses occurred until well into 1940. Rather, much of early work involved sharing materials. Though seemingly trivial, it was this very delicate time early in the life of the Cooperative Study when many connections were made and goodwill – and to some extent, trust – was forged between individuals across institutions.

The central staff made successful attempts to organize regional conferences that happened to transcend denominational boundaries in the first year of the Cooperative Study. For instance, they brought together faculty members from "Hendrix College, Little Rock Junior College, Stephens College, Park College, and the College of St. Catherine" to work on ideas related to survey courses in the natural sciences.[119] Additionally, the central staff worked to advertise the experiments occurring within the cooperating colleges to others institutions across the country.[120] This too, occasionally transcended denominational boundaries and involved institutions not directly involved in the Cooperative Study. After requesting and receiving the CSC freshman handbook, an administrator at the Methodist driven Alabama Polytechnic Institute (later Auburn University) wrote to Sister Annette "to acknowledge the receipt of a copy of your freshman handbook which I think is excellent, and, what is more important, is also delightful." "It was handed to a committee of our girls," the administrator continued, "who are working on a system of government for their new dormitories. They, too, were delighted with it."[121] Similarly, the president of Hamilton College (originally Presbyterian but deliberately secular since the 1890s) requested and received questionnaires from the CSC that had been developed for a variety of curricular purposes at the 1939 summer workshop.[122]

CSC professors were offered and accepted a "one-page questionnaire . . . used for the student evaluation of teaching by Professor Harold E. Davis of Hiram College."[123] Kenneth Wegner, a CSC professor of mathematics, was mailed a syllabus for the required terminal course in mathematics at Antioch College by Professor Max Astrachan.[124] Although not all resource sharing led to further cooperation, it did lead to a desire to seek out more information about the other cooperating institutions. Wegner, for instance, asked for a "conference of some of the mathematics teachers of the colleges in the Cooperative Study" to be held at the annual meeting of the American Mathematics Society.[125] This was granted.

Wegner's desire to work with others in the Cooperative Study was representative of many of the faculty at the CSC and other campuses. On October 28, 1939, Sister Annette wrote to Ralph Ogan to invite him to "discuss the work which is now going on in the other twenty-one colleges in the study."[126] This was not the first time that Sister Annette had written to Ogan. She had written earlier in the month to mention that the CSC "faculty would like to have joint conferences with the Macalester faculty when your staff visits St. Paul."[127] Ogan replied to this request by setting up a "miniature workshop" to be held on the CSC campus between December 8th and 10th. By November 24, the *Catherine Wheel* was able to report that the "entire staff" of the Cooperative Study would be present.[128] Central staff members held campus-wide discussions with faculty members and students.[129] Additionally, faculty and central staff members held more specific meetings organized around issues of humanities, social studies, and the natural sciences.[130] The work occurring at other schools was frequently cited in these meetings.

It was common for the central staff to visit individual campuses, particularly in 1939. As they did so, they began to identify promising projects that could be widely shared with others as examples. The central staff sought to loosely organize their work around the topics of sciences, student personnel, social sciences, and the humanities. Among these topics, the central staff found that humanities tended to simultaneously raise the most interest, and cause the most consternation among faculty members. As such, a large percentage of central staff's working hours were devoted to the issue of reforming humanities courses.[131] During the first year of the Cooperative Study, the central staff identified a very promising experiment in the humanities curriculum at the College of St. Catherine. Indeed, in the first summer workshop, Sister Mona Riley had come to work on a survey-type humanities course that might replace separate courses in art, literature, music, and so forth at the CSC. Survey courses reflected the cutting edge of curriculum development and were of great interest to many in the general education movement. Indeed, just two years earlier, several individuals representing institutions that would soon participate in the Cooperative Study contributed to an edited volume on survey courses. However, relatively little was published about survey courses in the humanities in this volume.[132] This was indicative of the larger lacuna in the literature.

Sister Mona reflected on her experiences at the 1939 summer workshop in the widely available workshop proceedings. She also kept in touch with the central staff and asked for material related to humanities courses at other institutions.[133] However, she was reluctant to share any further information on her experimental course with anyone involved in the Cooperative Study as she felt the course was too embryonic.[134] This created an issue for central staff members who were inundated with requests for more information about Sister Mona's experiment. By October 3, 1939, central staff member Harold B. Dunkel implored Sister Mona to share more information and to allow members of the central staff to report on her project. Dunkel acknowledged that "nearly every college" in the Cooperative Study and "many" not in the Cooperative Study "wants to 'do something about the Humanities course.'" "The type of course you are working on is a new development," Dunkel pled, "and one in which the other schools are particularly interested. Yet there is no place to which we can refer them for the possible workings of such a course as yours." Dunkel concluded his letter in a whimsical manner characteristic of his correspondence during this time period. "In fact," he proclaimed, "I feel so keenly that it is your duty to let those who dwell in darkness see the light that I am going to be very difficult. Immediately upon mailing this letter, I shall begin to assume that silence gives consent and shall continue to assume so unless I hear definitely to the contrary. If you do not have overwhelming objections, we shall consider silence more than golden."[135] Neither objections nor materials were immediately forthcoming.

Nearly one month later, Dunkel and other central staff members were at Muskingum College meeting over two days with faculty on "the advisability of having a freshman orientation course in the Humanities instead of offering separate introductory courses in the various arts."[136] The central staff provided information about projects at several participating colleges, with emphasis on the CSC and Sister Mona's work. At the end of the meeting, the faculty members of Muskingum decided to pursue the following questions: "What further evidence do we want to collect, how much further do we want to study before we make our decision?" while opting to "have some more meetings and get material and see what these other colleges have done in their humanities course."[137] This helped to lay the groundwork for a major meeting between the CSC and Muskingum on the issue of humanities. Contact between the two schools had thus far been limited, though cordial.

Around the same time as the meeting at Muskingum, Ralph Ogan visited the CSC and saw them engaged in, among other projects, an effort to reform their courses in religion. He recommended that CSC faculty get in touch with Muskingum faculty to collaborate on religious coursework. Sister Annette and other faculty members were open to this idea and wrote to a Muskingum faculty member, noting that Ogan had "called the attention of our faculty to the significant work you are doing in the teaching of Bible" and asking for a "a copy of your objectives and of any other material on the subject which you would be willing to send us."[138] The faculty member obliged and sent along a copy of a syllabus for a course called "Life and Religion." Sister Annette acknowledged that the CSC faculty were "finding it very interesting and helpful."[139] The CSC also provided some material from their courses on religion (particularly on teaching the Old Testament) that eventually assisted Muskingum in introducing their course "Human Living: An Integrated Course in Psychology, Philosophy and Religion."[140]

Shortly thereafter, a Muskingum faculty member sent a faculty news bulletin "devoted entirely to a report of some of our activities in relation to the Cooperative Study" to Sister Annette.[141] An impressed Sister Annette responded that she had read the report and was "turning it over to our Committee on Experimentation for consideration at its next meeting." "It is the most stimulating bulletin of its kind that I have yet read," she extolled, "and one suggestive of activities which might well be carried on in our own college." Envisioning future cooperation between CSC and Muskingum, Sister Annette inquired "If you have one or two extra copies of this edition, I could use them to our advantage. Please put me on your mailing list for future editions of the Faculty News Bulletin. Allow me to congratulate you and your faculty on the splendid leadership you are taking in this study, I look forward with great interest to your future publications."[142] These two events solidified the working relationship between the CSC and Muskingum.

Collaboration between the CSC and Muskingum continued along various fronts throughout the first half of 1940. However, it was not until

November when Muskingum faculty members planning a week-long visit to St. Paul reached out to CSC faculty. "Your work in the Humanities is so favorably known that we hope that you will permit us to come at some time during the week. If possible, we should like to spend a whole day at St. Catherine's," one Muskingum faculty member wrote to Sister Annette.[143] Sister Annette responded that should "would be delighted" and asked Sister Mona to clear her schedule for a day so that she could share her work on the humanities course.[144] Though very little evidence exists related to what was said during the visit beyond the evidence cited in the introduction of this chapter, it was largely influential on the two resulting survey courses in humanities at the CSC and Muskingum, to be sure.[145]

Cooperation Without Consensus in Action: Negotiating Divergent Religious Beliefs

To this point, it may seem that I have presented cooperation without consensus as though engaging in curricular reform was or is a value-less endeavor. All curricula, particularly religious curricula, is laden with values, however. And cooperation without consensus was a process that largely respected and celebrated that fact. Indeed, the denominational colleges in the Cooperative Study in General Education did more than simply exchange syllabi and share ideas on assignments. Rather, they actively considered the types of (religious) values, and not just skills, they wished to sharpen within their students. As one professor at Macalester would note, the objective of general education at his institution involved the "Development of a Christian PHILOSOPHY OF LIFE."[146] Similarly, a dean at Centre College reflected, "*Christian* education, we believe at Centre, must first be *education*, and our ideal must be *Christian education*."[147] Colleges were extraordinarily different in how they defined this. As one central staff member recalled

> Our colleges were . . . very diverse . . . but nowhere were [their] differences greater or more basic than in those area necessarily involved in determining an adequate philosophy of life. To take but a single example, some of our colleges were church-related. They were naturally committed to the belief that any adequate philosophy of life must have a Christian or religious orientation.[148]

Many central staff members and faculty in the Cooperative Study in General Education referred to these objectives as "intangible." That did not mean, however, that they did not wish to evaluate the values of their students and gauge their change over time. To do so, they worked to build "inventories."[149] These were often short questionnaires designed to "assess student attitudes toward justice, social responsibilities, and religious ideals."[150] Ideally, they would allow colleges to "expand greatly [their] means of collecting information about the student and of interpreting that information so that [they] might better serve student needs."[151] Focusing on the creation of these inventories reveals that denominational institutions were willing to discuss religious values, but would adapt the inventories for their own use or protest if they felt their values were being compromised in any way.

The College of St. Catherine was instrumental in creating three major inventories used by institutions within and beyond the Cooperative Study: The Life Situations Questionnaire, the General Goals for Life Inventory, and the Religious Attitudes scale. Sister Annette wrote about her institution's early experiences in the Cooperative Study and the need for inventories to measure student values and growth. "A scrutiny of the commonly used instruments for evaluating achievement in our college gave convincing evidence that some of the most important aspects of growth, such as the increase in Christian and scholarly attitudes, were not being adequately appraised" she began. "Although there was indirect evidence that students were growing in these respects," she continued, "such evidence had not been recorded as systematically as had achievement in other areas. Appraisal was difficult because attitudes are extremely intangible, and such paper and pencil tests as were in existence were not deemed adequate for measuring our objectives." This suggested the desire to build more objective instruments to measure student growth. "Nevertheless," she concluded "the realization that these 'intangibles' are the most important outcomes of Catholic higher education seemed to warrant experimenting in this area."[152] This suggests that the inventories themselves were written to gauge religious values in the way that its authors saw them. The CSC was also cautious to not allow working with Protestant colleges to affect their commitment to Catholicism or providing a Catholic education. This is evidenced by CSC leaders asking instructor Agnes E. Keenan early in the Cooperative Study to prepare and deliver an essay entitled "The Differences Between Catholic and Non-Catholic Education" to a CSC faculty meeting. This essay was then published in the *Journal of Religious Instruction* in late 1939.[153]

The central staff was aware that no college would want to relinquish the ability to choose the values of their curriculum. Indeed, the very reason for cooperation without consensus was to maintain those values in a hostile environment. However, the central staff did believe in the ability of individuals to borrow *methods and means* from others without ensuring a similar outcome. This was the very heart of cooperation without consensus: institutions can cooperate without sacrificing individuality or autonomy.

In this spirit, the central staff asked if Sister Annette would present the draft of her Life Situations Questionnaire in the 1939 summer workshop. This was a project that Sister Annette had been working on in relation with religious questionnaires for the purposes of sectioning freshman since the early 1930s. Following her presentation, Ralph Ogan commented

> Development of Christian character seems pretty intangible. But Sister Annette and her colleagues have analyzed this objective to the point that to a significant extent they can estimate the success of the student in achieving it. Other colleges might, of course, have different viewpoints as to the nature of a good philosophy of life, but it still remains a fact that we would be better educators if we were to clarify this and other objectives.[154]

Immediately, faculty at Protestant colleges in the Cooperative Study requested copies of the Life Situations Questionnaire. A faculty member at Allegheny College asked for a copy and acknowledged receipt by saying "I feel that you have something here which is very worthwhile."[155] A faculty member at Hendrix also requested a copy as well as any other "materials regarding evaluation of religious growth and philosophy."[156] He would later acknowledge receipt by noting his "very great appreciation for the material." "It will be of much benefit to us in our studies" he continued, and concluded by saying, "I want to again express my admiration of the way your group is going about their study."[157]

This was not a one-sided conversation. Sister Annette also requested information on other religious inventories being created, including a "plan for the procedure in the study of religious attitudes" developed by Bethany College.[158] Later, Sister Annette would see all inventories as the central staff leaned on her to join a committee that would review and report on all inventories at the cooperating colleges.[159] These were used to adjust the inventories. Though the institutions agreed on the basics of the questionnaire, their interpretation of student responses varied based on their religious beliefs. A similar situation occurred with the General Goals of Life Inventory. Comparing Sister Annette's use of the inventory to that of a faculty member from Park College reveals that they placed different emphases on the values.[160]

While the Life Situations Questionnaire did measure religious values, it did not do so as much as the Religious Attitude Scale. The religious attitude scale grew out of Sister Marie Philip's teaching of religion at the CSC. She was convinced by the central staff to provide her preliminary scale for wide distribution. It would not be, a central staff member assured her "offered with an expectation that others will use them as they stand or copy them in detail. [The scale is] expected rather to show interested teachers what others are doing and what procedures they are finding useful." This simply reemphasized the argument that people were more interested in the method rather than the content of the scale.

"Your test, of course," the staff member continued, "was designed for your own purposes, and none of the other colleges would find it suited to their purposes. However – and this is the important point – your purposes and theirs are not entirely dissimilar. I think it might be very interesting and helpful to see how you went about the job."[161] This provocative argument convinced Sister Marie who went on to publish the piece in the *Journal of Religious Instruction*.[162] She would work with others to revise their own inventories, but no Protestant college used Sister Marie's inventory as such. Rather, they relied upon a similar inventory by Irwin R. Beiler of Allegheny College that was published in the *Journal of Bible and Religion*.[163] As Harold Dunkel would recall, Beiler's inventory was "intended for use with Protestant students, [and] was much less useful for studying the beliefs of Catholics."[164] The two inventories were developed cooperatively, but adjusted for the particular needs of the clientele and faculty member.

Though much of this cooperation went on with very little conflict, there was one particular area that caused some controversy. It involved ways in which the central staff scored the tests, particularly as they related to social issues surrounding the Second World War. The central staff consisted of evaluators who believed very strongly in objectivity and neutrality. Harold Dunkel described his work nearly fifty years later: "what is the student to do; set up the situation where the student does what you say he should be able to do, see whether he can do it. Now, this is completely free of content, purpose, thrust; this is a very neutral thing. I just come in and say, 'I'm an evaluator. Now, tell me what you're doing, and I'll help you find out how well you're doing it. I don't care what you're doing.' "[165] But, by placing too much faith in neutrality and objectivity, members of the central staff occasionally ran afoul of the CSC and other faculty members.

A scoring of an inventory disturbed two CSC faculty members and Sister Annette so much so that they considered pulling out of a 1943 inter-collegiate conference organized by the Cooperative Study to discuss adapting general education to deal with issues related to the Second World War. "The war has tended to accentuate tremendously the difference between our philosophy of life and that of non-Catholic colleges, even though we have much in common with the non-Christian humanist." Sister Annette began her charged letter to Ralph Ogan, "The faculty is united in its rejection of anything savoring of pragmatism and relativism, and feels it cannot do business with anyone who does not recognize the existence of a natural law."[166] Interestingly, this suggests more an aversion to the non-Christian colleges represented at the conference than the Protestant ones. "I call this to your attention," Sister Annette continued "so that you can advise us about sending representatives to the social studies committee meeting. Sister Teresa and Sister

Mary Edward, who are planning to attend, are both excellent teachers and leaders of social thought on our campus. They are tolerant and cooperative, but have very strong moral conviction, which I am sure are not shared by the staff nor by the majority of representatives who will be present from other colleges." It is difficult to tell which representatives are being suggested. "They (and I, too) took exception" Sister Annette concluded, "to the scoring of a number of the items on Mr. Levi's preliminary inventory on the grounds that they were unethical and immoral."[167] Ogan acknowledged Sister Annette's frustration and addressed her concerns. Once his letter was shared with Sister Teresa and Sister Mary Edward, they decided to attend the conference.[168] This particular moment demonstrates the power that each individual had to walk away from collaborative projects and processes. Ultimately, this situation proved to be more of an anomaly as sufficient trust had been built in the past four years of cooperating.

Conclusion

At the end of the Second World War, as the Cooperative Study in General Education, was concluding its work and publishing its final reports, few denominational colleges had closed. On the contrary, many were optimistic about the postwar world and what opportunities this time period – now marked by historians as academia's golden age – afforded their institutions. Cooperation without consensus, or the idea that individuals and institutions with different values and objectives would engage in interinstitutional cooperation as long as the general autonomy of each was respected, was a key innovation that helped high schools and colleges react to a tumultuous time for American society and schooling. Philanthropic groups, administrators, faculty, and students were keen to continue engaging in cooperation without consensus to meet the new (often curricular) challenges of the postwar world. An example comes from two veterans of the Cooperative Study in General Education: the College of St. Catherine and Macalester College. Inundated with new students on the GI Bill and federal pressure to respond to global threats, they joined in cooperative program with nearby Hamline University and the University of St. Thomas to work on an "area studies" program. Their work was funded by the Louis W. and Maude Hill Family Foundation and continued well into the early 1960s.[169] New social contexts will always call for new approaches to curriculum. The recurrent periods of economic retrenchment will always create anxieties and imperatives for institutions to offer quality education in the most "efficient" manner. Though contexts will shift, cooperation without consensus does seem to have staying power and is worth further historical exploration.

Notes

1. "Teachers Study Course Techniques," *The Catherine Wheel*, November 22, 1940, 3. Both institutions changed their names in 2009. The College of St. Catherine became St. Catherine's University while Muskingum College became Muskingum University. This chapter will refer to both institutions by their historical namesakes.
2. This broad definition of general education acknowledges the many attempts during the mid-twentieth century to define the term. For a descriptive listing of the many definitions of general education during this time period, see George J. Bergman, "Definitions of General Education," *Journal of Educational Administration and Supervision* 33 (1947): 460–68.
3. R. W. Ogan to Sister Annette 22 November 1940 B: 345 F: 7 St. Catherine's University Archives, St. Paul, Minnesota. Hereafter cited as CSC Papers. Ogan was granted a leave of absence from serving as the Dean of Muskingum College the year before to become associate director of the Cooperative Study. Ogan continued to stay in touch with his former colleagues at Muskingum. On this move, see "Dean R.W. Ogan is Given Leave of Absence: Plans to go to University of Chicago to Head Research," *The Black and Magenta*, May 30, 1939.
4. Sister Annette to Ralph W. Ogan, 29 November 1940, Box: 345 F: 7 CSC Papers. Biographical information on Sister Annette Walters, a key figure in this chapter, is available in Eileen A. Gavin, "Sister Annette Walter's Unfinished Dream: 'To Make the Universe a Home,'" in *Women of Vision: Their Psychology, Circumstances, and Success*, eds. Eileen A. Gavin, Aphrodite Clamar, and Mary Anne Siderits (New York: Springer, 2007), 159–176.
5. This chapter uses "interinstitutional cooperation" and "cooperation" interchangeably. It defines these terms as activity between the representatives of two or more institutions where a common problem is considered, and physical and/or intellectual resources are shared. These activities can occur in unstructured settings (e.g. two faculty members exchanging syllabi) or structured ones (e.g. a joint conference sponsored by the institutions or an outside entity). This definition is purposely left broad for two reasons. The first, as scholar Daniel W. Lang suggests, is that "the terminology of cooperation is confused and imprecise." See his article "A Lexicon of Inter-Institutional Cooperation," *Higher Education* 44 (2002): 153–183. The second reason is that a broad definition allows for a greater incorporation of collaborative activities that Catholic and Protestant institutions engaged in.
6. Histories of Catholic higher education emphasizing conflict include Philip Gleason, *Contending with Modernity: Catholic Higher Education in the Twentieth Century* (New York: Oxford University Press, 1995); Anne Hendershott, *Status Envy: The Politics of Catholic Higher Education* (New Brunswick, NJ: Transaction Publishers, 2009); William P. Leahy, *Adapting to America: Catholics, Jesuits, and Higher Education in the Twentieth Century* (Washington, DC: Georgetown University Press, 1991); John Whitey Evans, *The Newman Movement: Roman Catholics in American Higher Education, 1883–1971* (Notre Dame: University of Notre Dame Press, 1980); Edward J. Power, *Catholic Higher Education in America: A History* (New York: Appleton-Century-Crofts, 1972); David J. O'Brien, *From the Heart of the American Church: Catholic Higher Education and American Culture* (Maryknoll, NY: Orbis Books, 1994), 97–98; Alice Gallin, "American Catholic Higher Education: An Experience of Inculturation," in *Trying Times: Essays on Catholic Higher Education in the 20th Century*, eds. William M. Shea and Daniel Van Slyke (Atlanta: Scholars Press, 1999), 99–120; Alice Gallin, *Negotiating Identity: Catholic Higher Education Since 1960* (Notre Dame,

IN: University of Notre Dame Press, 2000); Peter M. Collins, *A Twentieth-Century Collision: American Intellectual Culture and Pope John Paul II's Idea of a University* (Lanham, MD: University Press of America, 2010), chapter 1. Histories of Protestant higher education emphasizing conflict include George M. Marsden, *The Soul of the American University: From Protestant Establishment to Established Nonbelief* (New York: Oxford University Press, 1994); esp. chapter 21; Douglas Sloan, *Faith and Knowledge: Mainline Protestantism and American Higher Education* (Louisville, KY: Westminster/John Knox Press, 1994); Julie A. Reuben, *The Making of the Modern University: Intellectual Transformation and the Marginalization of Morality* (Chicago: University of Chicago Press, 1996); William C. Ringenberg, *The Christian College: A History of Protestant Higher Education in America*, 2nd ed. (Grand Rapids, MI: Baker Academic, 2006).

7. Kathleen A. Mahoney, *Catholic Higher Education in Protestant America: The Jesuits and Harvard in the Age of the University* (Baltimore: Johns Hopkins University Press, 2003), 2. Marsden, *The Soul of the American University*, 5. Kathleen A. Mahoney makes a point similar to Marsden in a review essay of the aforementioned works of Marsden, Reuben, and Sloan. See her article "The Rise of the University and the Secularization of the Academy: The Role of Liberal Protestantism," *History of Higher Education Annual* 16 (1996): 125.

8. Reasons for the lack of cooperation are provided by Roy J. Deferrari, "Cooperation in Catholic Higher Education," *National Catholic Educational Association Bulletin* 42 (1946): 13–26; Charles E. Ford and Edgar L. Roy, *The Renewal of Catholic Higher Education* (Washington, DC: National Catholic Educational Association, 1968), 17; Paul A. FitzGerald, *The Governance of Jesuit Colleges in the United States, 1920–1970* (South Bend: University of Notre Dame Press, 1984). Examples of Catholic cooperation after 1950 include: Sister Hilda Gleason, "Co-Operation of Six Small Colleges in Non-Western Studies Program," *Catholic Educational Review* 61 (1963): 470–474; "Inter-institutional Cooperation," Special Issue. *National Catholic Educational Association Bulletin* 60 (1964): 1–31; Sister M. Dolores Salerno, "Patterns of Interinstitutional Co-operation in American Catholic Higher Education – 1964," (PhD Dissertation, The Catholic University of America, 1966); Arthur Dennis Sullivan, "Patterns of Inter-institutional Cooperation in Canadian Catholic Higher Education," (PhD Dissertation, The Catholic University of America, 1966); Carl Alan Trendler, "Inter-institutional Cooperation for Academic Development Among Small Church-Related Liberal Arts Colleges," (EdD diss., Indiana University, 1967); Kathryn Miller, "The Sisters of St. Joseph College Consortium: Mission and Image," *Occasional Papers on Catholic Higher Education* 1 (1995): 3–24; James A. Patterson, *Shining Lights: A History of the Council for Christian Colleges and Universities* (Grand Rapids, MI: Baker Academic, 2001).

9. Examples include Lansing W. Bulgin, "The Associated Christian Colleges of Oregon: Cooperation Among Three Small Institutions," *Liberal Education* 52 (1966): 466–469; J. Lynn Leavenworth, "Toward Seminary Merger," *Christian Century* 83 (1966): 527–534; Harold William Berk, "The Christian College Consortium in a Social Context," (PhD Dissertation, University of Toledo, 1974).

10. There is, however, a short paragraph notice entitled "Two Catholic Institutions Join Pact with Protestant Colleges," *College and University Business* 40 (1966): 108 that informs readers that Mundelein College (IL) and St. John's University (MN) had joined the Central States College Association. Obstacles to interfaith cooperation are discussed in Seymour A. Smith, *Religious Cooperation in State Universities* (Ann Arbor: Published Privately by the University of Michigan, 1957), 67–72. Some instances of cooperation are covered

briefly in this book, yet the author claims on page vii that "The study concentrates on the larger state universities, for it is here that the problems of cooperation have risen most acutely, and it is here that the most creative attempts have been made to find workable patterns. Other colleges and universities, of course, have their robles and a development of their own. Another volume, however, is needed for them."

11. Deferrari, "Cooperation in Catholic," 16.

12. On the increasing secularization of colleges and universities in the late nineteenth and early twentieth century see Marsden, *The Soul of the American University*; Sloan, *Faith and Knowledge*; Reuben, *The Making of the Modern University*; Ringenberg, *The Christian College*.

13. Mother Eucharista Galvin, "College Teachers Meeting, January 28, 1939," Box 345, Folder 2, CSC Papers.

14. "President's Report to the Board of Trustees of Muskingum College, June 13, 1938, 1" Class: B-3, Box 13, Folder 5, Muskingum University Library Archives and Special Collections, Muskingum University, New Concord, Ohio. Hereafter cited as "MUSC Papers."

15. Ibid, 5.

16. The religious nature of the College of St. Catherine and its faculty is emphasized in the following works: Karen Kennelly, "The Dynamic Sister Antonia and the College of St. Catherine," *Ramsey County History* 14 (1978): 3–18; Sister Karen M. Kennelly, "Faculties and What They Taught," in *Catholic Women's Colleges in America*, eds. Tracy Schier and Cynthia Russett (Baltimore: Johns Hopkins University Press, 2002), 98–122; Rosalie Ryan and John Christine Wolkerstorfer, *More Than a Dream: Eighty-Five Years at the College of St. Catherine* (St. Paul, MN: Privately Published by the College of St. Catherine, 1992); Jane Lamm Carroll, Joanne Cavallaro, and Sharon Doherty, eds., *Liberating Sanctuary: 100 Years of Women's Education at the College of St. Catherine* (Lanham, MD: Lexington Books, 2012). At Muskingum, occasional challenges by faculty and students threatened the institution's commitment to religion. However, the historians who have studied these challenges have argued that "conservative" forces prevailed in the battle over the religious ideals that drove Muskingum. Information on Muskingum's battles over religious values is presented in A. William Hoglund, "Muskingum College Student Rebels in the 'Jazz Age,'" *Ohio History* 76 (1967): 147–58, 178–79; William L. Fisk, *A History of Muskingum College* (New Concord, OH: Privately Published by Muskingum College, 1978); Bradley J. Longfield and George M. Marsden, "Presbyterian Colleges in Twentieth-Century America," in *The Pluralistic Vision: Presbyterians and Mainstream Protestant Education and Leadership*, eds. Milton J. Coalter, John M. Mulder, and Louis B. Weeks (Louisville: Westminster/John Knox Press, 1992), 107.

17. Linda Eisenmann, "Reclaiming Religion: New Historiographic Challenges in the Relationship of Religion and American Higher Education," *History of Education Quarterly* 39 (1999): 304.

18. Mahoney, *Catholic Higher Education*, 2.

19. Comparative data and analysis of Protestant and Catholic institutions is available in Fred J. Kelly and Ella B. Ratcliffe, *Privately Controlled Higher Education in the United States, Bulletin, 1934, No. 12* (Washington, DC: United States Government Printing Office, 1934).

20. This topic is thoroughly covered in the aforementioned works by Reuben and Marsden as well as Christian Smith, ed., *The Secular Revolution: Power, Interests, and Conflict in the Secularization of American Life* (Berkeley: University of California Press, 2003). Robert Kenneth Wilson-Black has traced the

anxieties of Protestant collegiate educators toward the loss of religious ideals being reflected directly in the college curriculum. See his work "Uses of Religion: The Dual Role of College Religion Departments at Midcentury," (PhD Dissertation, University of Chicago, 2002), esp. chapter 1.

21. On standardization and its "scientific" undertones in society and universities see Bruce A. Kimball, *The "True Professional Ideal" in America: A History* (Cambridge, MA: Blackwell, 1992); William M. Sullivan, *Work and Integrity: The Crisis and Promise of Professionalism in America*, 2nd ed. (San Francisco: Jossey-Bass, 2005). For a broader discussion of how "scientific" educational research was helping to drive standardization efforts see Ellen Condliffe Lagemann, *An Elusive Science: The Troubling History of Educational Research* (Chicago: University of Chicago Press, 2000). On the earliest efforts to accredit institutions and curricula see Hugh Hawkins, *Banding Together: The Rise of National Associations in American Higher Education, 1887–1950* (Baltimore: Johns Hopkins University Press, 1992); Harland G. Bloland, *Creating the Council for Higher Education Accreditation (CHEA)* (Phoenix: Oryx Press, 2001), chapter 1; Richard J. Shavelson, *Measuring College Learning Responsibly: Accountability in a New Era* (Stanford: Stanford University Press, 2010), chapter 3.

22. On the decline in higher education budgets see Malcolm M. Willey, *Depression, Recovery, and Higher Education: A Report by Committee Y of the American Association of University Professors* (New York: McGraw-Hill Book Company, 1937); Mary Garwood Reeves, "Economic Depression in Higher Education: Emory University, the University of Georgia and Georgia Tech, 1930–1940," (PhD Dissertation, Georgia State University, 1985); Kevin P. Bower, " 'A Favored Child of the State': Federal Student Aid at Ohio Colleges and Universities, 1934–1943," *History of Education Quarterly* 44 (2004): 364–387.

23. R.W. Ogan, "The Program of Muskingum College," Class: E1BA B: 184 F: RW Ogan Correspondence 1932–1937, MUSC Papers.

24. Floyd W. Reeves, et al., *The Liberal Arts College: Based Upon Surveys of Thirty-Five Colleges Related to the Methodist Episcopal Church* (Chicago: University of Chicago Press, 1932); Jordan R. Humphrey, "Liberal Arts Colleges in the Tumultuous 1940s: Institutional Identity and the Challenges of War and Peace," (PhD Dissertation, Pennsylvania State University, 2010). See also the individual case studies in John J. Laukaitis, ed., *Denominational Higher Education During World War II* (New York: Palgrave Macmillan, 2018).

25. " 'Not Built for a Day:' Allegheny College 125th Commemorative Publication, 1940," B 16, Folder, 'Not Built for a Day:' Allegheny College 125th Commemorative Publication, 1940, William Pearson Tolley Papers, Syracuse University Special Collections and Research Center, Syracuse, New York.

26. See the discussion of secularization's effects on the smaller colleges in comparison to major research universities in Ringenberg, *The Christian College*, 125–137; Robert Lynn Wood, " 'The Survival of Recognizably Protestant Colleges:' Reflections on Old-Line Protestantism, 1950–1990," in *The Secularization of the Academy*, eds. George M. Marsden and Bradley J. Longfield (New York: Oxford University Press, 1992), 170–194; Anthony J. Dosen, *Catholic Higher Education in the 1960s: Issues of Identity, Issues of Governance* (Charlotte, NC: Information Age Publishing, 2009), esp. 33.

27. Richard Novak and David Leslie, "A Not So Distant Mirror: Great Depression Writings on the Governance and Finance of Public Higher Education," *History of Higher Education Annual* 20 (2000): 59–78.

28. David O. Levine, *The American College and the Culture of Aspiration, 1915–1940* (Ithaca: Cornell University Press, 1986), 186; Hugh Hawkins, "The Making of the Liberal Arts College Identity," *Daedalus* 128 (1999): 8–12. It should be

noted that the anxieties and the rhetoric did not often match the reality. On this fact, see Bruce A. Kimball, "Revising the Declension Narrative: Liberal Arts Colleges, Universities, and Honors Programs, 1870s-2010s," *Harvard Educational Review* 84 (2014): 243–264.

29. Archie M. Palmer, "Introduction," in *The Liberal Arts College Movement,* ed. Archie M. Palmer (New York: J.J. Little and Ives Company, 1930), 5.
30. Herbert Hoover, "From the President," in *The Liberal Arts College,* 1.
31. William S. Bovard, "The Church and the College," in *The Liberal Arts College,* 149.
32. Ibid., 149–150.
33. Ibid., "Appendix A: Minutes of the Conference, March 18–20, 1930" in *The Liberal Arts College.*
34. Ibid., "Appendix A: Minutes of the Conference, March 18–20, 1930" in *The Liberal Arts College.*
35. J. R. McCain, "Pressing Problems of Independent Colleges: Discussion," in *Educational Conference Under the Auspices of The Association of American Colleges: Richmond, Virginia, October 21–22, 1938* (New York: The Consolidated Reporting Co., 1938), 58–59.
36. This conclusion also features in Robert L. Campbell, "New Paths for the Liberal Arts College," *Journal of the American Association of College Registrars* 13 (1938): 203–212.
37. Robert N. Montgomery to Frank Howard, 26 December 1940, B: D-2d F: 1940, MUSC Papers. The same letter was sent to several potential donors, and these have been collected in this archival folder.
38. Examples of interfaith cooperation between religious groups have been documented in numerous works including Benny Kraut, "A Wary Collaboration: Jews, Catholics, and the Protestant Goodwill Movement," in *Between the Times: The Travail of the Protestant Establishment in America, 1900–1960,* ed. William R. Hutchison (New York: Cambridge University Press, 1989), 193–230; Wendy L. Wall, *Inventing the "American Way:" The Politics of Consensus from the New Deal to the Civil Rights Movement* (New York: Oxford University Press, 2008); Kevin M. Schultz, *Tri-Faith America: How Catholics and Jews Held Postwar America to its Protestant Promise* (New York: Oxford University Press, 2011); David A. Hollinger, "After Cloven Tongues of Fire: Ecumenical Protestantism and the Modern American Encounter with Diversity," *Journal of American History* 98 (2011): 21–48; Sarah Griffith, *The Fight for Asian American Civil Rights: Liberal Protestant Activism, 1900–1950* (Urbana: University of Illinois Press, 2018).
39. Some examples of interfaith cooperation in educational projects during this time period are discussed in Diana Selig, *Americans All: The Cultural Gifts Movement* (Cambridge: Harvard University Press, 2008), chapter 4; Harold S. Wechsler, "Making a Religion of Intergroup Education: The National Conference of Christians and Jews, 1927–1957," *Journal of Ecumenical Studies* 47 (2012): 3–40; Matthew S. Hedstrom, *The Rise of Liberal Religion: Book Culture and American Spirituality in the Twentieth Century* (New York: Oxford University Press, 2013).
40. For a discussion of the liberal and fundamentalist split, see George M. Marsden, *Fundamentalism and American Culture,* 2nd ed. (New York: Oxford University Press, 2006), esp. part three; Elesha J. Coffman, *The Christian Century and the Rise of the Protestant Mainline* (New York: Oxford University Press, 2013).
41. David A. Hollinger, *Protestants Abroad: How Missionaries Tried to Change the World but Changed America* (Princeton: Princeton University Press, 2017), 10.

Each of the Protestant institutions in the Cooperative Study in General Education represents a mainline denomination.

42. Marsden, *The Soul of the American University*, 14. However, it is imperative to note that "more tolerant" is in no way synonymous with "tolerant." See the discussion on the overall issues of image that the Catholic colleges have always faced in Andrew M. Greeley, *From Backwater to Mainstream: A Profile of Catholic Higher Education* (New York: McGraw-Hill, 1969), 109–111.

43. Anthony Burke Smith, *The Look of Catholics: Portrayals in Popular Culture from the Great Depression to the Cold War* (Lawrence: University Press of Kansas, 2010), 6. Examinations of agreements and disagreements among Protestants, as well as between Catholics and Protestants can be found in Alison Collis Greene, *No Depression in Heaven: The Great Depression, the New Deal, and the Transformation of Religion in the Delta* (New York: Oxford University Press, 2016); Kenneth J. Heineman, *A Catholic New Deal: Religion and Reform in Depression Pittsburgh* (University Park: Pennsylvania State University Press, 1999).

44. Andrew Jewett, *Science, Democracy, and the American University: From the Civil War to the Cold War* (New York: Cambridge University Press, 2012).

45. David P. Baker, "The Politics of American Catholic School Expansion, 1870–1930," in *The Political Construction of Education: The State, School Expansion, and Economic Change*, eds. Bruce Fuller and Richard Rubinson (New York: Praeger, 1992), 189–206; James L. Heft, *Catholic High Schools: Facing New Realities* (New York: Oxford University Press, 2011), chapter 2.

46. On the CSJ and their work in education, see Carol K. Coburn and Martha Smith, *Spirited Lives: How Nuns Shaped Catholic Culture and American Life, 1836–1920* (Chapel Hill: University of North Carolina Press, 1999), chapter 6. Educational historians have recently uncovered a pattern that suggests that Catholic nuns were more willing to accept progressive or newer forms of education so long as they were certain their doctrinal commitments were not in any danger. This pattern also applies to the CSC. On this pattern see Ann Marie Ryan, "Catholic Women Educators' Discourse and Educational Measurement in the Early Twentieth Century United States," *Paedagogica Historica* 55 (2019): 416–28; K.M. Gemmell, " 'Living a Philosophical Contradiction?' Progressive Education in the Archdiocese of Vancouver's Catholic Schools, 1936–1960," *History of Education Quarterly* 59 (2019): 351–378.

47. Levine, *The American College*, 77.

48. Ann Marie Ryan, " 'The Straight Road': Promoting Catholic Higher Education in Early-Twentieth Century Chicago," *American Educational History Journal* 33 (2006): 65–75; Ann Marie Ryan, "Keeping 'Every Catholic Child in a Catholic School' During the Great Depression, 1933–1939," *Catholic Education: A Journal of Inquiry and Practice* 11 (2007): 157–175; For specific enrollment data as well as insight on this phenomenon see Leahy, *Adapting to America*, chapter 1. For enrollment data and analysis of the growth of public secondary schooling see John K. Folger and Charles B. Nam, *Education of the American Population* (New York: Arno Press, 1976), 5–10; David B. Tyack, Robert Lowe, and Elizabeth Hansot, *Public Schools in Hard Times: The Great Depression and Recent Years* (Cambridge: Harvard University Press, 1984), 144–150.

49. On the growth of women's Catholic higher education see Mary J. Oates, "The Development of Catholic Colleges for Women, 1895–1960," *U.S. Catholic Historian* 7 (1988): esp. 416–420; Kathleen A. Mahoney, "American Catholic Colleges for Women: Historical Origins," in *Catholic Women's Colleges in America*, 25–54. For a more localized case study see Ann Marie Ryan,

"Meeting Multiple Demands: Catholic Higher Education for Women in Chicago, 1911–1939," *American Catholic Studies* 120 (2009): 1–26.

50. "College Notes," *Ariston* 15 (1920): 19.

51. "On the Campus," *Ariston* 29 (1934): 45.

52. "St. Paul's Leads with 83 girls, Minneapolis Follows with 34," *The Catherine Wheel*, February 5, 1937.

53. On national accreditation trends, see Michael C. Johanek, ed., *A Faithful Mirror: Reflections on the College Board and Education in America* (New York: College Entrance Examination Board, 2001); Marc A. VanOverbeke, *The Standardization of American Schooling: Linking Secondary and Higher Education, 1870–1910* (New York: Palgrave Macmillan, 2008). The imperative for Catholic high schools is discussed in Ann Marie Ryan, "Negotiating Assimilation: Chicago Catholic High Schools' Pursuit of Accreditation in the Early Twentieth Century," *History of Education Quarterly* 46 (2006): 348–381. On Catholic attempts to reconcile public school reform efforts and scientific measurements, see Thomas E. Woods, Jr., *The Church Confronts Modernity: Catholic Intellectuals and the Progressive Era* (New York: Columbia University Press, 2004), chapter 4; Ryan, "Catholic Women Educators'," It should be noted as well that there were failed attempts for Protestant organizations to engage in institutional organization centered around issues of accreditation. Following this failure, accreditation took on a more scientific and secular tone. On this, see John Frederick Bell, "When Regulation was Religious: College Philanthropy, Anti-slavery Politics, and Accreditation in the Mid-Nineteenth-Century West," *History of Education Quarterly* 57 (2017): 68–93.

54. John Tracy Ellis, "Accreditation and the Catholic College," *Catholic Educational Review* 34 (1936): 589.

55. Gleason, *Contending with Modernity*, 184; Lester F. Goodchild, "The Turning Point in American Jesuit Higher Education: The Standardization Controversy between the Jesuits and the North Central Association, 1915–1940," *History of Higher Education Annual* 6 (1986): 81–116. For a discussion of the NCA's modernizing effect on a religious college see Michael S. Hamilton, "The Fundamentalist Harvard: Wheaton College and the Continuing Vitality of American Evangelicalism, 1919–1965," (PhD Dissertation, University of Notre Dame, 1994), 90–96. Histories of the North Central Association include Calvin O. Davis, *A History of the North Central Association, 1895–1945* (Ann Arbor, MI: The North Central Association of Colleges and Secondary Schools, 1945); David Williams, "A Historical Study of the Involvement of the North Central Association with Higher Education in the United States," (PhD Dissertation, Wayne State University, 1972).

56. Constance Logue, "History of the College of St. Catherine," College of St. Catherine, *La Concha 1920 Yearbook* (St. Paul, MI: Graduating Class of 1920, 1920), 54.

57. Ibid.

58. "Faculty Speak Before Educational Meeting," *The Catherine Wheel*, April 26, 1935, 1.

59. See Antonia McHugh, "Funding Experience," *Journal of Higher Education* 6 (1935): 149–154.

60. Sister Annette Walters to Ralph W. Ogan, 30 October 1941. Box 345, Folder 6, CSC Papers.

61. Gleason, *Contending with Modernity*, 184; Kennelly, "The Dynamic Sister," 13.

62. "On the Campus," *Ariston* 27 (1933): 38.

63. Catholic sisters, including those who founded and worked for CSC, seeking further education during this time period is discussed in Darra Mulderry,

" 'What Human Goodness Entails:' An Intellectual History of U.S. Catholic Sisters, 1930–1980," (PhD Dissertation, Brandeis University, 2006), 37–63. Broader context is provided in Kathleen Sprows Cummings, *New Women of the Old Faith: Gender and American Catholicism in the Progressive Era* (Chapel Hill: University of North Carolina Press, 2009), chapters 2 and 3.

64. Karen M. Kennelly, "An Immigrant Drama: The College of St. Catherine and Phi Beta Kappa," *U.S. Catholic Historian* 28 (2010): 43–63.

65. Historian Mary J. Oates found that, by and large, wealthy Catholic donors, while open to supporting Catholic colleges did not have the desire nor the financial ability to sustain these institutions. See her book, *The Catholic Philanthropic Tradition in America* (Bloomington: Indiana University Press, 1995), 135–137. On the diverse sources of funding that the CSC enjoyed, see Kennelly, "An Immigrant Drama," esp. 46. Many of the institutions in the Cooperative Study in General Education faced similar difficulties and sought out philanthropic funds actively.

66. Sister Antonia to Trevor Arnett 10 March 1931, Series 1, Sub-Series 1, Box 91, Folder 810, General Education Board Archives, Rockefeller Archives Center, Sleepy Hollow, New York. Hereafter cited as "GEB Papers."

67. Ernest Victor Hollis, *Philanthropic Foundations and Higher Education* (New York: Columbia University Press, 1938), 121. Although Marybeth Gasman and Katherine V. Sedgwick, eds., *Uplifting A People: African American Philanthropy and Education* (New York: Peter Lang, 2005) has challenged the notion of a small monopoly of philanthropic bases, CSC's tendency was to seek out foundations as often, if not more often, than "informal" donors.

68. For the relationship between the General Education Board and the University of Chicago see John W. Boyer, *The 'Persistence to Keep Everlastingly at it': Fund-Raising and Philanthropy at Chicago in the Twentieth Century* (Chicago: Published privately by the College of the University of Chicago, 2004).

69. See Kennelly, "The Dynamic Sister Antonia," 13–14. McHugh was also able to secure smaller grants from the Carnegie Corporation. Kennelly's article covers the earliest grants received in the late 1910s and early 1920s.

70. "Of General Interest," *Ariston* 24 (1930): 40.

71. "On the Campus," *Ariston* 27 (1933): 39–40.

72. On the religious affiliations of members of the General Education Board see Raymond B. Fosdick, *Adventure in Giving: The Story of the General Education Board* (New York: Harper & Row, 1962).

73. On the influence of the Baptist religion on the philanthropists who founded of the University of Chicago see Willard J. Pugh, "A 'Curious Working of Cross Purposes' in the Founding of the University of Chicago," *History of Higher Education Annual* 15 (1995): 93–126; Kenneth W. Rose, "Why a University for Chicago and Not Cleveland? Religion and John D. Rockefeller's Early Philanthropy, 1855–1900," (Unpublished Research Report, Rockefeller Archives Center, 1995); Conrad Cherry, *Hurrying Toward Zion: Universities, Divinity Schools, and American Protestantism* (Bloomington: Indiana University Press, 1995); Michael Lee, "Higher Criticism and Higher Education at the University of Chicago: William Rainey Harper's Vision of Religion in the Research University," *History of Education Quarterly* 48 (2008): 508–533; John W. Boyer, *The University of Chicago: A History* (Chicago: University of Chicago Press, 2015).

74. Wallace Buttrick to Frederick P. Keppel, 30 April 1924. Series 1, Sub-Series 1, Box 91 Folder 809 GEB Papers.

75. "Editorial: Honorary Degree," *Ariston* 30 (1936): 29.

76. M. Elizabeth LeBlanc, "The Concept of General Education in Colleges and Universities: 1945–1979," (PhD Dissertation, Rutgers University, 1980), 25; For a discussion on the growth of American higher education and its relationship to general education see Roland L. Guyotte, III, "Liberal Education and the American Dream: Public Attitudes and the Emergence of Mass Higher Education, 1920–1952," (PhD Dissertation, Northwestern University, 1980).

77. David R. Russell, *Writing in the Academic Disciplines: A Curricular History*, 2nd ed. (Carbondale: Southern Illinois University, 2002), 137. The irony of Russell referring to general education as a "god-term" should not be lost on readers.

78. Kevin S. Zayed, "Cooperation Without Consensus: National Discussions and Local Implementation in General Education Reform, 1930–1960," (PhD Dissertation, University of Illinois at Urbana-Champaign, 2016). On the widespread belief in experimentation by members of the general education movement, see Gail Aileen Koch, "The General Education Movement in American Higher Education: An Account and Appraisal of its Principles and Practices and their Relation to Democratic Thought in Modern American Society," (PhD Dissertation, University of Minnesota, 1979), esp. chapters 2, 4–5. The theories underlying experimentation are discussed in Leon Alirangues, "The Experimentalist Curriculum Paradigm," (PhD Dissertation, Rutgers University, 2002); William H. Schubert, et al., *Curriculum Books: The First Hundred Years*, 2nd ed (New York: Peter Lang, 2002), chapter 4.

79. Henry M. Wriston, "Critical Appraisal of Experiments in General Education," in *The Thirty-Eighth Yearbook of the National Society for the Study of Education: Part II: General Education in the American College*, ed. Guy Montrose Whipple (Bloomington, IL: Public School Publishing Company, 1939), 309.

80. J. Harold Goldthorpe, "Trends in Philanthropy: Summary of Gifts to a Selected Group of Institutions of Higher Education in the Last Twenty Years," *Journal of Higher Education* 12 (1941): 73–80; J. Harold Goldthorpe, *Higher Education, Philanthropy, and Federal Tax Exemptions* (Washington, DC: American Council on Education, 1944); various chapters in John Dale Russell, ed., *The Outlook for Higher Education* (Chicago: University of Chicago Press, 1939) deal with issues related to endowment, philanthropy, and federal support of institutions of higher learning.

81. Earl J. McGrath, "The Cooperative Study in General Education," *Junior College Journal* 9 (1939): 501.

82. Roger L. Geiger, *To Advance Knowledge: The Growth of American Research Universities, 1900–1940* (New York: Oxford University Press, 1986); Rebecca S. Lowen, *Creating the Cold War University: The Transformation of Stanford* (Berkeley: University of California Press, 1997), 26–66; Kersten Jacobson Biehn, "Improving Mankind: Philanthropic Foundations and the Development of American University Research between the World Wars," (PhD Dissertation, Rice University, 2006). A useful comparison between elite and non-elite institutions may be seen through the case study of the state of Massachusetts in Richard M. Freeland, *Academia's Golden Age: Universities in Massachusetts, 1945–1970* (New York: Oxford University Press, 1992), esp. 51–69.

83. Zayed, "Cooperation Without Consensus."

84. Sister Hildegarde Marie, "Initiating a Cooperative Study Among Catholic Women's Colleges," *National Catholic Educational Association Bulletin* 49 (1952): 238. For a list and analysis of many of the cooperative studies see Wilford M. Aikin, "Co-operative Studies of Education," *Journal of Higher Education* 11 (1940): 379–382, 400; William G. Wraga, "Clinical Technique, Tacit

Resistance: Progressive Education Experimentation in the Jim Crow South," *History of Education Quarterly* 59 (2019): 227–256.

85. The NCA did take general education seriously both on the secondary level and within institutions of higher learning. On the former, see Will French, "Curriculum Responsibilities of the North Central Association: What Initiative Shall the North Central Association Take in Relation to the Secondary School Curriculum?" *North Central Association Quarterly* 9 (1934): 317–321. On the latter, the NCA would suggest in a promotional pamphlet that institutions that operated on a for-profit basis or "do not include among their major functions the provision of general education" were the only two criteria that rendered an institution "not eligible for accreditation." See North Central Association of Colleges and Secondary Schools, *Know Your North Central Association* (Ann Arbor, MI: Author, 1951), 14. Also, see Davis, *A History of the North Central Association*, esp. 22–23, 211–218.

86. Mary Glenn Wiley and Mayer N. Zald, "The Growth and Transformation of Educational Accrediting Agencies: An Exploratory Study in Social Control of Institutions," *Sociology of Education* 41 (1968): esp. 42–46, quote on 45; C.R. Maxwell, "Value of Past Educational Experiments," *North Central Association Quarterly* 10 (1935): 445–47; H.M. Wriston, "The North Central Method of Evaluating Colleges," in *Educational Conference Under the Auspices of the Association of American Colleges, Atlanta, GA, November 1–2, 1935* (New York: The Consolidated Reporting Co., 1935), 72–79; Davis, *A History of the North Central Association*, 100–101, 126–130.

87. "Proceedings of the Commission on Institutions of Higher Education," *North Central Association Quarterly* 9 (1934): 41–42.

88. William P. Tolley, "Twenty-One Colleges Examine Themselves," *Educational Record* 22 (1941): 306.

89. On the relationship of the NCA and the ACE during the 1930s and 1940s, see *The American Council on Education: History and Activities* (Washington, DC: American Council on Education, 1938), 50; Davis, *A History of the North Central Association*, esp. 168; Williams, "A Historical Study of the Involvement," esp. chapter 6; Hawkins, *Banding Together*, 93, 122.

90. A discussion of secondary school reform during the Great Depression by the methods of Cooperative Studies is available in David L. Angus and Jeffrey E. Mirel, *The Failed Promise of the American High School, 1890–1995* (New York: Teachers College Press, 1999), esp. 63–67; Kevin S. Zayed, "Striving for a Unity of Opposites: The General Education Movement, Vocationalism, and Secondary Education," in *Educating a Working Society: Vocationalism in 20th Century American Schooling*, ed. Glenn P. Lauzon (Charlotte, NC: Information Age Publishing, 2019), 135–153. For an interpretation of the relationship between high schools and the general education movement see William G. Wraga, *Democracy's High School: The Comprehensive High School and Educational Reform in the United States* (Lanham, MD: University Press of America, 1994), 77–81.

91. These committees are listed in National Education Association, *A Directory of National Deliberative Committees in Education: Prepared for the Joint Commission on the Emergency in Education* (Washington, DC: Author, 1934).

92. Robert J. Havighurst, "Assistance Given to Cooperative Educational Experiments by Foundations," *Educational Method* 20 (1941): 331–34, esp. Tables 1 and 2.

93. Examples include Wilford F. [sic] Aikin, "The Experiment as Directed by the Progressive Education Committee," *North Central Association Quarterly*

9 (1934): 350–52; H.H. Ryan, "Experimenting with the Curriculum," *North Central Association Quarterly* 11 (1936): 222–226.

94. Craig Kridel and Robert V. Bullough Jr., *Stories of the Eight-Year Study: Reexamining Secondary Education in America* (Albany: State University of New York Press, 2007).

95. Robert J. Havighurst, "Interviews: Ralph W. Tyler," (December 27, 1939); S 102, B 285, F 2972 General Education Board Papers, Rockefeller Archive Center, Sleepy Hollow, New York quoted in Kridel and Bullough, *Stories of the Eight-Year Study*, 95.

96. "The American Council on Education: A Cooperative Study in General Education" Box 345 Folder 7 CSC Papers; "Proposed Emphases for the Study During 1939–40" Box 115, Folder 1, American Council on Education Archives, Hoover Institution Library and Archives, Stanford, California. Hereafter Cited as "ACE Papers."

97. Tolley, "Twenty-One Colleges," 304–305.

98. In the late 1930s, just as the Cooperative Study was getting underway, representative or generalizable sampling was accepted and widely being applied to many social surveys and other sociological research projects. On the history of representative sampling and its application to sociological research, see Frederick F. Stephan, "History of the Uses of Modern Sampling Procedures," *Journal of the American Statistical Association* 43 (1948): 12–39; Alain Desrosieres, "The Part in Relation to the Whole: How to Generalise? The Prehistory of Representative Sampling," in *The Social Survey in Historical Perspective, 1880–1940*, eds. Martin Bulmer, Kevin Bales, and Kathryn Kish Sklar (New York: Cambridge University Press, 1991), 217–244; Sarah E. Igo, *The Averaged American: Surveys, Citizens, and the Making of a Mass Public* (Cambridge: Harvard University Press, 2007).

99. Ralph W. Tyler, "Education: Curriculum Development and Evaluation," an oral history conducted 1985–1987 by Malca Chall, Regional Oral History Office, The Bancroft Library (Berkeley: University of California Berkeley, 1987), 122.

100. Sister Annette, "The Program of Faculty Studies at the College of St. Catherine," in *Proceedings of the Workshop in General Education, 1940, Volume IV: Educational Administration* (Chicago: Cooperative Study in General Education, 1941), 115.

101. Sister Eucharista to George A. Works, November 10, 1938, B: 345 F: 7 CSC Papers.

102. Sister Annette Walters, "The Program of Faculty Studies at the College of St. Catherine," in *Proceedings of the Workshop in General Education, 1940*, 113.

103. "College Teachers Meeting, January 28, 1939" B: 345 F: 2 CSC Papers; Eucharista Galvin, "Annual Report of the President of the College of St. Catherine to the Board of Trustees, June 1939" Administrative Annual Reports, St. Catherine University Archives and Special Collections, http://content.clic.edu/cdm/ref/collection/annrpt/id/21 Accessed April 21, 2019.

104. President's Report to the Board of Trustees, Muskingum College, October 21, 1938, 6–7." Class: B-3, Box 13, Folder 5, MUSC Papers.

105. Much of this work was documented in a nationally distributed volume, Muskingum College Faculty, *A College Looks at its Program* (Columbus, OH: The Spahr & Glenn Company, 1937). On the history of general education reform at Muskingum, see John Harold Bright, "An Historical Development of Present-Day Problems of Muskingum College" (PhD Dissertation, University of Cincinnati, 1950).

106. R.W. Ogan to Members of the Teaching Staff, May 20, 1939, Class: E-4b, Box 218, F: Faculty Meeting, 1933–1949, MUSC Papers.

107. R.W. Ogan to Members of the Teaching Staff, December 3, 1938, Class: E1B. B: 184, F: R.W. Ogan Correspondence 1938–1939, MUSC Papers.

108. "The Workshop Group in Problems of Educational Administration," in *Proceedings of the Workshop, 1940*, 10.

109. Ralph W. Ogan, "The Cooperative Study in General Education," *Educational Record* 23 (1942): 692–693.

110. "Proposed Emphases for the Study During 1939–40" Box 115, Folder 1, ACE Papers.

111. J. L. McCreight, "Toward Improvement in General Education: Values Derived from Participation in the Cooperative Study in General Education, Muskingum College, New Concord, Ohio," 32. Class F-1, Box 269, Folder: General Education Studies, 1930–1942" MUSC Papers.

112. Ibid.; "Cooperative Group Draws Summer Workshop Plans," *The Catherine Wheel*, April 19, 1940.

113. "Workshop in General Education Conducted by the Cooperative Study in General Education of the American Council on Education, the University of Chicago, 1944," B: 345 F: 5 CSC Papers.

114. Benjamin Fine, "Colleges Unite in Broad Study of Own Needs: Resources Pooled by 21 to Survey Problems and Aid Education," *New York Times*, June 8, 1941. A small bulletin was even put out in the *Journal of Higher Education* that noted that college personnel outside of the Cooperative Study had joined the conference and found it useful. See "The Reporter," *Journal of Higher Education* 12 (1941): 280.

115. Louis M. Heil to Sister Annette, February 7, 1939, B: 345 F: 7 CSC Papers.

116. A surviving example is "Directory of Interests of Faculty Members in the Colleges: September, 1940," (Chicago: Cooperative Study in General Education, 1940). A copy is available at the Joseph Regenstein Library, University of Chicago, Chicago, Illinois.

117. Sister Annette, "A Program of Research in General Education," *The Catholic Educational Review* 39 (1941): 89.

118. "What the Seminars are Doing" Class E1B B: 184 F: RW Ogan Correspondence, 1938–1939, MUSC Papers.

119. Louis M. Heil to Sister Annette, May 6, 1939 B: 345 F: 7 CSC Papers.

120. John L. Bergstresser to Sister Annette September 22, 1939, B: 345 F: 7 CSC Papers.

121. R. B. Draughon to Sister Annette Walters December 4, 1939 B: 345 F:7 CSC Papers.

122. Sister Annette to W.H. Cowley, December 19, 1939 B: 345 F: 7 CSC Papers.

123. John L. Bergstresser to Sister Annette, December 30, 1940 B: 345 F: 7 CSC Papers.

124. Max Astrachan to Sister Annette, December 9, 1939 B: 345 F: 7 CSC Papers.

125. Louis M. Heil to Kenneth W. Wegner February 14, 1940 B: 345 F: 7 CSC Papers; Paul L. Dressel to Kenneth Wegner, February 27, 1940 B: 345 F: 7 CSC Papers; Louis M. Heil to K.W. Wegner April 1, 1940 B: 345 F:7 CSC Papers; "Sister Mona Attends Meet," *The Catherine Wheel*, April 19, 1940, 6.

126. Sister Annette to Ralph W. Ogan, October 28, 1939 B: 345 F: 7 CSC Papers.

127. Sister Annette to R.W. Ogan, October 4, 1940, B: 345 F: 6 CSC Papers.

128. "Cooperative Study Staff Has Workshop: Study Problems of Curriculum; Evaluation of Student," *The Catherine Wheel*, November 24, 1939. "Study Staff, Faculty Hold Conferences," *The Catherine Wheel*, December 8, 1939.

129. "Cooperative Study Leaders Address Faculty Members," *The Catherine Wheel*, April 19, 1940.
130. "Study Staff, Faculty Hold."
131. Harold B. Dunkel, *General Education in the Humanities* (Washington, DC: American Council on Education, 1947), chapter 6.
132. B. Lamar Johnson, ed., *What About Survey Courses?* (New York: Henry Holt, 1937).
133. Harold B. Dunkel to Sister Mona, September 19, 1939, B: 345 F 5 CSC Papers.
134. "Staff Writes for Bulletin," *The Catherine Wheel*, December 8, 1939.
135. Harold B. Dunkel to Sister Mona, October 3, 1939 B: 345 F: 7 CSC Papers.
136. "Group Conference: Literature, Arts, and Language Faculty of Muskingum College Meeting with the Following Members of the Central Staff of the Co-Operative Study in Education, Mr. Barton – Humanities, Mr. Dunkel – Language, Mr. Hill – Philosophy, Thursday Evening, November 2, 1939" Class F-1, Box 269, Folder: General Education Studies, 1930–1942" MUSC Papers.
137. Ibid.
138. Sister Annette to J. L. McCreight, November 21, 1939 B: 345 F: 7 CSC Papers.
139. Sister Annette to J. L. McCreight, November 28, 1939 B: 345 F: 7 CSC Papers.
140. James L. McCreight, "Human Living: An Integrated Course in Psychology, Philosophy, and Religion," *The Journal of the American Academy of Religion* 16 (1948): 151–154.
141. S. H. McGuire to Sister Annette, December 6, 1939, B: 345 F: 7 CSC Papers.
142. Sister Annette to S. H. McGuire, December 13, 1939 B: 345 F: 7 CSC Papers.
143. T. A. Barnhart to Sister Annette, November 4, 1940 B: 345 F: 7 CSC Papers.
144. Sister Annette to T. A. Barnhart, November 7, 1940 B: 345 F: 7 CSC Papers.
145. McCreight, "Toward Improvement in General Education."
146. C. E. Ficken, "The Problem of Formulating Institutional Objectives," in *Proceedings of the Workshop*, 1940, 81.
147. James H. Hewlett, "True Christian Education is Real Education – Plus," Series 1, Sub-Series 1, Box 76 Folder 663 GEB Papers.
    "Editorial: Honorary Degree," *Ariston* 30 (1936): 29.
148. Dunkel, *General Education*, 22.
149. A more thorough discussion of inventories appears in Dunkel, *General Education*, esp. 21–24. The CSC's relationship with inventories can be seen in "Cooperative Study in General Education: Reports of liaison Officers, November 5, 1942, 51–57." Series 1, Sub-Series 3, Box 562 Folder 6009 GEB Papers.
    "Editorial: Honorary Degree," *Ariston* 30 (1936): 29.
150. Ryan and Wolkerstorfer, *More than a Dream*, 34.
151. McCreight, "Toward Improvement in General Education," 33.
152. Sister Annette, "A Program of Research," 90. The goals of the CSC are written out in this article as well.
153. "A. Keenan Writes Study," *The Catherine Wheel*, November 24, 1939; Agnes E. Keenan, "The Differences Between Catholic and Non-Catholic Education," *Journal of Religious Instruction* 9 (1939): 249–256.
154. Annette, "The Program of Faculty Studies," 116.
155. G. E. Buckingham to Sister Annette, November 16, 1939 B: 345 F: 7 CSC Papers.
156. O. T. Gooden to Sister Annette, November 2, 1939 B: 345 F: 7 CSC Papers.

157. O. T. Gooden to Sister Annette, November 17, 1939 B: 345 F: 7 CSC Papers.

158. R. H. Eliassen to Sister Annette, November 27, 1940 B: 345 F: 7 CSC Papers.

159. J. L. Bergstresser to Sister Annette, December 6, 1941 B: 345 F: 7 CSC Papers.

160. Dunkel, *General Education*, 55–69.

161. W. H. Hill to Sister Marie Philip, November 6, 1940 B 345 F 7 CSC Papers.

162. "Sister Marie Philip Publishes Articles," *The Catherine Wheel*, May 9, 1941.

163. Dunkel, *General Education*, 80.

164. Ibid.

165. Harold B. Dunkel, interview by Thomas Roby, December 18, 1987, transcript published as *The Reminisces of Harold B. Dunkel*, 54, Special Collections Research Center at the University of Chicago, Joseph Regenstein Library, Chicago, Illinois.

166. Sister Annette to Ralph W. Ogan 23 January 1943, B: 345 F: 5 CSC Papers. It is difficult to know what Sister Annette meant precisely by "natural law" as one scholar of the term recently noted that "There is no way to give a definition without running afoul of one school of natural law or another." Micah Watson, "Natural Law in *The Abolition of Man*," in *Contemporary Perspectives on C.S. Lewis' The Abolition of Man*, eds. Tim Mosteller and Gayne John Anacker (New York: Bloomsbury, 2017), 25–46 Quote from 27.

167. Sister Annette Walters to Ralph W. Ogan, January 23, 1943. B: 345 F: 5, CSC Papers.

168. "Two Sisters at Education Meet," *The Catherine Wheel*, February 12, 1943.

169. Jeanne Halgren Kilde, *Nature and Revelation: A History of Macalester College* (Minneapolis: University of Minnesota Press, 2010), 203.

7 "Desegregated but Not Integrated"

Race and the Politics of Student Housing in American Higher Education History

Kate Rousmaniere

Long after American colleges and universities were forced to admit students of color into their classrooms, they continued to maintain barriers to those students by refusing them places to live. Institutions did this by restricting on campus housing for students of color, and then ignoring racist barriers to off-campus housing. Well after the legal barriers to admission to higher education were toppled, African American students' limited access to off-campus housing served as the "Mason Dixon line between town and gown."[1]

African American students' exclusion from the most basic of services to allow for education – a place to rest their head at night – was one that Black students consistently identified as the most pressing problem that they faced after registration, and that Black and White anti-racist community efforts often galvanized around. Through the 1950s and 60s, African American college student activists focused on accessible housing both on and off campus, in addition to the more legendary civil rights struggles to integrate local restaurants, movie theaters, and public services, and, eventually campus issues of curriculum, staffing and resources.[2]

This study explores African American students' experiences of off-campus housing in American higher education after the Second World War as part of a larger discussion about the meaning of educational desegregation. In her study of racial and gender integration at three American colleges in the late 19th century, Christi Smith cautions historians to not equate "educational access with greater inclusivity and egalitarian progress."[3] Access is not the same thing as inclusion, an experience well understood by the first African American students admitted to predominantly White college campuses. As one of the first Black women students at the University of North Texas described her experience: "they desegregated but didn't integrate: they let you go, but they won't treat you equally."[4]

The topic of racially integrated housing cuts to the core of a racial conflict in higher education, intersecting both deeply personal experiences of race and racism and the relationship of higher education institutions to their local communities. Surveys of White college students in the postwar years noted that even as White youth gradually became more accepting of their Black peers' civil rights, they remained unwilling to associate with their Black classmates in social and personal situations, including dating and housing.[5] Black students' access to off-campus housing also cut to the core of town-gown relations: when a predominately White higher education institution was court ordered to racially desegregate its campus, it claimed no legal authority over the local community, thus effectively permitting the continuance of racist community practices.

The case of off-campus housing also aligns with the larger history of racial segregation in the American real estate industry. Housing, the most intransigent, pervasive, and persistent domain of racial segregation, is traditionally explained away by the term *de facto* – or the result of private practices and individual preferences and not governmental law and policy. But scholars have recently shown how the long history of racial segregation in residential housing is in fact the result of intentional policies and practices by government and private industry.[6] So, too does racial segregation in university housing have a legislative policy history, a history of intentional prohibition and segregation. From the mid-19th century well through the 1970s, students of color suffered the indignities of social exclusion and the burden of finding their own housing while their purportedly liberal colleges permitted academic registration. Even when their classrooms became legally "integrated," Black students faced continued racial segregation in on and off-campus housing and social activities in a daily atmosphere of hostility. Having won the battle to attend college, these students then had to figure out how to survive it, find places to sleep, eat, socialize, and study. As one historian of African American women in higher education has written, the act of "creating space within academic institutions and demanding quiet time to study was no small feat."[7]

Early Restrictions

The first Black students who integrated higher education institutions faced continued housing exclusion both on and off campus once they passed the registration desk. One early example from Oberlin College is notable because of the pride with which the College held its founding abolitionist roots and the increasing disjuncture between that vision and its housing policies. Two decades after the Civil War, African American Oberlin College students faced great difficulties in finding private housing off campus, even in a community where one fifth of the population was African American, albeit increasingly located in segregated parts of town.[8] By the turn of the century, race relations in the town and college had deteriorated to "an impassable line between Black and White" reported one African American Oberlin student, where the College offered limited and segregated dormitory space to Black students, and sponsored racially segregated boarding houses in town.[9] In 1920, the Dean of Women allowed White women students to claim the dormitory rooms that Black women had won in a lottery. Through the 1940s, White students and alumni at Oberlin and other purportedly liberal campuses objected to even marginally integrated dormitories.[10]

The first students who broke through admissions barriers in the early 1950s were denied on campus housing or were assigned housing in notably segregated dormitories. When Authurine Lucy enrolled at the University of Alabama as the first African American student in 1956, she commuted sixty miles because she was refused a room in a dormitory.[11] Charlene Hunter Gault at the University of Georgia in 1961 and James Meredith at the University of Mississippi in 1962 were assigned to their own wing of a dormitory to prevent their interaction with White students; Meredith shared his wing with federal marshals.[12] When Raymond L. Johnson enrolled in a PhD program in mathematics at Rice University in 1963, he was able to rent an apartment in Houston only because his landlord thought he was an international student from India, not African American.[13] Harry Edwards, recruited to San Jose State University in the early 1960s as an athlete, slept in the lobby of a men's dormitory until he was able to move into a two-bedroom apartment with sixteen other Black athletes, an act which was possible only because the absentee landlord did not know that the residents were Black.[14] Other Black students lived with and worked as domestics for White families to help pay for their education.

Even after some universities lifted restrictions on African American students' access to dormitories, that housing remained largely off limits because White students could request roommate changes for any reason, or the dormitories were configured so that common areas and bathrooms remained segregated.[15] Two years after African American students were permitted to apply to the University of Arkansas in 1955, they were prohibited from living in residence halls when, in response the integration of Little Rock High School, state governor Oval E. Faubus required University administrators to eject all African Americans from dormitories. Until 1967, the University of Arkansas, like many other universities, maintained racial identification on applications for student housing, thus allowing White students to reject Black roommates.[16]

Civil Rights victories in the courts in the 1940s and 50s offered only false hope. Two Supreme Court cases in 1950 – *McLaurin v. Oklahoma* and *Sweatt v. Painter* – expanded the scope of educational accessibility to differential treatment outside of the classroom. Neither case spoke specifically to housing, yet they both opened up the argument that sheer admission to a university classroom was not enough and that differences in experiential and physical facilities must be considered as part of "substantive equality."[17]

But the impact of those cases eluded Black college students in search of places to live. Indeed, when in November 1961, three Black students at the University of Texas (the site of the *Sweatt* decision) filed suit against the university to desegregate dormitories, the University resisted, arguing that since only 14 percent of its total student body lived in dormitories, the topic was not significant enough to be covered by the *Sweatt* and *McLaurin* cases. The administration then threatened to fire any law faculty who helped the plaintiffs in the case.[18]

Universities' exclusion of Black students from housing and other social aspects of campus was an intentional strategy to abide by court rulings while maintaining racial order on campus. When two dozen African American students entered the University of Kentucky in 1954, the goal of what one historian described as keeping "students separate within the efforts to integrate" meant that Black and White students were effectively isolated from each other except for sitting in the same classes.[19] As one of those first Black students at the University of Kentucky recalled: "I felt that I wasn't attending college . . . I was attending, being ignored, and going home."[20] Upon her retirement in 1957, University of Kentucky Dean of Women Sarah Holmes praised "the quietness" with which racial integration had been carried out at the university where no Black student had applied to live in a dormitory in the previous three years. Dean Holmes encouraged Black women students to attend the state Historically Black College, Kentucky State University at Frankfort, where they would have dormitory access.[21]

Seven years later at the University of Kentucky, only 6.5 percent of 100 apartment landlords surveyed rented to Black students and only 61.4 percent rented to foreign students. In 1965, many Black students reported that they had been refused housing by White landlords, although many students simply didn't even ask White landlords, suspecting their answer.[22] In 1965, all 15 Black University of Kentucky students living off campus, and random samples of White and foreign students indicated "widespread reluctance by landlords to rent their apartments or rooms to Negroes." It was, the survey concluded, an "especially trying situation for the Negro."[23]

The case of University of Kentucky law student Richard Harding in 1955–1958 offers an example of an early individual struggle for housing. Harding, who would become the second African American graduate of the University of Kentucky College of Law, completed the three-year curriculum in two and a half years, while holding a full time job. In October, 1955, Harding, then a first year law student living 60 miles away in Frankfort, applied to housing in the newly opened Cooperstown Housing complex for married students in Lexington. Funded and managed by the University, the complex was built specifically to house University of Kentucky married students and their families.[24] University President Dickey replied to Harding that "at the present time," the University did not have available any "housing for married Negro students."[25] In August 1956 Harding applied again to married student housing and was informed that the policy had not changed.[26] Harding completed his law degree in spring 1957, and in December 1957 applied for housing again, indicating that he was preparing to begin another graduate degree. He was refused again. But Harding knew the law that any campus building funded by federal loans must admit students of color and the construction of Cooperstown had relied on just such loans.

University of Kentucky President Dickey also knew the law because Harding's on-going request overlapped the case of another African American couple that had applied for family housing on campus while attending a summer 1957 workshop. The president and dean of students strategized that it would be safer to house this married couple on campus for a few summer months, and thereby "postpone the time when we would need to accept these students" into Cooperstown.[27]

That postponement lasted only one year, as in August 1958, Robert Harding applied for housing a fourth time, and noted that he had requested both the State NAACP and Senator to investigate the situation. Within a week, housing in the community, although not in the Cooperstown complex, was secured for Robert Harding and his family. President Dickey noted his pleasure with the settlement to the Harding case to the President of the State NAACP, commenting on the University's "pride in the smoothness of the integration process" with a "minimum of publicity."[28] Such avoidance was not unique to Southern campus communities: similar accommodation was articulated in 1910 by President King of Oberlin College, still the figurehead of racial equity, who argued that personal and social relations are "essentially questions of personal privilege" – a statement designed to appease racist students, alumni, and community members who objected to integrated housing – and characterized by later historians as the "Oberlin Compromise," echoing the theme of Booker T. Washington's 1895 "Atlanta Compromise" that Blacks and Whites should co-exist, but not co-mingle.[29]

Restrictions on housing facing Black college students remained so severe through the early 1960s that many civil rights activists felt that access to residential facilities remained the final barrier to racial equity in higher education.[30] The 1960 *US Commission on Civil Rights Equal Protection of the Laws in Public Higher Education* noted that while access to on campus housing had largely improved in recent years, off-campus housing remained a problem for students at both recently desegregated and historically integrated colleges.[31]

Race and the Off-Campus Housing Economy

Prohibitions against African American students living on campus inadvertently furthered an off-campus housing economy that sustained some local African American communities financially and culturally. In some college towns, universities established a separate approval system for Black students to rent rooms from identified families in local, segregated, residential communities. In other communities, Black families took on the initiative themselves. For example, in early 20th century Iowa City, the local Ku Klux Klan worked with White landlords to prevent Black housing ownership through restricted covenants, and the University of Iowa maintained an unwritten policy that prevented Black students from on-campus housing. In response, in 1919, the Iowa State Federation of Colored Women's Clubs bought, renovated, and staffed a 12-room house in Iowa City for Black women students at the University of Iowa.[32] At some campuses, an African American staff member took on the responsibility of identifying homes and advising students. At the University of Illinois, Albert Lee, employed by the University President as a messenger, clerk or doorman for over fifty years beginning in 1895, acted as the unofficial "Dean of Black Students," in official university matters, connecting students with available off-campus housing, and serving as a unifying resource and support for on and off campus African American life.[33]

Such off-campus housing arrangements with the local Black community provided both income and support for local families, as students bolstered the local Black community, participating in the local church and community activities.[34] Black families often rearranged their own household for students: in the late 1940s in Champaign Illinois, home of the University of Illinois, 20 percent of all African American households had lodgers or more than one family group, although most of those dwellings had only one or two bedrooms.[35] As one host recalled about the experience: "we were all poor but the students were poor too. . . . they were good company and they were like family, and we took them in as part of the family."[36]

Such households also provided students with mentorship, familial support, and social and professional networks as well as access to services denied them in the town, such as meals, hair care, religious services, and study space. The isolation of the classroom, where White students and faculty ignored and insulted Black students, and the absence of accessible campus life outside of the classroom meant that home stays might provide well needed warmth and support. The house mothers of some boarding houses gained reputations as powerful and nurturing social mentors who monitored students' health and social life. In Iowa City in the 1940s, two women kept boarding houses for Black students that gained such a reputation that when Duke Ellington came to play at the

University, he would also play at one of the houses. African American students and alumni collaborated to create an information network and welcome service for students.[37] In Denton Texas in the mid-1950s, a mother and two grown daughters kept a number of apartments and rental houses for Black students at the recently integrated University of North Texas, and "embraced" the students in ways that compensated for the neglect and hostility experienced on campus.[38] Such supports helped the minority of Black students survive the isolation of their experience. As one student at the University of Arkansas recalled: "We didn't feel like we were away from home, almost."[39]

But such community support was not ideal. The university inspection and approval system for off-campus housing for students of color required specific provisions that could interfere with independent households, while effectively exempting the university from its own responsibility to house students of color. University approval could also lead to favoritism of a few local Black families: in the Oberlin College case described earlier, the Dean of Women ostensibly rejected Black women from the dormitory in part because of support from a few local Black families who stood to profit from operating a segregated boarding house approved of by the College.[40] And because racially segregated neighborhoods were often far from a university campus (in Denton Texas, the Black community that was popularly called "Shack Town" was a few miles from campus), students had to rely on public transportation or car pools to get to class, sacrificing their own time, money, and physical safety, given the danger facing African Americans in public transportation at the time.[41] Class, culture and generational fissures emerged when Black middle-class college students lived with working class Black families. This was the impression of a White faculty member who served on a University of Kentucky campus committee that studied housing challenges for Black students in 1965 and who observed that "middle and upper class Negroes" could only find off-campus housing in unacceptable neighborhoods, a problem that would only increase when the university started to hire Black faculty.[42] When historically Black all women's Spelman College assigned students to live off campus due to a housing shortage on campus, some parents objected to the inconvenience and risks of commuting in the increasingly urbanized Atlanta area.[43] Spelman College administrators also noted "a great deal of friction" between their Black students and Black landladies, who were "forever displeased with the students' poor housekeeping, staying out late, and delinquent rent payments."[44]

In some off-campus communities, liberal Whites sponsored multiracial housing or community centers for students to support Black students, further inter-racial dialogue and to support students as they faced discrimination on and off campus.[45] But for all the radical impetus of these community ventures, such offerings continued to relieve the university of its responsibility to provide housing for enrolled students of color.

Approved Housing

Beginning in the 1950s, some universities developed an inspection process of off campus properties that designated university approval for student housing with the provision that the unit not discriminate on the
basis of race, religion, color, or national origin.[46] This practice furthered
university compliance with emerging federal prohibitions on racial segregation, thus permitting institutions' applications for federal grants. But
in most college towns, only a minority of available local housing sought,
or gained such approval and universities rarely enforced the provisions.
In 1959, only 17 of 43 northern public universities that promised non-
discrimination in admissions also held non-discriminatory regulations
of landlords registered with those universities. In that same year, only
57 (or 13 percent) of 447 landlords on Ohio State University's approved
housing list indicated their willingness to accommodate students without
regard to race or color.[47] Even though a 1960 Ohio law prohibited racial
discrimination in public accommodations, and Ohio State University
approved a non-discrimination policy in housing, it was not until 1968
that the University forbad students to rent from landlords who discrimi-
nated.[48] In 1963, only 7.5 percent of University of Iowa students live in
approved housing that promised to not discriminate, and the University
did not require approval of off-campus housing for married students or
students over 21, even though many complaints were made by graduate students of color.[49] In 1965, the University of Kentucky offered no
special help to international or Black students, arguing that it treated
everybody equally and offered no "special lists" for groups of students.[50]
At the University of Kansas in 1961, when a university-community Civil
Rights Council demanded that the university ensure that landlords on
the approved rental list prohibit racial discrimination, the Chancellor
rejected the request, arguing that to do so would interfere with private
citizens' rental rights.[51]

At the University of Illinois, on campus housing officially desegregated in 1945 after a public campaign by the Chicago *Public
Defender*, but its non-discrimination policy for off-campus housing was
not adopted until 1960.[52] Two years later, 51 percent of local rooming
houses continued to discriminate.[53] And at some institutions, the University regulation applied only to some types of rental properties. At
Ohio's Kent State University in 1961, the anti-discrimination requirement adopted by the university that year applied to only 15 percent of
over 2000 off-campus housing units available to Kent students.[54] And
listings also had adverse effects: at the University of Texas, the Off-
Campus Housing office list of approved off-campus facilities that were
racially integrated allowed White students the opportunity to avoid
renting in integrated housing, while still offering only limited offerings for Black students.

Housing as a Civil Right

Access to housing for students of color was a leading concern of early civil rights activists whose work in the 1960s centered on the integration of on-campus housing and the adoption of non-discrimination policies of university approved off-campus housing.[55] As one observer noted, while Black student activists faced many struggles, "the adversity of hous- ing discrimination, financial difficulties, and social isolation in particu- lar are issues which caused many Black students to protest."[56] The issue was heightened in the 1960s with the increasing presence of African American students on campus – African American student enrollment increased by over 100 percent between 1964 and 1969, compared to a 5-percent growth in White student enrollment.[57]

In the early 1960s the Congress of Racial Equality (CORE) began to investigate housing conditions for Black students at a number of high profile institutions, including UCLA where in 1962, CORE picketed a housing development that had denied housing to a African American doctoral student who worked as a physicist at a local defense firm. In response, the builders asserted that they reserved the right to refuse a home sale to anybody. Students reported that, "despite clearly stated university policies against racial or religious discrimination in student housing and employment, reports of discrimination persist."[58] At the University of Chicago that same year, students and community members affiliated with CORE conducted paired rental applicant testing, where a Black potential tenant attempted to rent an apartment, followed by a White potential tenant: activists noted when Black applicants were rebuffed and White applicants were approved. In January 1962, CORE organized a sit-in protest at the university's administration building and a picket outside the real estate company's office, with the support of stu- dent government leaders.[59]

When in 1962, University of Iowa officials claimed no bias in approved off-campus housing, students picketed the administration building and called for more proactive leadership.[60] Student activists at Ohio State University focused on the problem of off-campus housing for the entirety of the 1960s decade, conducting four surveys of local housing and find- ing in each case that most local landlords refused to rent to Black stu- dents.[61] The 1960 survey found that of the 347 landlords contacted by the University, only 71 pledged not to discriminate.[62] The 1963 survey found that the owner of a discriminatory apartment building was a for- mer Ohio State football star, and a prominent community philanthropist and real estate developer. But in spite of student demonstrations, OSU administration neither prosecuted nor intervened with the landlord out of concerns of bad publicity and alienating White alumni.[63] The 1965 survey found that only 26 percent of the rooming houses registered with the Dean of Men's Housing Office said they were open to renting to

Black students. Another 26 percent said they were "undecided" on the issue, and 42 percent flat out refused to rent to Black students, violating university policy. The Administration's response was to stop maintaining a list of apartments available to students, claiming that off campus apartments were not the university's business.[64] The November 1968 survey found that in the case of 129 of 411 off campus rental units, Black students were told that the apartment was unavailable or that it would cost more than the White applicants had been told.[65]

Other campus activists took more direct action. In March 1968, University of Kansas campus activists led a sit in at the Chancellor's office, demanding that the university housing office refuse to list racially segregated rentals for off-campus housing. The university complied, although the University Greek system did not.[66] In spring 1968, Black students at Eastern Kentucky University submitted a petition to the Student government demanding that the university's approved housing lists must include a pledge of non-discrimination.[67]

In a number of college communities, students filed law suits, sometimes in coordination with the local NAACP. Through the 1960s, at the University of North Carolina in Chapel Hill, campus and community civil rights groups protested discriminatory practices in off-campus housing and fought for a city ordinance that would prohibit racial segregation.[68] In August 1964, two Black students sued the University of Arkansas alleging discrimination in a range of issues including athletics, the hiring of instructors, social organizations, recruitment of students, and on campus housing. In early September, the court ordered the university to integrate dormitories, basing its ruling largely on the *McLaurin v. Oklahoma* decision that required Black students to be treated in the same fashion as Whites at integrated schools.[69] A few days after the signing of the Federal Fair Housing Act in spring 1968, the University of Alabama Afro American Association filed suit against a local realtor who had refused two African American student housing.[70]

Activists' demand for non-discrimination clauses for off-campus housing intersected with emerging debates in American higher education on institutions' legal purview over students, or what was commonly called *in loco parentis*. The 1961 *Dixon v. Alabama* federal court decision arose when the leadership of the Historically Black Alabama State College summarily expelled six students for their participation in Civil Rights demonstrations off campus. The court held that a public college could not expel students without at least minimal due process, and subsequent court decisions further restricted the right of higher education authorities to discipline students for activities conducted off campus. These actions triggered other legal challenges to the constitutionality of higher education regulations off campus, including parietal, residence and disciplinary regulations.[71] In 1971, the 26th amendment lowered the age of majority from 21 to 18, further undermining higher education's authority over young people.

Central to these legal debates was whether the delisting of a discriminatory landlord from an approved housing list unconstitutionally deprived the landlord of property without due process, and whether universities which did not enforce policies against such discrimination with landlords were violating students' fourteenth amendment's guarantee of equal protection. In 1958, the Dean of Men at the University of Kentucky raised the range of issues at play when he sketched a proposal on "Housing for Negro Students." Were all students guaranteed housing? At the time of the writing, less than half of all married students and barely a quarter of all unmarried men students had university housing. What was the university's obligation to provide housing for all students? What would be the financial implications of racially integrating housing if the acceptance of African American students led to White students' abandonment of university housing on which the university held loans? Would the admittance of African American students jeopardize "the rights of bondholders" if a large number of White students left the housing because of its integration? If the apartments were racially integrated, what would be the effects on the value of neighboring residential property? What would be the effect on the "morale of other student families" if the apartments were integrated?[72]

To avoid some of these legal complications, universities rid themselves of off-campus housing offices that had connected the university to regulatory practices over the independent housing market and replaced them with voluntary faculty and student civil rights committees that were assigned to develop community education programs. As an educational institution, the University's position must be to "inform, persuade, and ultimately convince with the facts" argued University of Iowa President Hancher in 1963 in the midst of the community debate about discriminatory housing.[73] Hancher recommended individual outreach to landlords to assure landlords that White students would still rent rooms in racially integrated housing, an effort that the University of Iowa Student Senate took on with support of the local League of Women Voters. Such efforts had broad scope but little authority. As Willard Boyd, Professor of Law and chair of the Human Rights Committee at the University of Iowa described the committee's approach to landlords: "We will tell them that they ought not to discriminate."[74] According to the plan, each household on the approved list would receive a letter explaining the university position on racial discrimination and invite landlords to a meeting to discuss the program.[75]

At the University of Florida, an off-campus housing anti-discrimination policy was not approved until after the passage of the federal Fair Housing Act of 1968 and until that time the off-campus housing staff handled cases individually and on its own initiative, drawing as much as possible on their own interpretation of the 1964 Civil Rights Act and support from the City of Gainesville Human Relations Advisory Board. In this work, the office felt frustrated and inadequate. Subsequent county and city regulations against discrimination in housing through the 1970s helped bolster the office's efforts, but in 1978, the office campus housing office closed and all official university supervision over housing ceased.[76]

Conclusion

When Billie Mohair enrolled at the University of North Texas in Denton in the fall of 1959, five years after the institution officially integrated, she enjoyed her classes but felt in other areas of campus life "an invisible line" that kept her and other Black students separate. A native of Denton, Mohair lived at home where her family rented out rooms to other Black students.[77] Many scholars have shown that this "invisible line" of racial and cultural isolation for students of color has extended long past legal and policy mandates for desegregation, and remains embedded in the implicit practices of student life in higher education today. Recent studies have shown a persistent pattern of Predominantly White Institutions' neglect of off-campus housing experiences, failure to address racial conflict in residence life, and the continence of "racist stereotypes and unjustified perceptions of incompetence, excessive expectations for racial representation, and the racially inconsistent enforcement of standards and consequences" in student life.[78]

A study of the experiences of students of color historical exclusion from campus life raises the question of the ways in which the legacy of racial exclusion remains embedded in purportedly liberal institutions today. Only by recognizing the historical durability of racism on White campus contexts can institutions begin to move beyond them and, instead of acquiescing to dominant racial practices in the community, mobilize as allies with their students and local communities of color.[79] Such recognition must hold for both on and off campus interactions, as university life has always and continues to expand far beyond the classroom and residence hall. As an African American university staff member at Penn State University reported in 2001, "This is rural central Pennsylvania. And when you step off campus you are colored again."[80]

Notes

1. Guy B. Johnson, "Racial Integration in Public Higher Education in the South," *Journal of Negro Education* 23, no 3 (Summer 1954): 327.
2. Joy Ann Williamson, *Black Power on Campus: The University of Illinois, 1965–75* (Urbana: University of Illinois Press, 2003), 7–8, 13–14; Joy Ann Williamson-Lott, "Campus Life for Southern Black Students in the Mid-Twentieth Century," in *Rethinking Campus Life: New Perspectives on the History of College Students in the United States*, eds. Christine A. Ogren and Marc A. VanOverbeke (London: Springer, 2018).

3. Christi M. Smith, *Reparation and Reconciliation: The Rise and Fall of Integrated Higher Education* (Chapel Hill: University of North Carolina Press, 2016), 143.

4. University of North Texas Oral History collection #1850, Interview with Dr. Maxine Thornton Reese, March 24, 2014, 15.

5. Guerdon D. Nichols, "Breaking the color barrier at the University of Arkansas," *The Arkansas Historical Quarterly* 27, no 1 (1968): 20; Donal E. Muir and C. Donald Mc Glamery, "Trends in integration attitudes on a deep-South campus during the first two decades of Desegregation," *Social Forces* 62, no 4 (1984): 963–972.

6. Richard Rothstein, *The Color of Law: A Forgotten History of How our Government Segregated America* (New York: Liveright Publishing, 2017); Stephen Grant Meyer, *As Long as They Don't Move Next Door: Segregation and Racial Conflict in American Neighborhoods* (Lanham: Rowman & Littlefield, 2000); James W. Loewen, *Sundown Towns: A Hidden Dimension of American Racism* (New York: The New Press, 2018).

7. Stephanie Evans, *Black Women in the Ivory Tower, 1850–1954: An Intellectual History* (University Press of Florida, 2008), 8.

8. William E. Bigglestone, "Oberlin College and the Negro Student, 1865–1940," *The Journal of Negro History* 56, no 3 (1971): 207–11; Gary Kornblith and Carol Lasser, *Elusive Utopia: The Struggle for Racial Equality in Oberlin, Ohio* (Baton Rouge: Louisiana State University Press, 2018), 171, 175, 194.

9. Kornblith and Lasser, *Elusive Utopia*, 227, 236–237.

10. Raymond Wolters, *The New Negro on Campus: Black College Rebellions of the 1920s* (Princeton: Princeton University Press, 1975), 322–323; Bigglestone, "Oberlin College and the Negro Student," 207; Cally L. Waite, "The Segregation of Black Students at Oberlin College after Reconstruction," *History of Education Quarterly* 41, no. 3 (2001): 344–364; Henry, B. et al., eds., *Blacks at Harvard: A Documentary History of African-American Experience at Harvard and Radcliffe* (New York: NYU Press, 1993); Jerome Karabel, *The Chosen: The Hidden History of Admission and Exclusion at Harvard, Yale, and Princeton* (Boston: Houghton Mifflin Harcourt, 2005).

11. Robert A. Caro, "Autherine Lucy at the University of Alabama: How the Mob Won," *The Journal of Blacks in Higher Education* 37 (2002): 124.

12. Charlayne Hunter-Gault, *In My Place* (New York: Vintage, 1992); W. Ralph Eubanks, "A Black Student Confronts the Racial Legacy of Ole Miss," *The Journal of Blacks in Higher Education*, no. 43 (Spring, 2004): 106–111; Evans, *Black Women in the Ivory Tower*, 48.

13. "The Black Students Who Overturned the Whites-Only Clause in the Charter of Rice," *The Journal of Blacks in Higher Education*, no. 43 (Spring, 2004): 72.

14. Harry Edwards, *The Struggle That Must Be* (New York City: Macmillan, 1980), 184.

15. Kelly Sartorius, *Deans of Women and the Feminist Movement: Emily Taylor's Activism* (London: Springer, 2014), 128; University of North Texas Oral History collection #1850, Interview with Dr. Maxine Thornton Reese, March 24, 2014, 13.

16. Mordean Taylor Moore, "Black Student Unrest at the University of Arkansas," (Master's thesis, University of Arkansas, 1972), 33; Gordon D. Morgan and Izola Preston, *The Edge of Campus: A Journal of the Black Experience at the University of Arkansas* (Fayetteville: University of Arkansas Press, 1990), 24–25; Charles F. Robinson and Lonnie Williams, *"Remembrances in Black": Personal Perspectives of the African American Experience at the University of Arkansas, 1940s – 2000s* (Fayetteville: University of Arkansas Press, 2015), 46–47.

17. Gary M. Lavergne, *Before Brown: Heman Marion Sweatt, Thurgood Marshall, and the Long Road to Justice* (Austin: University of Texas Press, 2010).

18. Dwonna Goldstone, *Integrating the Forty Acres: The Fifty Year Struggle for Racial Equality at the University of Texas* (Athens: University of Georgia Press, 2006,), 106–107; Beverly Burr, "History of Student Activism at the University of Texas at Austin, 1960–88," (1988).

19. Sharon Barrow Childs, "The Integration of the First African American Undergraduates at the University of Kentucky," (PhD Dissertation, University of Kentucky, 2000), 49.

20. Quoted in Childs, "The Integration of the First," 101, 112.

21. Yvonne Eaton, "Dean Holmes to Retire July 1 If Replacement Can Be Hired," February 26 1957, *Kentucky Leader*, University of Kentucky Archives.

22. Frank Browning, "Color Bar is Real to Many," *The Kentucky Kernel*, April 29, 1965.

23. Kenneth Hoskins, "Survey indicates Housing Discrimination," *The Kentucky Kernel*, April 29, 1965; "Chairmen Report Rights Activities," *The Kentucky Kernel*, November 25, 1964.

24. Robert E. Harding to President Frank G. Dickey September 14, 1956, President Frank G. Dickey papers, Box 7, Folder: Dean of Men, 1956–1957, University of Kentucky Archives.

25. President Frank G. Dickey to Robert E. Harding, September 17, 1956, President Frank G. Dickey papers, Box 7, Folder: Dean of Men, 1956–1957, University of Kentucky Archives.

26. "Housing for Negro Students," Frank G. Dickey Presidential Papers, Box 7, Folder: Dean of Men, 1957–1958, "Dean of Men," University of Kentucky Archives.

27. President Frank G. Dickey to Dean Leslie L. Martin, June 17, 1957, University of Kentucky Archives.

28. President Frank G. Dickey to Mr. James A. Cumlin, September 27, 1958, President Frank G. Dickey papers, Box 7, Folder: Dean of Men, 1957–1958, University of Kentucky Archives.

29. Kornblith and Lasser, *Elusive Utopia*, 240.

30. Johnson, "Racial Integration in Public Higher Education in the South," 323.

31. 1960 *US Commission on Civil Rights Equal protection of the Laws in Public Higher Education*, 168–170.

32. Richard M. Breaux, "'Maintaining a Home for Girls': The Iowa Federation of Colored Women's Clubs at the University of Iowa, 1919–1950," *The Journal of African American History* 87, no 2 (2002): 236–255.

33. Deirdre Cobb-Roberts, "Student-Community Voices: Memories of Access versus Treatment at University of Illinois," in *Schools as Imagined Communities: The Creation of Identity, Meaning, and Conflict in U.S. History*, eds. Deirdre Cobb-Roberts, Sherman Dorn, and Barbara J. Shircliffe (New York: Palgrave Macmillan, 2006), 84–86, 98.

34. Cally Lyn Waite, *Permission to Remain Among Us: Education for Blacks in Oberlin, Ohio, 1880–1914* (Westport: Praeger, 2002), 119.

35. Cobb-Roberts, "Student-Community Voices," 96.

36. Lucy J. Gray as quoted in Cobb-Roberts, "Student-Community Voices," 96–97.

37. Ted Wheeler, "Going the Distance," 137; Dianna Penny, "I Never Thought of Myself as an Outsider," and Richard M. Breaux, "'Tireless Partners and Skilled Competitors': Seeing UI's Black Male Athletes, 1934–1960," in *Invisible Hawkeyes: African Americans at the University of Iowa During the Long Civil Rights Era*, eds. Lena M. Hill and Michael D. Hill (Iowa City: University of Iowa Press, 2016).

38. University of North Texas Oral History collection #1583, Interview with Virginia Huey You, May 2, 2006, 27.

39. Robinson and Williams, "*Remembrances in Black*," 146–148.
40. Wolters, *The New Negro on Campus*, 322–23; Bigglestone, "Oberlin College and the Negro Student," 212.
41. Greer C. Stanford-Randle, "The Black Student Movement at the Ohio State University: 'Black, Scarlet and Gray,' " (Master's thesis, Georgia State University, 2010), 136–37; University of North Texas Oral History collection #1583, Interview with Virginia Huey You, May 2, 2006, 7.
42. Judy Grisham, "Instructor Feels UK Should Help," *The Kentucky Kernel*, April 29, 1965.
43. Report from the Supervisor of the Off-Campus Students, 1966–67, Spelman College Archives, Atlanta, Georgia; Joshua F.J. Inwood, "Constructing African American Urban Space in Atlanta, Georgia," *Geographical Review* 101, no. 2 (2011): 147–63.
44. Report from the Supervisor of the Off-Campus Students, 1966–67, Spelman College Archives.
45. Oakley C. Johnson, "The Negro-Caucasian Club: A History," *Negro History Bulletin* 33, no 2 (1970): 40 (Reprinted from *Michigan Quarterly Review* 8, no 2 (April 1969); Elaine McNeil, "White Members of a Biracial Voluntary Association in Arkansas," (PhD Dissertation University of Kansas, 1967) (as cited in Morgan and Preston, *The Edge of Campus*, 25); Dorothy Dawson Burlage, "Truths of the Heart," in *Deep in Our Hearts: Nine White Women in the Freedom Movement*, eds. Joan C. Browning and Dorothy Dawson Burlage (Athens: University of Georgia Press, 2002); Glenda Alice Rabby, *The Pain and the Promise: The Struggle for Civil Rights in Tallahassee, Florida* (University of Georgia Press, 1999), 92.
46. "Policy Announced on Discrimination in Private Housing," *Daily Iowan*, January 17, 1961; Milton L. McGhee and Ann Fagan Ginger, "The House I Live In: A Study of Housing for Minorities," *Cornell Law Review* 46, no 194 (1960–61): 245.
47. William W. Van Alstyne, "Discrimination in State University Housing Programs – Policy and Constitutional Consideration," *Stanford Law Review* 13, no 60 (1960): 60, 77.
48. McGhee and Ginger, "The House I Live In," 245; William J. Shkurti, *The Ohio State University in the Sixties: The Unraveling of the Old Order* (Columbus: The Ohio State University, 2016), 116, 266; Jay R. Smith, "Prompt Housing Action Pledged," *Lantern* May 9, 1969, 1; Stanford-Randle, "The Black Student Movement at the Ohio State University," 7.
49. "Committee Announces New Policies on Off-Campus Housing Discrimination," *Daily Iowan* May 28, 1963; "SUI Negroes Cooperate in DI Inquiry," *Daily Iowan*, February 22, 1962, 1, 8; "Huit to Investigate Race Bias Report," *Daily Iowan* February 27, 1962; "Iowa City Renter Denies Race Bias," *Daily Iowan* March 2, 1962.
50. "No Special Help is Offered to Negro, Foreign Student," *The Kentucky Kernel*, April 29, 1965.
51. Kelly Sartorius, *Deans of Women and the Feminist Movement*, 127.
52. Joy Ann Williamson, "The Snail-like Progress of Racial Desegregation at the University of Illinois," *The Journal of Blacks in Higher Education*, no. 42 (Winter, 2003–2004): 116–20; Cobb-Roberts, "Student-Community Voices," 95–99.
53. Williamson, *Black Power on Campus*, 21.
54. Dan Warner, "No Fanfare for KSU's Ban on Housing Bias," *Akron Beacon Journal*, May 25, 1961, 30.
55. McGhee and Ginger, "The House I Live In," 244–45; Bruce L. Paisner, "University Denies Barring Negroes From Apartments," *Harvard Crimson*,

February 9, 1962; "GSA to Fight Discrimination," *Harvard Law Review* 35, no 6 (November 15, 1962): 9.

56. Stanford-Randle, "The Black Student Movement at the Ohio State University," 40–41.

57. Buell G. Gallagher, ed., *NAACP College and the Black Student: NAACP Tract for the Times* (NAACP, 1971), 17.

58. Eddie R. Cole, "College Presidents and Black Student Protests: A Historical Perspective on the Image of Racial Inclusion and the Reality of Exclusion," *Peabody Journal of Education* 93, no. 1 (2018): 84.

59. LaDale Winling, "Students and the Second Ghetto: Federal Legislation, Urban Politics, and Campus Planning at the University of Chicago," *Journal of Planning History* 10, no 1 (2011): 59–86.

60. "Editorial: Discrimination – Time for Strong Leadership," *Daily Iowan*, May 9, 1962.

61. Shkurti, *The Ohio State University in the Sixties*, 22.

62. Ibid., 21; "SLA Attacks Procedures in Housing Plan," *Lantern*, August 11, 1960.

63. Shkurti, *The Ohio State University in the Sixties*, 88–89.

64. William Shofner, "NAACP Probing Bias in Housing," *Lantern*, November 24, 1965, 1; William G. Shofner, "NAACP Unit Spurs Fight for Housing," *Lantern*, January 5, 1966, 1; Shkurti, *The Ohio State University in the Sixties*, 164–65.

65. Donald L. Cook, "Report City Black Housing Bias," *Lantern*, November 19, 1968, 1; Shkurti, *The Ohio State University in the Sixties*, 266.

66. Kelly Sartorius, *Deans of Women and the Feminist Movement*, 131–32; John L. Rury and Kim Cary Warren, *Transforming the University of Kansas: A History, 1965–2015* (Lawrence: University Press of Kansas, 2015), 228–31.

67. "EKU Negroes Submit Discrimination Petition," *The Kentucky Kernel*, March 7, 1968.

68. Jeffrey A. Turner, *Sitting in and Speaking Out: Student Movements in the American South, 1960–1970* (Athens: University of Georgia Press, 2010), 94, 210–11; John Ehle, *The Free Men* (New York: Harper & Row, 1965), 323.

69. Robinson and Williams, '*Remembrances in Black*', 46–47.

70. Turner, *Sitting in and Speaking Out*, 220–221, 221; University of Alabama President David Mathews, Afro American Association, 1968–1980, box 21, University of Alabama Archives; "Afros Reiterate Demands" University of Alabama *Crimson White*, April 5, 1968.

71. Scott Gelber, "Expulsion Litigation and the Limits of *in Loco Parentis*, 1860–1960," *Teachers College Record* 116, no 12 (2014); David J. Hanson, *The Lowered Age of Majority: Its Impact on Higher Education* (Washington, DC: Association of American Colleges, 1975).

72. "Housing for Negro Students," Frank G. Dickey Presidential Papers, Box 7, Folder: Dean of Men, 1957–1958, University of Kentucky.

73. "Committee Announces New Policies on Off-Campus Housing Discrimination," *Daily Iowan*, May 28, 1963.

74. "SUI Senate Resolution Asks Probe of Off-Campus Housing," *Daily Iowan*, September 24, 1963.

75. "Committee Announces New Policies on Off-Campus Housing Discrimination," *Daily Iowan*, May 28, 1963.

76. Carl B. Opp to Rev. Mr. Earle C. Page, Chairman, Human Relations Advisory Board, Gainesville, Florida, December 5, 1967; "Anti Discrimination Policies Affecting Off-Campus Housing," 6 January, 1976, Papers of Carl Opp, University of Florida Archives. Today, Off-Campus Housing offices at Universities tend to serve as an information source, with a disclaimer of university responsibility.

77. University of North Texas Oral History collection #713, Interview with Billie Mohair, February 25, 1988, 12.

78. Harper, Shaun R. et al., "Race and Racism in the Experiences of Black Male Resident Assistants at Predominantly White Universities," *Journal of College Student Development* 52, no 2 (2011): 197. See also Terrell L. Strayhorn, "Fittin' in: Do Diverse Interactions with Peers Affect Sense of Belonging for Black Men at Predominantly White institutions?" *NASPA Journal* 45, no 4 (2008): 501–527; William A. Smith, Walter R. Allen, and Lynette L. Danley, "Assume the Position . . . You Fit the Description:' Psychosocial Experiences and Racial Battle Fatigue among African American Male College Students," *American Behavioral Scientist* 51, no 4 (2007): 551–578; Terrell L. Strayhorn and Taris G. Mullins, "Investigating Black Gay Male Undergraduates' Experiences in Campus Residence Halls," *Journal of College & University Student Housing* (2012); William A. Smith, Tara J. Yosso, and Daniel G. Solórzano, "Racial Primes and Black Misandry on Historically White Campuses: Toward Critical Race Accountability in Educational Administration," *Educational Administration Quarterly* 43, no 5 (2007): 559–585; Harwood, Stacy A., et al. "Racial Microaggressions in the Residence Halls: Experiences of Students of Color at a Predominantly White University," *Journal of Diversity in Higher Education* 5, no 3 (2012).

79. Shaun R. Harper, "Am I My Brother's Teacher? Black Undergraduates, Racial Socialization, and Peer Pedagogies in Predominantly White Postsecondary Contexts," *Review of Research in Education* 37, no 1 (2013): 207; Sylvia Hurtado, et al., "Enhancing Campus Climates for Racial/Ethnic Diversity: Educational Policy and Practice," *The Review of Higher Education* 21, no 3 (1998): 279–302.

80. "Penn State University: Blacks are Unhappy in the Happy Valley," *Journal of Blacks in Higher Education* 32 (August 31, 2001): 20.

8 Transforming the Mission With a Nontraditional Presidency

David C. Hardesty's Land-Grant Leadership at the End of the Twentieth Century

Katlin Swisher

Amid shifts of the perception of higher education and the public's questioning of the role and value of public universities, West Virginia University (WVU) experienced institutional change through nontraditional presidential leadership in the late 20th century. Rather than following the typical academic administrative path through the faculty ranks, David Hardesty became WVU's 22nd president in 1995 after a distinct business, legal, and governmental career. From the moment he was hired, Hardesty faced critiques and doubts about his qualifications and his political intentions from the campus community, especially faculty. This chapter examines Hardesty's 12-year journey – more than twice the average duration of a university presidency – from outsider to hero, a leader who persevered and overcame much conflict as his administration attempted to modernize WVU's land-grant mission in response to privatization, changing technology, and market demands. With a reorganized leadership structure and a strategic plan that aspired to put students first and transform the institution's party school reputation, WVU became a national brand in the wake of privatization. Through document analysis of official University publications and speeches and interviews with administrators, faculty, and staff, this chapter illustrates an example of how leaders can engage with their institution's mission while navigating shifts in social, cultural, political, and economic contexts.

Leading from the Outside: The Nontraditional President

While most university presidents follow the traditional academic pathway of earning tenure and leading from academic leadership roles like department chairs, deans, and provosts, in recent decades, higher education institutions have increasingly been open to or sought presidential candidates with broader skillsets from industry, business, government, and law. As of a 2017 study,[1] nontraditional presidents made up one-third of university presidents, compared to 40.5 percent in a

2018 study of presidential career histories.[2] The advent of the nontraditional president has occurred in the wake of privatization, a period in higher education history where public institutions are responding to decreasing state appropriations with more reliance on student tuition, private fundraising, budget cuts, and other cost-savings measures, even taking on more corporate-like models.[3] This shift has evolved the expectations and characteristics of what is traditionally desired from the role of president, including transitioning institutional activity to emphasize business operations and fundraising, even being described as a "substantial threat to the status quo" of higher education leadership.[4]

This historical case examines how a nontraditional president overcame outsider status to innovate and implement several modern initiatives at a flagship, land-grant, and research university. Hired following a long-time traditional president, David Hardesty began the role of president at West Virginia University in 1995 after a distinct business, legal, and state government career.[5] Hardesty came into the role after working as an attorney at Bowles Rice in Charleston, West Virginia, and serving as West Virginia State Tax Commissioner.

Prior to being named president of WVU, Hardesty's only previous higher education experience was as an instructor at the WVU College of Law and as a member of WVU's governing board. But he was intertwined with the university itself following an extraordinary undergraduate experience, earning a bachelor's degree in 1967. While an undergraduate, he served as student body president and won the Rhodes Scholarship, which included an opportunity to study abroad at Oxford University in the United Kingdom. There Hardesty earned both bachelor's and master's degrees in philosophy, politics, and economics. He later went on to earn a Juris Doctorate from Harvard Law School. Hardesty also had the experience of being the parent of a legacy student as his daughter enrolled at WVU while he was president.[6] Because of this experience, throughout his presidency, he sought to improve the accessibility of these types of experiences for students.

A Turbulent Transition

In light of his nontraditional pathway to the presidency, from the moment he was hired as WVU's president, Hardesty faced a tumultuous environment because of his outsider status. Before he ever arrived on campus, he faced doubts about his qualifications and his intentions from the campus community, especially faculty. Many individuals did not have confidence in or support the hiring decision because he came from a legal and political background rather than a traditional career trajectory in academia.

One faculty member went as far as to file a lawsuit against Hardesty, which was eventually dismissed by the Kanawha County Circuit Court.[7] A former governing board member recalled this dissent:

> David Hardesty became an academic. He didn't start off as an academic. [Hardesty] was a lawyer when he was hired. . . . There was a lot of consternation when [Hardesty] became president from the faculty because he was not an academic.

This lack of confidence and support, especially from faculty, meant Hardesty started off his presidency with tensions and challenges that he had to overcome before his first day in the role, and he continued to face these critiques of being in the pocket of the politicians and the legislature for several years into his presidency.

Recognizing these tensions from the beginning, even in preparation for his interview for the role, Hardesty studied the situation he was entering and began conducting research and gathering feedback through his professional network. This preparation would become the foundation for his approach to the presidency. A faculty member and advisor to Hardesty explained that his leadership began before he was ever selected for the position:

> [Hardesty] asked several people that he knew in one capacity or another to help give him a sense of the on-campus situation. I was one of those that he called on to do that. He reached out to them . . . basically as part of his preparation for his on-campus interview process.

Hardesty himself acknowledged the uphill battle he faced:

> As a "nontraditional president" I needed to meet constituent expectations with regard to consultation and shared governance. I began by arranging a series of meetings with the various faculties on the Morgantown campus. . . . These meetings represent a significant commitment, given the number of campuses and colleges[8] within the University.[9]

That proactive, yet nontraditional information-gathering philosophy was an approach that Hardesty introduced to his new role that he carried over from his legal and business background and maintained throughout his presidency – consistently learning, seeking information, and researching trends. Pulling from a political leadership style, he recognized that gaining power is the source for making things happen and studied how individuals and groups, both internal and external to the university, navigated the power dynamics.[10] Hardesty's researched approach to leadership was a characteristic that a staffer in the Office of the President remembered, saying,

> Hardesty loved to use those sorts of think-tanks to stimulate thinking. He read; he always read. And sometimes when he had like a Saturday where he would just say he was going to take [the day] to read. We would always be like, "Ugh, he's going to come in Monday with some big ideas." He read everything he could about organizational development and planning.

Hardesty also described this information-gathering style in his book written with his wife Susan, *Leading the Public University*. "I constantly seek information that can help me do my job better. When I find it – whether in books, in journal articles, in reports from other universities, in news items, or just from insight – I make a point of sharing it with appropriate members of my management team."[11] He embodied this political leadership style as a response to the criticisms he faced, seeking ways to build relationships among the "rolling arenas" and "ongoing contests of individual and group interests"[12] in the university's naturally political setting.[13]

Convening the "Kitchen Cabinet"

To support this feedback-gathering approach and inform subsequent planning, Hardesty put together a "kitchen cabinet" – a small group of advisors to which he reached out individually for advice. This innovative step was another example of his non-traditional approach and was inspired by his political, legal, and business background. His goal was to encourage efficiency and seek out early victories. It was Hardesty's intention to quickly learn to navigate the unfamiliar aspects of the organizational structure and the internal politics of the university. One of his advisors remembered, "It was people who believed deeply in [WVU] and wanted to help him. And what happened is it didn't have any institutional bias . . . they would ask questions, and they would say well there's this issue and there's that issue and there's this issue." The "kitchen cabinet" would collect additional information and conduct research to see how the issues presented in the information gathering were making an influence elsewhere in higher education and how other universities navigated them. This advisor recalled how Hardesty would introduce possible issues to pursue with the "kitchen cabinet" and how the work on those issues would subsequently occur. He said, "[We] would go away, and [we] would really work on different ideas that the president had independently. [We] worked on the best findings in the field. And we'd come back, and [we'd] say here's the things we can do."

After the "kitchen cabinet" returned with its findings, they would determine what issues to pursue. Those issues were often addressed by task forces, a structure that allowed the administration to tackle issues as they occurred. This advisor explained that this model gave WVU the capacity to address issues that spanned the various administrative units of the university, saying, "They were burning problems. They were problems that didn't belong to a single dean, vice president, director, or some chief official. . . . And what happens is no one really owned it."

The issues addressed by the task forces did not necessarily have to connect or relate to each other, nor were they all presented comprehensively in one document or location. Instead, they were addressed as problems arose. However, that lack of connection or comprehensive approach was often evident to the campus community, and the strategy or reasoning behind why certain issues or initiatives were pursued were often questioned by both faculty-at-large and the Faculty Senate. The advisor recalled, "It was very much driven by a very strong-willed president, which in my mind was good. But if you were sitting on the outside you would say, 'I don't understand how those initiatives link together.'" Hardesty used his executive power to carry those initiatives through despite the questions and critiques. His strong-willed personality and approach to leadership reflected having a strong purpose,[14] while simultaneously suggesting a lack of understanding or disregard for the traditional dual governance structure of higher education,[15] a common challenge for nontraditional presidents not familiar with the organization of higher education.

One of the critiques of the "kitchen cabinet" model that arose from the interviews is that it did not often incorporate WVU's academic colleges and schools and their leadership in the planning process, another reflection of Hardesty's tendency to work outside official channels.[16] An example of this approach was the creation of WVU's Leadership Studies Program, a curricular change Hardesty pursued out of his passion for leadership development. When the program was first established, it did not have an academic home, belonging to no college or school, a faculty member with extensive strategic planning experience recalled,

> That may be a good example of how it was hard for [Hardesty's] model to work as effective as it needed to in a university. . . . Not a good formula for a curricular change to really take hold. It had trouble finding a home that would love it. But it was politically very attractive. . . . I think the leadership program was a good example of a good idea not effectively implemented because, in part, of the inexperience in dealing with how a university effectively implements and nurtures a change.

Because the "kitchen cabinet" was so small, concerns arose that the university's day-to-day operations were not always addressed as quickly, strategically, or comprehensively as possible because there was so much focus on special, signature projects or "niche" activities. This absence of comprehensive planning ascribed to decision-making was rejected in favor of more one-off, targeted victories for the majority of Hardesty's presidency until his administration was required to take a more comprehensive approach by its accreditors and the state government, discussed later in this chapter. The approach implies that the choice reflects not only Hardesty's legal and business background outside of higher education, but also his need to overcome the early criticism he faced by obtaining quick successes to gain more political capital and credibility among the campus community for future decisions.

Pursuing Transformation

The Hardesty administration used the task force approach to address the challenges facing WVU as a land-grant institution in the late 20th century: meeting the changing needs of students, gaining ground in research operations and funding, addressing shifts in technology, responding to new state governance and funding structures, and recommitting to community engagement. Many of these challenges were remnants of the effects of World War II on higher education institutions, particularly public, research universities.

Becoming a Student-Centered University

In the wake of massification following World War II,[17] there was an increasing expectation for higher education institutions to respond to the changing demands of students, especially as enrollments increased. Even after enrollments stagnated in the 1970s and 1980s and academics became standardized,[18] student life had become more than just the classroom experience. Universities transitioned to a holistic approach to education, connecting what was learned in the classroom with students' extracurricular activities, the beginnings of the administrative emphasis on student development.[19]

The Hardesty administration tended toward this holistic approach. On the first day of his presidency in his inaugural speech and subsequent press conference on July 1, 1995, he kicked off an initiative intended to transform WVU into what he described as a "student-centered" university. This followed higher education's phase out of the post-World War II philosophy of in loco parentis, or student personnel workers serving as caretakers "in place of parents," as the responsibilities became more nuanced beyond the classroom and professional, focusing on roles like advising, financial aid, housing, dining, health services, and the like.[20]

While the concept of educating the whole student, both embracing and implementing a philosophy that intersected students' academic, personal, and social experiences, came about in higher education over the course of the 20th century,[21] this focus on the student experience was more present at WVU than ever before during Hardesty's administration in the late 1990s and eventually became his legacy.

An Office of the President staffer recounts how Hardesty placed a podium on the lawn in front of E. Moore Hall, a campus building located in a highly trafficked area of campus and declared that WVU was to become more student-centered and announced plans for a student affairs task force. She reflected, "[Hardesty] basically put his flag in the ground that we want to become more student-centered. . . . He elevated that."

The Student Affairs Task Force aspired to exceed students' expectations by improving their living and learning environments, treating them with respect, and investing in their academic success.[22] They began with a redesign of the first-year experience. Dubbed "Operation Jump Start," it included a comprehensive set of programming focused on student learning and retention with initiatives like intensified academic advising, increasing technology resources for students, and making student services, such advising, scheduling, registration, financial aid, and student accounts, more efficient.

A Campus-Wide Commitment

In his inaugural speech, Hardesty charged that all WVU employees would play a role in retention, and that was the foundation that would help WVU "become one of the leaders in retention among land-grant universities".[23] Looking back on the initiative nine years later in WVU's 2004 Accreditation Self-Study Report, he claimed, "This student-centered philosophy now permeates the campus and includes a focus on critical inquiry in the classroom as well as an emphasis on responding to student needs in WVU's service units".[24] By including a call to action for all University employees, Hardesty was striving to gain buy-in from all across campus to engage with students.

Initially, Hardesty didn't gain that buy-in, especially from faculty. Faculty questioned the emphasis placed on students, not only because the focus took away from other more faculty-centric priorities, like research, but also because of the expectation placed on them to support retention initiatives and work more closely with students beyond their standard teaching responsibilities. Some faculty believed Hardesty, as a nontraditional president, did not understand their responsibilities as not only teachers, but also scholars, and that the scholarship and research aspects of their roles were devalued because of the additional expectations placed on them to more regularly interact with students.[25]

One of the ways Hardesty attempted to carry out this initiative was adding staff specifically with the responsibility of working with students, a common strategy in higher education as the role of student affairs personnel continued to be more professionalized in the late 20th century in response to growing enrollments as well as student and family demands.[26] Beyond the "kitchen cabinet" model described previously, Hardesty made several changes and additions to the executive leadership team. One new role was a dean of students who reported directly to the president, a progressive type of position at the time when university administrations were still relatively small and most administrative work was still decentralized in the hands of the faculty-at-large and the faculty senate. However, as the breadth of student life and student services continued to grow on college campuses through the 20th century, "dean of students" positions gained more agency and influence.[27] At WVU, this role had previously served as an associate provost reporting up to the provost, which Hardesty believed made it a forgotten or "lesser" position, according to an advisor. He said, "There were conversations about it and there were also faculty that [questioned], 'What *is* this?' " Many faculty reacted negatively to the administrative changes, questioning the purpose of the dean of students position in particular and the "administrative bloat" from the new positions and the costs of salaries and benefits associated with them.

Embracing Parents and Families

The philosophy of in loco parentis had been long buried by the late 20th century, and the student rights movement had given way to engaged parents seeking to be more involved in their students' daily lives.[28] This relationship has since evolved to become more of a partnership approach with parents and families offering more layers of support and guidance (e.g. academic, emotional, financial and personal), which was reflected at WVU. During this time, Hardesty launched, in partnership with his wife Susan, a Mountaineer Parents Club, one of the first of its kind in the country, to connect the parents and families of WVU students to the campus community and to each other. This part of the initiative also included a toll-free "Parents Helpline" that students' parents and families could call with questions, and on-campus fall and spring parents' weekends to engage families in activities on campus and around Morgantown. "The Parents Club, which has over 12,000 families, and toll-free Parents Help Line also speak to our commitment to student-centeredness.[29] The initiative sought to embrace students' primary opinion leaders, their families, into their experience, a shift in the late 20th century as students continued to become more reliant on their families' ideas and checkbooks.

This programming reflected Hardesty's desire to improve the experience he had as a WVU parent for other parents. He knew the administration must navigate the limitations in place with the Family Education Rights and Protection Act, a federal policy that protects the privacy of student records. Both the Mountaineer Parents Club and the Parent Helpline were established to support this effort.

Living and Learning Together

The Hardesty administration also sought to create a sense of belonging for new, first-year students by personalizing their first year on campus. The administration created the Resident Faculty Leader Program, living-learning communities that featured a faculty member residing in each residence hall to facilitate programming and offer mentorship, inspired by his time at the University of Oxford in the United Kingdom as a Rhodes Scholar, where a similar program existed. This initiative demonstrated the administration's aspiration to integrate students' residential experiences with their academic experiences, connecting students with well-respected faculty who could serve as resources and mentors.

This initiative highlights how the role of on-campus housing evolved in higher education during the 20th century overall. Once seen as a way to "[control] student behavior around the clock",[30] residence halls have since become a way to offer a more holistic approach to their development[31] and engage them in campus life,[32] which was reflected through the Residential Faculty Leader program and the living-learning communities that resulted from it.

Throughout Hardesty's presidency, these living-learning communities also evolved to include interest groups, where floors in the residence halls were dedicated to specific disciplines like engineering, nursing, and creative arts, and students took a course or courses together as a group. However, faculty in general were not supportive of the idea because of the extra time commitment, responsibility, and interaction with students that would be required. An Office of the President staffer recalled some complaints Hardesty received after introducing the idea in a faculty meeting:

> They were pushing back and grousing about the role of faculty and no business talking to the students and all that. And he said, "How many of you are parents of college students?" So, some hands go up. And he said, "How many of you are parents to students who go to WVU?" Some hands go down, some stay up. "How many of you have a student at WVU who lives in a residence hall?" And the way he tells the story, all but one hand goes down. This one person had their hand up. And he said, "What do you think?" And that person . . . said, "Implement this as fast as you can." And so, I think that gave

him the perseverance and had that real effect on folks that you may not think we need to do anything about this. . . . He felt like dorms were like warehouses where students were between classes.

While faculty in general did not support the Resident Faculty Leader program, Hardesty was able to gain enough interest and participation from influential faculty and administrators to launch it in some of the residence halls, and it grew over time.

This personalization of the student experience was also seen through New Student Convocation, launched in August 1995, a welcome event for all new WVU undergraduate students. At this event, Hardesty spoke on why he created the event and the goals he had for all WVU students, including embracing technology, learning communication skills, acquiring leadership skills, valuing diversity, preparing for society, making new friends, and connecting with the campus community, especially faculty and staff. He said,

> At WVU, most of you will begin a journey through the world of ideas. Your journey will truly transform you, and this convocation, this day, this event, reaffirms both our intent to help you make this journey and your commitment to make it through diligent study, exploration, and investigation.[33]

In 1998, three years after the student-centered initiative was first implemented, the administration established an academic standards and expectations committee to review the work of the student-centered university initiative and the goals and expectations WVU had set for undergraduates as part of it. The group conducted a study of undergraduate education literature and administered surveys to WVU faculty and students to assess the state of undergraduate education at WVU as it related to national trends. The Commission's most significant finding was that much more work needed to be done to revamp the first-year experience beyond just Operation Jump Start's initial efforts (see Becoming a Student-Centered University), and it recommended a required University orientation course for all new first-time, first-year students. The one-credit course, University 101, was intended to offer students resources and tools to aid their transition from high school to college. Initiatives were also established to help students writing and math skills, including the establishment of a Center for Writing Excellence and Institute for Math Learning.

Other new academic and student life initiatives included the relaunch of Festival of Ideas, a series bringing nationally known speakers to campus that was held in the 1960s when Hardesty served as student body president. According to the university's 2004 Accreditation Self-Study Report, speakers in the series at that time included Maya Angelou, Spike

Lee, and Kareem Abdul-Jabbar. WVUpAllNight, a weekly on-campus event for students on the weekends with free food and activities, was a new healthy entertainment option. In collaboration with the Student Government Association, the Mountaineer Maniacs was created as a student organization to promote positive school spirit and attendance at all University sporting events. The University also began a study of a long-term concern of addressing faculty, staff, and student day care concerns, and plans for a student recreation center were announced. An initiative was launched to address the needs of the university's growing nontraditional student population. The university also started collaborating with fraternities on national policies of their houses "going dry." These programs and activities represented all shared goals of elevating the university's scholarly reputation and overcoming its negative party school image, which is also engrained and celebrated in the university's tradition and culture by students and alumni alike, despite the negative publicity that abounds from the image it portrays, particularly through rankings from the Princeton Review and Playboy.

In his October 1998 State of the University Address, Hardesty shared some academic successes from the task force's work: the retention rate from freshman year to sophomore year retention improved to 80 percent, and academic suspensions decreased by 40 percent. From a campus culture perspective, he noted that residence hall occupancy was up from 80 percent in 1993 to full in 1998 and that the university dropped out of the Princeton Review's top 10 party school ranking after being ranked first the previous year. In terms of campus safety, total incident reports were down by 23 percent and vandalism reports were down by 30 percent in comparison to 1995 when his presidency began. Emergency room admissions of students during football weekends had also decreased by more than 50 percent in a year's time. This progress reflected his administration's initial motivations for putting the student experience first: "We must always remember to look to those we serve for guidance – students. Above all, we must remain student-centered. If we are to preserve the public trust, students must remain our primary focus."[34]

Hardesty came into the presidency with an immediate focus on the student experience with aspirations of increasing access to student experiences like he had in his own undergraduate career, from serving as student body president to winning the Rhodes Scholarship and studying at Oxford. This motivation is reflected through not only the administration's emphasis on student initiatives but the way they approached them – by gaining input from the students – and their families – directly. An advisor reflected,

> [Hardesty] came with some preconceived notions and some ideas, and that's not bad. If I'm interviewing you for a job, we hope you

come with some ideas. We don't just come and say wow, here, just lay here and grab the sun. What happened is [Hardesty] had an outstanding undergraduate career. His undergraduate experience was extraordinary for a lot of different reasons. What he tried to do was say how can every student at [WVU] have that same [experience].

Though the initiatives and programming evolved over time, students continued to be a priority for Hardesty and his administration throughout this time as president, even at the expense of other parts of the mission and University operations, including faculty and research. This change in campus culture reflected Hardesty's desire to emulate his unique undergraduate experiences and replicate those for as many students as possible and that his priority was on the student experience, even if that meant placing less emphasis and resources on other parts of the organization. It reflects the direction universities were pursuing in the 1990s and 2000s, seeking to make their campuses more appealing to a wider population of students (and their most influential opinion leaders – parents) and address their evolving needs with more resources, programs, and services.[35]

Raising the Standard in Research

WVU's research efforts were behind its peers by this time. Following World War II, WVU lost many opportunities to expand its footprint in higher education, including its research agenda and subsequent funding structure due to financial and governance restrictions from the state of West Virginia. State code prohibited West Virginia's public colleges and universities from accepting federally funded research grants and projects unless they could fund the contract up front. Because the federal government only reimbursed the research projects once they were complete, it was not financially feasible for WVU to fund these expensive research projects.

In addition, because the state, and subsequently the university, followed the fiscal calendar (i.e. July 1–June 30), it did not have the legal authority to commit beyond the funds currently available or carryover unspent balances into the next fiscal year because any available budget not spent was returned to the state treasury at the end of the current fiscal year.[36] Any federal grants coming to WVU were routed through the state treasurer's office, making any resources property of the state rather than the university.[37] These limitations hampered WVU from pursuing top-tier federal research funding, setting the institution back following World War II when other universities were gaining ground.

In contrast to other land-grant, research institutions, WVU had been trailing in research activity since World War II, when the federal government established research support through grant funding and infrastructure, including the establishment of the National Science Foundation.[38] While WVU's development and increasing enrollment mirrored national trends of postwar expansion toward massification during this time, a simultaneous trend was the separation between research universities and the undergraduate-focused colleges.[39]

With its research goals in place, WVU was caught in the middle of this separation. It sought to be among the major research universities but failed to make it into those ranks because of its inability to fund federal research grants and the lack of state support for those endeavors.

> Since WVU occupied a "muddled middle ground," not inconsequential but yet not among those institutions now "knocking on the door of greatness," competitors Penn State and Pittsburgh among them, the central issue facing WVU was how to position itself closer to that door of opportunity.[40]

The competition, particularly for research status and funding, is not unlike the competition seen in the higher education marketplace today not only for research status and funding, but enrollment and value in the public's view.[41]

Despite these challenges, Hardesty's administration viewed research as the foundation for carrying out the tenants of the land-grant mission and stressed the importance of connecting research's relevancy to state and national issues: "WVU's research mission cuts across every segment of the university and has increasingly been at the core of our land-grant institution's activities. It is our mechanism for learning and developing our knowledge base."[42] In response to these deficits, the administration established a research task force to review how WVU could continue growing and producing research focused research programs that aligned with the needs of West Virginians and contributed to the state's intellectual, social, cultural, and economic growth while also improving students' integration into the research process.[43]

The idea of focusing the university's research came about as a finding from the task force because the group believed "WVU can't be all things to all people" in its research efforts,[44] which was a stark contrast to the expansion of programming that "engaged society and serving West Virginia and the nation," identified later in the chapter, demonstrating how the administration prioritized each of these goals for carrying out its land-grant mission.

The research task force recommended that the university specialize in niche areas and target resources to those areas. Research was emphasized as the arm of the university that has most potential to make a difference in citizens' lives and in the economy. "The need for research has become more important to our security and economy. Therefore,

WVU must be increasingly aggressive to maintain a competitive edge in its research programs."[45]

The following focus areas were selected based on the university's existing strengths and resources, potential for funding, state industry needs, and potential for statewide economic and community development: Advanced Materials; Energy and Environment; Human Development and Culture; Information Technology; Local and Regional Economic Development; and Molecular and Biomedical Sciences. These focus areas were an opportunity to target specific research activities in ways that had an opportunity to influence and support economic development in the state, similar to the goals presented by Klein and Woodell[46] for land-grant, research universities aspiring to expand their economic development efforts, which demonstrated how research and innovation, human capital and talent development, and stewardship of place all intersect to inform the most potential for economic development activities between land-grant universities and their home communities:

> In this climate, we must make sure that as a land-grant institution, we are part of a culture of innovation. We must ask ourselves hard questions challenge the status quo and truly assess whether we can do more in or, to adapt to world changes.[47]

However, unsurprisingly, Hardesty's administration faced critique from faculty researching in disciplines not directly represented in the focus areas.

Other research goals included maintaining the university's status as a top 100 research university[48] and doubling research funding over a five-year period to ensure that continued designation. In 1997, WVU Research Corporation was established to streamline the university's research operations and support these goals. A former official from the Office of the Provost recounted,

> The Research Corp[oration] was set up as a way to quote circumvent state policies. It was a way to get more . . . flexibility with regard to our ability to hire. . . . The Research Corp[oration] was set up as a way to provide greater flexibility for our research faculty and the research projects and so it became the repository for grants and so forth.

The creation of WVU Research Corporation contributed to improving the university's organizational structure intended to make processes related to research more efficient.

A request-for-proposal was initiated in 1999 for a research park near the university's campus to support entrepreneurship and technological development. Its first phase was intended to have infrastructure for a

25,000 square foot business incubator to promote entrepreneurialism and provide services to small businesses, but it never materialized. The university's library repository and a federal building are currently located on the site. A former academic affairs administrator and dean discussed the delays in implementing the research park, saying,

> So, it never really took off. . . . We had many stops and starts with people who were going to help build the building. We were going to set up something, but we never got at the park initiated. It still sits there, and we've got money in the ground in terms of having all of the utilities and stuff ready to go. At some point in time somebody is going to figure out what to do with it. Right now, there's just no capacity to invest into it.

Despite the setback, research continued to grow in other ways. As of 2003,[49] the following increases had occurred in sponsored funding and research expenditures:

- 123 percent growth in total sponsored funding from 1999–2002
- 148 percent increase in funding from federal sources since 1998
- 53 percent increase in Health Sciences Center research expenditures from 1998–2002
- a research and development expenditures ranking of 121 out of 500 universities in 2000
- retention of the Carnegie Doctoral/Research University Extensive classification

Technology transfer was another way the Hardesty administration continued to expand research activities. While federal policies were passed several decades prior to "encourage the transfer of university technology to private industry," also called technology transfer,[50] WVU did not catch up to this shift until 1999, when the university created an Office of Technology Transfer. With the passage of the Bayh-Dohl Act in 1980, research universities began to capitalize by expanding resources to support tech transfer and "translating university research into innovations for economic development."[51] WVU eventually caught up to this trend. The office was staffed by business professionals trained to support the university's research and economic development activities. In four years, tech transfer activities on campus increased by 300 percent and two startup companies were founded.[52] A director of economic development role was added that same year. All of these tactics are comparable to the action items presented in Klein and Woodell's[53] recommendations for innovating research at public universities, reflecting new opportunities for faculty and staff to contribute to the university's research mission. They also contributed to elevating the university's national prestige because the rankings that accompanied them elevated the university's reputation and status.

Preparing for a New Millennium

As the year 2000 approached, colleges and universities recognized that their "viability would rest on building capacity for technology."[54] Without progress, every functional, operational aspect of the institution, such as enrollment, hiring, finances, data management, and infrastructure would be inhibited.

At WVU, the administration sought to improve businesses practices and data processing across campus and how those efforts were organized, including the Health Sciences Center and regional campuses, another strategy influenced by his business and legal background. The plan to reach this goal, Integration 2000, also reflected technical upgrades in preparation for the new millennium. A professor who worked on this plan shared how the plan operationalized the land-grant mission by connecting all parts of the university across the state. She recollected,

> It was really the first effort to say WVU needs to think of itself as a national player. . . . And that instead of being very strong regional presence, which certainly is part of the land-grant mission, that we should also be part of the sort of land-grant consortium and we should be a member at that table. That we as an institution were becoming more involved in that group that we wanted to see more of a network so that we weren't just the flagship university in this upper corner of the state but that we were really serving the entire state. And one of the ways we could do that would be by strengthening our connections with Keyser, Beckley, Parkersburg, and one of the things that made those connections more possible in the 1990s was technology so that it wasn't sort of a natural alliance to think about technology and a stronger alliance among regional campuses. . . . We've got these new technologies; we need to be embracing them. We need to be connecting as a whole network of campuses to serve our students.

This effort included email accounts for every student, library software updates, and the addition of Oracle software for all data processing, including payments. BANNER, a student information system, was implemented, which allowed for telephone registration and early progress toward web-based registration. All residence halls were wired for computer access, and various laptop computer programs were launched in academic units and the libraries. An interactive video network was added for remote classrooms to allow virtual students to communicate with their professors.

However, that faculty member is not confident Integration 2000 reached all of its intended goals due to budget challenges. She said, "But with the budget getting cut and cut again, it was hard to balance all those things. And it I don't know if the Integration 2000 project really achieved some of its goals. And I think part of the reason it may not have was that it was getting so hard to move forward on one front as the ground was getting undermined in terms of budget."

The financial strains placed on the university by the state's decreasing appropriations were just beginning. While the Hardesty administration attempted to move the university forward in terms of 21st-century technology and business practices across all campuses while navigating the scarce resources available, it came at a cost. At a time when high school graduates started to decrease nationally,[55] the university began to turn to out-of-state student recruitment for a larger student population and their accompanying greater tuition revenue, which directly resulted in critiques from in-state residents who eventually became nearly outnumbered in terms of enrollment. Simultaneously, that enrollment growth placed a strain on the one campus population that was not growing in size or in compensation – faculty. That would change, to a point, following more governance changes and mandates from the state government, discussed next.

Responding to Regulation and Privatization

Since World War II, WVU had been forced to "defend its status as the state's land-grant public university."[56] In contrast to many of the state's other higher education institution, by this point in history WVU had become a mature, complex land-grant university with a comprehensive mission and operation, differentiating itself from the state's other four-year colleges, many of which were first established as normal schools. However, the West Virginia State Legislature historically had a tendency to pursue a traditional centralized governance structure for all higher education institutions (modeled after the state's K–12 education system), which resulted in a homogenous approach to treating all higher education institutions the same, regardless of their missions, structures, enrollments, endowments, or other defining characteristics, demonstrating the state's inability to differentiate research institutions from state colleges and limiting WVU's operations, especially those related to finance and research.[57] This stratification was further complicated beginning in the mid-20th century as several West Virginia colleges received permission to rename themselves as universities. While WVU fought for autonomy,[58] this shift hindered for the institution for years to come as it faced obstacle after obstacle in pursuing its goal of becoming a premier national research university.

In the decades leading up to Hardesty's administration, state regulation, protest, and reform defined WVU as it struggled politically for less regulation and more autonomy while facing national pessimism about the efficacy of higher education. The movement toward massification after the post-World War II baby boom followed by stagnating enrollments resulting in revenue declines and consideration of reductions in employees and programs only added to the negative attitudes toward higher education nationally[59] as well as in West Virginia.

Simultaneously, the financial framework for funding American higher education began to shift in two ways: a steady decrease in state appropriations for public universities, coupled with an increasing dependence on tuition income and an increased burden on students through loans.[60] While these shifts took effect more slowly in West Virginia, most significantly in the 2000s and 2010s, the state eventually caught up. In fiscal year 2015, West Virginia cut higher education more than any other state except Wyoming, decreasing the per-student funding by more than 20 percent since the 2008 recession.[61]

As part of the first round of ongoing cuts to state appropriations in the early 2000s, new state legislation shaped the Hardesty administration's decision making by calling for improved efficiencies and emphasis on quality. With objectives of developing high quality and economically relevant educational opportunities statewide, focusing resources on programs and courses that offered the most viable career opportunities for students, and providing competitive salaries to all employees, new legislation, Senate Bill 547, called for the university to create a plan to reallocate $32 million of its existing budget over five years to meet legislative mandates.[62]

A subsequent policy change, Senate Bill 653, called for universities to create a campus compact describing how they were efficiently spending their state budget allocations. An Office of the President staffer reflected on the resource challenges:

> It's all of a sudden we get hit again, and we're like, "Ugh." We had already done some of what you call the low hanging fruit and some of those things. So that became difficult. . . . We just had cuts and cuts.

Meanwhile, WVU's accreditor, the Higher Learning Commission, mandated that the administration pursue a formal strategic planning process. This mandate was part of the nationwide movement during this time to justify the outcomes of higher education to the public to demonstrate how their tax dollars were being invested, with many policy institutes and governing bodies requiring assessments of learning outcomes.[63] In response to these policy changes, the Hardesty administration pursued organizational initiatives to make the day-to-day operations of the university more efficient, especially in the context of preparing the institution's technology for the next millennium (see previous section) and navigating the decreases in state appropriations. This strategy reflected Hardesty's business-oriented and legal background, which continued to reflect a political leadership style characterized by navigating situations with scarce resources.[64] As these initiatives were implemented, Hardesty also called on other higher education leaders in West Virginia to do respond accordingly.

> To insure WVU will be poised to serve the state and nation in the next millennium, we must continue to invest in our future. . . . During this time of rapid change, West Virginia University must remain an agile, responsive, and flexible institution which views these challenges as opportunities to increase its role and maximize its contribution to the ever-changing needs of society. . . . During this time of change, it will be important for those of us at West Virginia University to establish clear priorities and focus our resources on meeting objectives which directly reflect these priorities. . . . If WVU is to remain a strong and healthy institution, we must manage and administer, efficiently and effectively at every level. Institutions which continually evaluate their administrative performance and identify opportunities for improvement will be better prepared to face the challenges of change.[65]

The "challenges of change" Hardesty referenced included decreasing federal and state appropriations; the decreasing West Virginia population, including high school enrollment; changes to technology, especially in preparation for the year 2000; state mandates for salary increases; the increasing number of nontraditional students; increased calls for accountability (from students, parents, and government officials); and ongoing changes to the global economy. These fit into challenges facing higher education nationally at the time as identified by Duderstadt,[66] which included the hypercompetitive, global, knowledge-driven economy that requires a highly skilled, trained, and educated workforce (that only a college education can provide); continuing to define higher education as a public good amid decreasing public support and funding; and the nation's changing demographics and growing diversity without the appropriate mobilization of educational opportunities for the entire workforce. Forest and Kinser[67] echoed these challenges, identifying several factors that constrain presidents and limit the degrees of freedom in their leadership, including competing and conflicting organizational goals, federal and state policy and/or governance; expanding internal governance, public criticism, accountability, changing student markets, among others.

To address these obstacles, Hardesty's administration made recommendations for organizational structures and processes and internal and external collaborations. He reflected that this more customer-centered approach to leadership and organization reflected the university's striving to flatten layers of the administration and consolidate overlapping units for consistency,[68] another example of his leadership response inspired by his political, business, and legal background to address scarce resources for the university.[69]

Many of the cost-savings initiatives were met with dissent from faculty, staff, and students who felt that the decisions were made from the top-down rather than with input from the campus community. A faculty senator was quoted to this effect in WVU's campus newspaper, *The Daily Athenaeum*, "The tradition at the University is that they make the decision with the input of faculty, staff, and students. In this process, people felt left out."[70]

The biggest loser in the budget cuts may have very well been one of the most famed traditions in WVU history – the national championship rifle team. The sport was celebrated as a reflection of the state's rural, pro-Second Amendment heritage and further espoused by the university's mountaineer mascot image. One of five Division I-A athletic teams to be cut in 2003 as a cost savings due to the athletic department running on a deficit,[71] the elimination of the sport tarnished Hardesty's otherwise "heroic" presidency.[72] While the rifle team was restored in 2009 during James Clements's presidency with support from a line item in the state's budget[73] and has since produced an Olympic gold medalist in Ginny Thrasher, its initial disbanding wreaked havoc across the state of West Virginia, causing an outcry from alumni, donors and fans alike from Wheeling to Welch and everywhere in between.

> The backlash was immediate. Students fired off e-mails. Alumni collected 9,000 signatures on a petition demanding the team's return. The National Rifle Association wrote letters disputing the university's claim that the sport was too costly. (The team's $163,000 budget accounted for less than 1 percent of the athletic department budget.) And most team members refused to stop practicing and formed a club instead.[74]

This was just one example of the Hardesty administration's strategies for cost-savings and improved efficiencies. Because of the pressures from the purse-strappings of the state government, the idea of "focus"[75] permeated this period of Hardesty's presidency, reflecting the strategy of focusing the university's operations as a way of navigating through the budget challenges and governance expectations. The University responded by establishing Executive Business Offices to streamline financial operations, reorganizing human resources, combining food operations in the residence halls and student union, merging the facilities planning and physical plant units, merging computer science and computer engineering programs, and refinancing auxiliary bonds.

These examples of the state's disinvestment in public higher education highlights what Peters[76] describes as a counter-narrative to the land-grant mission. These competing ideas and interests take away from the potential impact land-grant institutions can have in their respective states, WVU included.

A strategy the Hardesty administration employed to continue seeking operational efficiencies and cost-savings in response to this period of scarce resources[77] due to decreasing state support was reorganizing the university's administrative structure. Two major organizational changes occurred at the university within two years of this initiative's release. The acquisition and merger of West Virginia Technical Institute in Montgomery, West Virginia, to become part of the WVU system was completed in 1997, which was met with significant discontent from that institution and community.[78] This effort was also managed by a task force approach. A faculty member who was a part of it reflected on the experience: "I would honestly say I don't think that the implementation was very successful because I don't think the Tech people were willing to make the commitment that needed to be done. It was a very unfriendly student environment, and they were not willing to make it more student friendly." Also in 1997, WVU formed a partnership with United Hospital Center in Clarksburg, West Virginia, which eventually evolved and expanded to what is known today as WVU Medicine. Hardesty reflected on the latter as an opportunity to increase access to healthcare for more West Virginia residents: "We are better serving West Virginians through access to higher education and healthcare while bolstering our support around the state."[79]

These organizational initiatives focused on administrative efficiencies represented Hardesty's innovative infusion of his legal and business background, characterized by organizational and operational efficiency, into the traditionally decentralized organization of higher education.[80] In response to ongoing cuts to state appropriations for higher education by the West Virginia State Legislature, he sought to frame WVU as a leader and model in business practices by sharing recommendations with not only leaders at WVU but higher education leaders across the state about how to restructure their operations to be more flexible and adaptable and, simultaneously, less bureaucratic. These recommendations offer a contrast to some critiques of his administration, which focused on the growing size of Hardesty's own leadership team and increasing reporting lines to the presidency, commonly seen in leadership teams during this period through the idea of "administrative bloat."[81] Similar recommendations would continue to be presented and employed throughout Hardesty's presidency as the university faced continued cuts to its state appropriations, requiring more resourceful-ness in budget management.

Engaging Society and Expanding the Extension Service

Despite the strained relations with the state government, the Hardesty administration still sought to bolster its relationship with and support of communities around the state. An integral part of the university's land-grant mission, one of the ways WVU carried it out was through community partnerships, including through the Extension Service. As McDowell[82] was calling for a change in direction in the relationship between land-grant universities and their communities because of what he saw as a failed Extension Service system, and others called for public universities to recommit to community engagement,[83] WVU attempted to innovate and expand the work of its Extension Service and establish more community partnerships.

Hardesty often publicly shared his perspective of the university's role in society in speeches by quoting former WVU President Irvin Stewart, saying "The state is our campus." For example, in a state of the university address[84] he remarked, "We must demonstrate to all of West Virginia our clear intention to view the state as our campus and to become more valuable to our state and the nation." He also said the following year,

> In a state where mountainous terrain creates formidable natural bar-riers between regions, the concept of remoteness is very real. Yet WVU serves all the people of West Virginia, not just those living in a particular region or a few population centers.[85]

These quotations reflect the motivation behind the administration's long-term goal of "engaging society."

Just like in the earlier sections about students, research, technology, and finance, the first major initiative toward pursuing this goal was establishing an Extension task force. Hardesty brought in Lawrence Cote from Pennsylvania State University to lead WVU Extension Ser-vice, who added new areas of focus for the Extension Service: work-force education and job accommodation, sustainable agriculture and agromedicine, food safety and nutrition, and child care. A staffer in the Office of the President reflected on the work of the task force and its efforts to improve Extension's operational efficiency and commu-nications. She shared that one of the most significant changes was reorganizing the infrastructure in the WVU Extension Service from a regional office format to focus more on programming in specialized subject matter areas, particularly after the advent of email connected the county offices with the Morgantown campus more than ever before. She explained,

> If I work in [agriculture], I'd rather have a really good subject matter expert that I can call upon. Youth development and health. Whatever their areas are. I'd rather call upon that and not have this money spent in the bureaucratic infrastructure. And so that was one of the bigger recommendations was that those offices went away. And they did try to create some more specialists in those areas.

While the reorganization was intended to save money and improve the efficiency of WVU Extension's operations in response to the ongoing budget restraints, the decision to eliminate the regional offices was met with criticism because there were fewer leadership positions around the state. This change is a direct contradiction to some recommendations for how public universities can serve their communities[86] and how land-grant universities can continue to engage with their communities, such as the campus doing more than sharing "physical space" with the town by meeting with community leaders to identify their needs.[87] The decision to move Extension Service personnel out of their home communities is also comparable to what McDowell[88] describes as abandoning the social contract with the communities.

However, despite the structural limitations from removing the regional offices, 90 percent of the task force's 95 recommendations were accomplished by 2000.[89] By 1998, 4-H, the Extension Service's youth development and leadership program, was serving more than 40,000 youth around the state annually, and that number grew to more than 56,000 by 2003.[90] The Extension Service introduced a Youth Entrepreneurship Program for elementary school-age 4-H members, which was facilitated by elementary school teachers.[91] During this time, the Extension Service increased its sponsored research funding from just under $1 million in FY 1998 to $5.3 million in FY 2003, which featured a tourism project linked to forest heritage assets across the state, flood recovery and disaster prevention efforts, and risk management strategies for farmers.[92]

In addition to the Extension Service's programmatic expansion, healthcare was another way the university "engaged society" during this time. Tens of thousands of patients were served annual through WVU's hospitals, regional campuses, and a new partnership with a regional hospital center.[93] These partnerships and collaborations reflected the Hardesty administration's expansion of university community engagement to include partnerships West Virginia citizens, local businesses, nonprofit organizations, other higher education institutions, and government entities, striving to overcome the negative "ivory tower" perception of the university around the state.

Investing in the Land-Grant Mission: Navigating External and Environmental Issues

Throughout their tenure, Hardesty and his leadership team identified several broad external issues impacting decision-making at higher education institutions, especially WVU: the globalizing economy, increasing job market competitiveness for college graduates, communications and technology revolution, erosion of social responsibility and loss of civic responsibility among young adults, emergence of educational competitors (e.g. for-profit institutions, industry, etc.), and healthcare reform costs.[94] These challenges were consistent with those Duderstadt[95] acknowledged in his descriptions of societal challenges facing higher education leaders.

These challenges reflect the state of higher education during this time period, one ridden with changing market demands and external environmental influences.[96] The administration framed many of their initiatives and task forces in response to these issues. Hardesty called for WVU to become a "high-performance university," identified characteristics of high-performance organizations, and made recommendations for how leaders should act on them.[97] This included becoming other-centered, or focused more on the campus community that the university serves (e.g. students, customers, patients, clients, community members, and research sponsors); engaging with and continually learning from society (through areas like job creation, economic development, welfare reform, healthcare, education, and technology); narrowing research focus to areas that reflect the university's strength and opportunities for research development; emphasizing human development and teamwork through initiatives like improving internal communication and encouraging collaboration and appreciation; and differentiating from the competition. One executive leadership team member recalled how Hardesty's experience in law and business framed his motivations for efficient management of University operations in response to these external contexts: "I think that the effort there was to try to get us to sort of think outside the box about how we can become more efficient and more effective. And I think those words efficiency and effectiveness have, have just ridden through the change of time because we still talk about it today."

Hardesty often spoke of how engaging with the land-grant mission could help WVU navigate these external and environmental challenges facing higher education, similar to Crow and Dabars's perspective in their conceptualization of the "New American University".[98] For instance, in his inaugural address, Hardesty said, "It has always had the same mission: teaching, research, and service. The manner in which it has met its mission, however, has in large measure been determined in the context of events influencing it at various times in its history. Our generation of leadership at West Virginia University is challenged today, just as prior generations of leadership have been challenged."[99] This quote captures the way Hardesty and his leadership team continued to frame their approach to addressing challenges through the lens of the land-grant mission throughout their tenure.

Conclusion

With the public confidence in higher education continuing to decline,[100] it is more important than ever for public universities to demonstrate their value to their communities and citizens. Because of their inherent mission of community engagement and service, land-grant universities, in particular, are responsible for taking the lead in redefining this social contract with the public[101] and identify new ways to work with, rather than for, the community through their research, teaching, and service missions. "The Morrill Act funded an idea – the pursuit of an ideal to expand access to quality higher education and to purpose higher education with the responsibility to advance community and social prosperity through all of its meanings."[102] An intentional assessment of mission, leadership, and community engagement strategies is an opportunity to carry out that responsibility.

Coming into the presidency as an outsider, someone whose curriculum vitae did not reflect that of what was typical or expected of a university president, Hardesty faced many of these challenges from the start. His recognition of this outsider status and the criticism he faced, especially from faculty, was important for navigating the early part of his administration as he kicked off a major initiative, namely, becoming a student-centered university, on the first day of his presidency.

Despite the transitional challenges, Hardesty used his nontraditional political, business, and legal background to empower his leadership team to shift WVU's focus from reactive, status-quo operations to embodying and innovating the tripartite land-grant mission, which reflected how the administration sought to innovate and transform WVU into a modern land-grant university focused on the future. However, these efforts were still met with criticism, especially from faculty who were expected to do "more" beyond their traditional workload as the university shifted to a more student-centered culture. The new student-focused initiatives modernized retention, safety, and processes like financial aid, advising, and registration while building relationships with parents and improving WVU's reputation for prospective students across the state.

The establishment of WVU Research Corporation gave faculty the flexibility to pursue major funding opportunities from the federal government and national organizations, making WVU a research competitor in the national marketplace for the first time. Organizational changes to WVU Extension Service, despite facing many criticisms, helped identify programming needs and focus priorities in West Virginia communities, making WVU a more familiar partner in the communities around West Virginia. Simultaneously, a comprehensive strategic plan featuring modernized technology and facilities and a focus on efficient business operations reflected a modern university becoming a player in the national arena while responding to austerity and frequent state governance changes.

Broadly, this case could be used as a model for other land-grant universities and presidents of those institutions to inform their own approaches to mission-building and strategic planning. It also contributes to the broader literature on community engagement and universities in terms of how higher education institutions define their relationships with their communities and contribute to them.

In terms of leadership, this study highlights the importance of maintaining an awareness of institutional history and current situational analysis for new leaders – not just presidents, but other executive and academic leadership as well as governing board members. This study demonstrates the role of qualitative research and perspectives within a given institution that go beyond learning what the university appears to be like via a website, brochure, or video to convey the genuine pulse and direction of the campus. For leaders broadly, it also informs possible strategies for navigating the expectations of different stakeholders with differing priorities.

This study also contributes to the leadership literature in terms of the way the role of the president has evolved over time, especially the expectations of nontraditional presidents. Especially amid the pressures of budget strains and reliance on tuition dollars and private funding, the assumed roles and responsibilities of the university presidency have changed, becoming more externally focused. University presidents are expected to be the face of the institution, representing it to a variety of external stakeholders, including alumni and donors, community leaders, federal, state, and local government officials, and more. As a result, presidents have also become more reliant on their executive leadership team members, particular the provost, to manage the internal, day-to-day responsibilities. For example, the provost in Hardesty's administration was relied on to assume many of the strategic planning responsibilities, and the administration began expanding the role and power of the student affairs division by moving the locus of control as the student affairs leader was moved into its own reporting line to the president rather than the provost. This position has since evolved to the title of dean of students/vice president of student affairs. All of these shifts reflect administrative bloat, with the expanding roles and responsibility of leadership in the organization.

While this presidency was initially framed by significant criticism and doubt, Hardesty is remembered on WVU's campus today by many of the participants interviewed as an innovative, heroic leader,[103] someone who persevered and overcame much conflict as he sincerely attempted to modernize WVU and put the "student-centered" university on the national map, particularly in the wake of declining state support and market changes.

Notes

1. Scott Beardsley, *Higher Calling: The Rise of Nontraditional Leaders in Academia* (Charlottesville, VA: University of Virginia Press, 2017).
2. Tressie McMillan Cottom, Sally S. Hunnicutt, and Jennifer A. Johnson, "The Ties That Corporatize: A Social Network Analysis of University Presidents as Vectors of Higher Education Corporatization," *SocArXiv*, May 2018, https://doi.org/10.31235/osf.io/wpcfq.
3. Roger Geiger, *American Higher Education Since World War II* (Princeton, NJ: Princeton University Press, 2019).
4. Beardsley, *Higher Calling*.
5. Predecessor Neil Bucklew had served for nine years prior.
6. West Virginia University College of Law, "David C. Hardesty, Jr," www.law.wvu.edu/faculty-staff/emeriti-faculty/david-c-hardesty Accessed January 22, 2020.
7. Ron Lewis, *Aspiring to Greatness: West Virginia University Since World War II* (Morgantown, WV: West Virginia University Press, 2013).
8. At this time, WVU's organizational structured included three regional campuses (i.e. Potomac State College, WVU Institute of Technology, and WVU-Parkersburg), as well as 12 academic colleges and schools.
9. David C. Hardesty, *Statement of Presidential Assessment in Connection with the Board of Trustees' Presidential Evaluation* (Morgantown, WV: West Virginia University, 1999).
10. Lee G. Bolman and Terrance E. Deal, *Reframing Organizations: Artistry, Choice, and Leadership* (San Francisco, CA: Jossey-Bass, 2013); Kathleen Manning, *Organizational Theory in Higher Education Policy* (New York, NY: Routledge, 2013).
11. David C. Hardesty, *Leading the Public University: Essays, Speeches, and Commentary* (Morgantown, WV: West Virginia University Press, 2007), 43.
12. Bolman and Deal, *Reframing Organizations*, 188.
13. Scott E. Masten, "Authority and Commitment: Why Universities, Like Legislatures, are Not Organized as Firms," *Journal of Economics & Management Strategy* 15, no. 3 (January 2005): 649–684, http://dx.doi.org/10.2139/ssrn.224624.
14. Burton R. Clark, "Belief and Loyalty in College Organization," *The Journal of Higher Education* 42, no. 6 (June 1971): 449–515, https://doi.org/10.1080/00221546.1971.11774879; Burton R. Clark, "The Organizational Saga in Higher Education," *Administrative Science Quarterly* 17, no. 2 (June 1972): 178–184, https://doi.org/10.2307/2393952.
15. Jack Knott and A. Abigail Payne, "The Impact of State Governance Structures on Management and Performance of Public Organizations: A Study of Higher Education Institutions," *Journal of Policy Analysis and Management* 23, no. 1 (December 2004): 13–30, https://doi.org/10.1002/pam.10176.
16. John R. Thelin, *A History of American Higher Education* (Baltimore, MD: The Johns Hopkins University Press, 2011).
17. Geiger, *American Higher Education Since World War II*.

18. Roger L. Geiger, "The Ten Generations of American Higher Education," in *American Higher Education in the 21st Century: Social, Political, and Economic Challenges*, eds. Philip G. Altbach, Patricia J. Gumport, and Robert O. Berdahl (Baltimore, MD: Johns Hopkins University Press, 2011), 37–68.

19. Gwendolyn Dungy and Stephanie A. Gordon, "The Development of Student Affairs," in *Student Services: A Handbook for the Profession*, eds. John H. Schuh, Susan R. Jones, Shaun R. Harper, and Associates (San Francisco, CA: Jossey-Bass, 2011), 61–79.

20. Ibid.

21. Ibid.

22. West Virginia University Student Affairs Task Force, *Student Affairs Task Force Report* (Morgantown, WV: West Virginia University, 1996).

23. David C. Hardesty, "State of the University Address," (speech, West Virginia University, Morgantown, WV, January 16, 1996).

24. West Virginia University, *Self-Study Submitted to the Higher Learning Commission of the North Central Association of Colleges and Schools* (Morgantown, WV: West Virginia University, 2004), https://accreditation.wvu.edu/files/d/94dc0a40-7db7-4c25-a4c1-e4f1e73f0440/hlc-wvu-self-study-2004.pdf.

25. Associated Press, "WVU Creates Panel to Raise Standards," *Weirton Daily Times*, May 14, 1998, 3A; Lewis, *Aspiring to Greatness*.

26. Dungy and Gordon, "The Development of Student Affairs."

27. Ibid.

28. Ibid.

29. West Virginia University, *Self-Study Submitted to the Higher Learning Commission*.

30. Kristen A. Renn and Lori D. Patton, "Campus Ecology and Environments," in *Student Services: A Handbook for the Profession*, eds. John H. Schuh, Susan R. Jones, Shaun R. Harper, and Associates (San Francisco, CA: Jossey-Bass, 2011), 242–256.

31. Robert D. Reason and Ellen M. Broido, "Philosophies and Values," in *Student Services: A Handbook for the Profession*, eds. John H. Schuh, Susan R. Jones, Shaun R. Harper, and Associates (San Francisco, CA: Jossey-Bass, 2011), 80–95.

32. Linda J. Sax and Cassandra E. Harper, "Using Research to Inform Practice," in *Student Services: A Handbook for the Profession*, eds. John H. Schuh, Susan R. Jones, Shaun R. Harper, and Associates (San Francisco, CA: Jossey-Bass, 2011), 499–514.

33. David C. Hardesty, "Building a High-Performance Organization at West Virginia University," (speech, West Virginia University, Morgantown, WV, March 5, 1997).

34. David C. Hardesty, "State of the University Address," (speech, West Virginia University, Morgantown, WV, October 6, 1998).

35. Dungy and Gordon, "The Development of Student Affairs."

36. Irvin Stewart, *West Virginia University 1946–1958: A Report Covering the Administration of Irvin Stewart as president of the University July 1, 1946–June 30, 1958* (Morgantown, WV: West Virginia University, 1958); Lewis, *Aspiring to Greatness*.

37. Lewis, *Aspiring to Greatness*.

38. Thelin, *A History of American Higher Education*.

39. Roger L. Geiger and Nathan M. Sorber, *The Land-Grant Colleges and the Reshaping of American Higher Education* (New Brunswick, NJ: Transaction Publishers, 2013).

40. Lewis, *Aspiring to Greatness*, 74; Paul Miller, "WVU Council of Administration Retreat Remarks," (lecture, West Virginia University, Morgantown, WV, April 13, 1964).

41. James J. Duderstadt, "Creating the Future: The Promise of Public Research Universities for America," in *Precipice or Crossroads?* eds. Daniel Mark Fogel and Elizabeth Malso-Huddle (Albany, NY: SUNY Press, 2012), 221–240.
42. David C. Hardesty, "State of the University Address," (speech, West Virginia University, Morgantown, WV, February 10, 1997).
43. West Virginia University, *Self-Study Submitted to the Higher Learning Commission.*
44. Ibid.
45. West Virginia University, *Overview of West Virginia University for New Members of the University System Board of Trustees* (Morgantown, WV: West Virginia University, 1999).
46. Eva Klein and Jim Woodell, *Higher Education Engagement in Economic Development: Foundations for Strategy and Practice* (Washington, DC: Association of Public and Land-Grant Universities, 2015), www.aplu.org/library/higher-education-engagement-in-economic-development-foundations-for-strategy-and-practice/file.
47. David C. Hardesty, "State of the University Address," (speech, West Virginia University, Morgantown, WV, 2005).
48. West Virginia University, *Overview of West Virginia University for New Members.*
49. David C. Hardesty, *Statement of Presidential Assessment in Connection with the Four-Year Presidential Evaluation* (Morgantown, WV: West Virginia University, 2003).
50. Geiger, "The Ten Generations of American Higher Education."
51. Geiger, *American Higher Education Since World War II*, 273.
52. Hardesty, *Statement of Presidential Assessment in Connection.*
53. Klein and Woodell, *Higher Education Engagement in Economic Development.*
54. Daryl G. Smith, "The Diversity Imperative Moving to the Next Generation," in *American Higher Education in the 21st Century: Social, Political, and Economic Challenges*, eds. Philip G. Altbach, Patricia J. Gumport, and Robert O. Berdahl (Baltimore, MD: Johns Hopkins University Press, 2011), 465–490.
55. Geiger, *American Higher Education Since World War II.*
56. Lewis, *Aspiring to Greatness*, 52.
57. Lorimer Victor Cavins and David Kirby, *A Study of the Clientele of the Institutions of Higher Education in West Virginia* (Charleston, WV: State Board of Education, 1939).
58. Lewis, *Aspiring to Greatness.*
59. Geiger and Sorber, *The Land-Grant Colleges and the Reshaping of American Higher Education.*
60. Geiger, *American Higher Education Since World War II.*
61. Michael Mitchell, Vincent Palacios, and Michael Leachman, "States are Still Funding Higher Education Below Pre-Recession Levels," *Center on Budget and Policy Priorities*, May 1, 2014, www.cbpp.org/research/states-are-still-funding-higher-education-below-pre-recession-levels?fa=view&id=4135.
62. West Virginia University, *Self-Study Submitted to the Higher Learning.*
63. Geiger, *American Higher Education Since World War II.*
64. Bolman and Deal, *Reframing Organizations*; Manning, *Organizational Theory in Higher Education Policy.*
65. David C. Hardesty, *Administrative Organization Initiatives* (Morgantown, WV: West Virginia University, 1995).
66. James J. Duderstadt, "Aligning American Higher Education with a Twenty-First-Century Public Agenda," *Higher Education in Europe* 34, no. 3–4 (2009): 347–366, https://doi.org/10.1080/03797720903355612.
67. James J.F. Forest and Kevin Kinser, *Higher Education in the United States: An Encyclopedia* (Santa Barbara, CA: ABC-CLIO, 2002).

68. David C. Hardesty, "West Virginia Higher Education and West Virginia University: Driving Forces that Propel the Development of West Virginia," (speech, Executive with Executive Conference, West Virginia, April 11–13, 1996).

69. Bolman and Deal, *Reframing Organizations*; Manning, *Organizational Theory in Higher Education Policy.*

70. Jill Sieracki, "COMER/COE Merger Discussed at Meeting," *The Daily Athenaeum*, April 19, 1995.

71. Shelly Anderson, "WVU Cuts: We Feel 'Lost,' " *Pittsburgh Post-Gazette*, April 20, 2003, http://old.post-gazette.com/sports/wvu/20030420wvucuts0420p4. asp.

72. Lloyd Moman Basham, "Transformational and Transactional Leaders in Higher Education," *SAM Advanced Management Journal* 77, no. 2 (Spring 2012): 15–37.

73. Liz Clarke, "Buoyed by Public Support, West Virginia Rifle Team Returns to NCAA Prominence," *Washington Post*, December 15, 2009, www.washingtonpost. com/wp-dyn/content/article/2009/12/14/AR2009121401462.html.

74. Ibid.

75. Hardesty, *Administrative Organization.*

76. Scott J. Peters, "Storying and Restorying the Land-Grant System," in *The Land-Grant Colleges and the Reshaping of American Higher Education*, eds. Roger L. Geiger and Nathan M. Sorber (New Brunswick, NJ: Transaction Publishers, 2013), 335–354.

77. Karl E. Weick, "Educational Organizations as Loosely-Coupled Systems," *Administrative Science Quarterly* 21, no. 1 (March 1976): 1–19, http://doi. org/10.2307/2391875; Bolman and Deal, *Reframing Organizations.*

78. James M. Owston, "Survival of the Fittest? The Re-Branding of West Virginia Higher Education," *International Journal of Educational Advancement* 9, no. 3 (December 2009): 126–146, https://doi.org/10.1057/ijea.2009.37.

79. David C. Hardesty, "State of the University Address," (speech, West Virginia University, Morgantown, WV, September 8, 1997).

80. Duderstadt, "Aligning American Higher Education with a Twenty-First-Century Public Agenda."

81. Knott and Payne, "The Impact of State Governance Structures on Management and Performance of Public Organizations."

82. George R. McDowell, *Land-Grant Universities and Extension Into the 21st Century: Renegotiating or Abandoning a Social Contract* (Ames, IA: Iowa State University Press, 2001).

83. Kevin P. Reilly, "The Engaged Institution, the Twenty-First Century, and the New University Extension," *Journal of Higher Education Outreach and Engagement* 8, no. 1 (Fall 2002/Winter 2003): 29–35, https://openjournals.libs.uga. edu/jheoe/article/view/804; Stephen M. Gavazzi, "Engaged Institutions, Responsiveness, and Town-Gown Relationships: Why Deep Culture Change Must Emphasize the Gathering of Community Feedback," *Planning for Higher Education Journal* 43, no. 4 (July–September 2015): 1–9, www.scup.org/ resource/engaged-institutions-responsiveness-and-town-gown-relationships; Klein and Woodell, *Higher Education Engagement in Economic Development*; Sarah M. Brackmann, "Community Engagement in a Neoliberalism Paradigm," *Journal of Higher Education Outreach and Engagement* 19, no. 4 (Spring 2015): 115, http://openjournals.libs.uga.edu/index.php/jheoe/article/ view/1533; Hiram E. Fitzgerald, Karen Bruns, Steven T. Sonka, Andrew Furco, and Louis Swanson, "The Centrality of Engagement in Higher Education," *Journal of Higher Education Outreach and Engagement* 16, no. 3 (September 2012): 7–27, https://openjournals.libs.uga.edu/jheoe/article/ view/949.

84. David C. Hardesty, "State of the University Address," (speech, West Virginia University, Morgantown, WV, February 10, 1997).

85. David C. Hardesty, "State of the University Address," (speech, West Virginia University, Morgantown, WV, February 1998).

86. Clark, "Belief and Loyalty in College Organization"; Clark, "The Organizational Saga in Higher Education."

87. Gavazzi, "Engaged Institutions, Responsiveness, and Town-Gown Relationships."

88. McDowell, *Land-Grant Universities and Extension Into the 21st Century.*

89. Hardesty, *Statement of Presidential Assessment in Connection.*

90. Ibid.

91. Ibid.

92. Ibid.

93. David C. Hardesty, "State of the University Address," (speech, West Virginia University, Morgantown, WV, February 1998).

94. Hardesty, "Building a High-Performance Organization at West Virginia University."

95. Duderstadt, "Aligning American Higher Education with a Twenty-First-Century Public Agenda."

96. Geiger, *American Higher Education Since World War II.*

97. David C. Hardesty, "Building a High-Performance Organization at West Virginia University," (speech, West Virginia University, Morgantown, WV, March 5, 1997).

98. Michael M. Crow and William B. Dabars. *Designing the New American University* (Baltimore, MD: Johns Hopkins University Press, 2015).

99. David C. Hardesty, "State of the University Address," (speech, West Virginia University, Morgantown, WV, September 8, 1997).

100. Jeffrey M. Jones, "Confidence in Higher Education Down Since 2018," *Gallup,* October 9, 2018, https://news.gallup.com/opinion/gallup/242441/confidence-higher-education-down-2015.aspx.

101. McDowell, *Land-Grant Universities and Extension Into the 21st Century.*

102. John Hudzik and Simon, Lou Anna K, "From a Land-Grant to a World-Grant Ideal," in *Precipice or Crossroads?* eds. Daniel Mark Fogel and Elizabeth Malso-Huddle (Albany, NY: SUNY Press, 2012), 159–196.

103. Rita Bornstein, "Redefining Presidential Leadership in the 21st Century," *The Presidency* 5, no. 3 (Fall 2002): 16–19, https://search.proquest.com/docview/216471800?accountid=2837.

Notes on Contributors

Editor

Nathan M. Sorber is Department Chairperson and Associate Professor of higher education at West Virginia University. He is the author of *Land-Grant Colleges and Popular Revolt: The Origins of the Morrill Act and the Reform of Higher Education* (Cornell University Press, 2018), coeditor of *American Higher Education in the Postwar Era* (Routledge, 2017), and coeditor of *Land-Grant Colleges and the Reshaping of American Higher Education* (Transaction Press, 2013). He is the series editor of *Perspectives on the History of Higher Education* and has published pieces in the *Higher Education Handbook of Theory and Research, International Encyclopedia of Higher Education, Handbook of Universities and Regional Development, History of Education Quarterly, Agricultural History,* and other journals.

Contributors

Bryan McAllister-Grande received his EdD from the Harvard Graduate School of Education, where he studied intellectual history and higher education with Julie Reuben and Andrew Jewett. He is the assistant director for curriculum integration at Northeastern University. His interests include intellectual and cultural history, internationalization of higher education, and research methodology. His work has appeared in the *Society for U.S. Intellectual History Blog*, in publications on the future of International Higher Education, and in the *History of Knowledge Blog.*

Christine A. Ogren is an associate professor in the Department of Educational Leadership and Policy Studies at the University of Iowa. She is a former president of the History of Education Society, coeditor of *Rethinking Campus Life: New Perspectives on the History of College Students in the United States* (2018), and author of *The American State Normal School: "An Instrument of Great Good"* (2005) and articles in *Paedagogica*

Historica, History of Education Quarterly, Higher Education: Handbook of Theory and Research, and other journals.

Ethan W. Ris is an assistant professor in the College of Education at the University of Nevada, Reno. His work on the history of higher education has appeared in the *Journal of Higher Education, Teachers College Record*, and *History of Education*. He is the recipient of a 2020 Fellowship from the National Endowment for the Humanities. Ris holds a PhD from Stanford University.

Kate Rousmaniere is a professor of the social foundations of education who teaches the history and philosophy of education to K–12 educators and higher education staff. She has published widely on the history of American teachers and school principals, and on methodological issues in the history of education. A former City Council member and Mayor of the City of Oxford Ohio (2011–2019), she is currently engaged in the work of furthering town-gown relations in college towns, addressing high conflict issues of off campus student housing, student alcohol use, and economic development.

Sam F. Stack Jr. is a professor of social and cultural foundations at West Virginia University where he teaches history of American education, philosophy of education, and philosophy of research. His research interests include the history of progressive education, democratic theory, community, and John Dewey. He is the author of *The Arthurdale Community School: Education and Reform in Depression Era Appalachia* (University of Kentucky Press), *Elsie Ripley Clapp (1879–1965): Her Life and the Community School* (Peter Lang), and coauthor of *Teachers, Leaders, and Schools: Essays by John Dewey* (Southern Illinois University Press), which won a 2012 American Educational Studies Critics Choice Award. He lives in Morgantown, West Virginia.

Katlin Swisher is an assistant director of marketing and communications and instructor of leadership studies and media at West Virginia University. She holds a PhD and MA in higher education from WVU and served as the managing editor for the Graduate Student Journal of Higher Education. In 2012, Swisher graduated summa cum laude and as a university honors scholar and WVU Foundation Outstanding Senior with a BS in journalism from WVU. Her research interests include land-grant universities, strategic planning, higher education policy, and organizational theory. Swisher has presented research at the American Educational Research Association, Association for the Study of Higher Education, and National Rural Education Association.

Kevin S. Zayed is Juliana Wilson Thompson Visiting Assistant Professor of Education at The College of Wooster where he teaches courses on the foundations of education, applied teacher ethics, educational law and policy, urban education, and classroom management. His research interests include the broader history of K-12 and higher education, curriculum reform, and more specifically, the history of general and liberal education. Dr. Zayed's research has appeared in several journals and edited volumes including the *Journal of Comparative and International Higher Education* and the *Journal of General Education*. His current book-length project explores the reform of general and liberal education in high schools and colleges during the mid-twentieth century.

Index

Taylor & Francis eBooks

www.taylorfrancis.com

A single destination for eBooks from Taylor & Francis
with increased functionality and an improved user
experience to meet the needs of our customers.

90,000+ eBooks of award-winning academic content in
Humanities, Social Science, Science, Technology, Engineering,
and Medical written by a global network of editors and authors.

TAYLOR & FRANCIS EBOOKS OFFERS:

A streamlined
experience for
our library
customers

A single point
of discovery
for all of our
eBook content

Improved
search and
discovery of
content at both
book and
chapter level

REQUEST A FREE TRIAL
support@taylorfrancis.com

Printed in the United States
By Bookmasters